ENCYCLOPAEDIA OF
JOURNALISM AND MASS COMMUNICATION

ENCYCLOPAEDIA OF

JOURNALISM
AND
MASS COMMUNICATION

(In 10 Volumes)
Radio and Television

(Volume 5)

OM GUPTA

ISHA

ISHA BOOKS
Delhi-110033

Encyclopaedia of Journalism and Mass Communication

ISBN : 81-8205-365-X (Set)
ISBN : 81-8205-370-6 (Vol. 5)

Published in 2006 in India by
Isha Books
D-43, Prithviraj Road,
Adarsh Nagar, Delhi - 110033
e-mail : ishabooks@hotmail.com

Laser Typesetting at : Vinayak Printers, Delhi
Printed at : Salasar Imaging, Delhi

CONTENTS

Preface

The radio and television are broadcast media which are often regarded as the guardians of modern democracy, defenders of the public interest. They supplies lots of valuable information, including speeches, documentaries, interviews, advertisements, daily news, financial markets, entertainment programmes and much more.

Radio and television programs are distributed through radio broadcasting or cable, often both simultaneously. By coding signals and having decoding equipment in homes, the latter also enables subscription-based channels and pay-per-view services. A broadcasting organisation may broadcast several programs at the same time, through several channels. Digital radio and digital television may also transmit multiplexed programming, with several channels compressed into one ensemble.

This book is an up-to-date practical guide for would-be reporters eager to enter the hectic arenas of radio and TV news. It offers a vivid insight into the world of electronic reporting, taking you behind the scenes at TV and the radio services. All the essential skills are covered, with instruction in reporting, recording and editing using the latest equipment. Coverage for radio and TV includes: newswriting, newsgathering, newsreading, interviewing and programme-making. Essential guidance is also given on how you can break into a career in radio and TV journalism.

Editor

1

History of Radio

Radio is the wireless transmission of signals, by modulation of electromagnetic waves with frequencies below those of light.

Radio waves are a form of electromagnetic radiation, created whenever a charged object (in normal radio transmission, an electron) accelerates with a frequency that lies in the radio frequency (RF) portion of the electromagnetic spectrum. In radio, this acceleration is caused by an alternating current in an antenna. Radio frequencies occupy the range from a few tens of hertz to a few hundred gigahertz.

Other types of electromagnetic radiation, with frequencies above the RF range, are infrared, visible light, ultraviolet, X-rays and gamma rays. Since the energy of an individual photon of radio frequency is too low to remove an electron from an atom, radio waves are classified as non-ionising radiation.

Electromagnetic spectrum and diagram of radio transmission of an audio signal. Electromagnetic radiation travels (propagates) by means of oscillating electromagnetic fields that pass through the air and the vacuum of space equally well, and does not require a medium of transport (such as the aether). When radio waves pass an electrical conductor, the oscillating electric or magnetic field (depending on the shape of the conductor) induces an alternating current and voltage in the conductor. This can be transformed into audio or other signals that carry information. The word 'radio' is used to describe this phenomenon, and television, radio, radar, and cell phone transmissions are all classed as radio frequency emissions.

Origin of the Word 'Radio'

Originally, radio technology was called 'wireless telegraphy', which was shortened to 'wireless'. The prefix radio- in the sense of wireless transmission was first recorded in the word radioconductor, coined by the French physicist Edouard Branly in 1897 and based on the verb to radiate. 'Radio' as a noun is said to have been coined by advertising expert Waldo Warren. The word appears in a 1907 article by Lee de Forest, was adopted by the United States Navy in 1912 and became common by the time of the first commercial broadcasts in the United States in the 1920s. The American term was then adopted by other languages in Europe and Asia, although Britain retained the term 'wireless' until the mid-20th century.

In Chinese, the term 'wireless' is the basis for the term 'radio wave' although the term for the device that listens to radio waves is literally 'device for receiving sounds'.

Invention of Radio

The identity of the original inventor of radio, at the time called wireless telegraphy, is contentious. Early radios ran the entire power of the transmitter through a carbon microphone. While some early radios used some type of amplification through electric current or battery, until the mid 1920s the most common type of receiver was the crystal set. In the 1920s, amplifying vacuum tube radio receivers and transmitters came into use.

The theoretical basis of the propagation of electromagnetic waves was first described in 1873 by James Clerk Maxwell in his paper to the Royal Society, A dynamical theory of the electromagnetic field, which followed his work between 1861 and 1865. Towards the end of 1875, while experimenting with the telegraph, Thomas Edison noted a phenomenon that he termed "etheric force", announcing it the press on November 28. He abandoned this research when Elihu Thomson, among others, ridiculed the idea.

In 1878 David E. Hughes was the first to transmit and receive radio waves when he noticed that his induction balance caused noise in the receiver of his homemade telephone. He demonstrated his discovery to the Royal Society in 1880 but was told it was merely induction. Between 1886 and 1888 Heinrich Rudolf Hertz first validated Maxwell's theory through experiment, demonstrating that radio radiation had all the properties of waves (now called Hertzian waves), and discovering that the electromagnetic equations could be reformulated into a partial differential equation called the wave equation.

Mahlon Loomis was issued U.S. Patent 129971 on July 30, 1872. Roberto Landell de Moura, a Brazilian priest and scientist, conducted experiments in 1893/1894. He did not publicize his achievement until 1900. Claims have been made that Nathan Stubblefield invented radio before either Tesla or Marconi, but his device seems to have worked by induction transmission rather than radio transmission.

Wireless Age

In 1893 in St. Louis, Missouri, Tesla made devices for his experiments with the electricity. Addressing the Franklin Institute in Philadelphia and the National Electric Light Association, he described and demonstrated in detail the principles of his work. The descriptions contained all the elements that were later incorporated into radio systems before the development of the vacuum tube. He initially experimented with magnetic receivers, unlike the coherers used by Marconi and other early experimenters. Tesla is usually considered the first to apply the mechanism of electrical conduction to wireless practices.

On 19 August 1894, British physicist Sir Oliver Lodge demonstrated the reception of Morse code signalling using radio waves, using a coherer. Edouard Branly of France and Popov of Russia later produced improved versions of the coherer.

Alexander Popov, who was the first to develop a practical communication system based on the coherer, is sometimes considered to have been the inventor of radio. In 1894 he built a coherer and presented it to the Russian Physical and Chemical Society on May 7, 1895. In March 1896, he transmitted radio waves between different campus buildings in Saint Petersburg, but did not apply for a patent.

Between 1894 and 1900 the Indian physicist Jagdish Chandra Bose performed pioneering research on radio waves and created waves as short as 5 mm. In November 1894, Bose ignited gunpowder and rang a bell at a distance using electromagnetic waves, confirming that communication signals could be sent without using wires, but he too did not patent his work.

The New Zealander Ernest Rutherford, 1st Baron Rutherford of Nelson was instrumental in the development of radio. In 1895 he was awarded an Exhibition of 1851 Science Research Scholarship to Cambridge. He arrived in England with a reputation as an innovator and inventor, and distinguished himself in several fields, initially by working out the electrical properties of solids and then using wireless waves as a method of signalling.

Rutherford was encouraged in his work by Sir Robert Ball, who had been scientific adviser to the body maintaining lighthouses on the Irish coast; he wished to solve the difficult problem of a ship's inability to detect a lighthouse in fog. Sensing fame and fortune, Rutherford increased the sensitivity of his apparatus until he could detect electromagnetic waves over a distance of several hundred metres. Thomson quickly realised that Rutherford was a researcher of exceptional ability and invited him to join in a study of the electrical conduction of gases. The commercial development of wireless technology was thus left for Guglielmo Marconi.

In 1896 Marconi was awarded what is sometimes recognised as the world's first patent for radio with British Patent 12039, Improvements in transmitting electrical impulses and signals and in apparatus there-for. In 1897 he established the world's first radio station on the Isle of Wight, England. The same year in the U.S., some key developments in radio's early history were made and patented by Tesla.

The U.S. Patent Office reversed its decision in 1904, awarding Marconi a patent for the invention of radio, possibly influenced by Marconi's financial backers in the States, who included Thomas Edison and Andrew Carnegie. Some believe this was made for financial reasons, allowing the U.S. government to avoid having to pay the royalties that were being claimed by Tesla for use of his patents.

In 1909, Marconi, with Karl Ferdinand Braun, was awarded the Nobel Prize in Physics for "contributions to the development of wireless telegraphy". However, Tesla's patent was reinstated in 1943 by the U.S. Supreme Court, shortly after his death. This decision was based on the fact that prior art existed before the establishment of Marconi's patent. Some believe the decision was also made for financial reasons, to allow the U.S. government to avoid having to pay damages that were being claimed by the Marconi Company for use of its patents during World War I.

"Wireless" Factories and Vacuum Tubes

Marconi opened the world's first "wireless" factory in Hall Street, Chelmsford, England in 1898, employing around 50 people. Around 1900, Tesla opened the Wardenclyffe Tower facility and advertised services. By 1903, the tower structure neared completion. Various theories exist on how Tesla intended to achieve the goals of this wireless system. Tesla claimed that Wardenclyffe, as part of a world system of transmitters, would have allowed secure multichannel transceiving of information, universal navigation, time synchronization, and a global location system.

The next great invention was the vacuum tube detector, invented by a team of Westinghouse engineers. On Christmas Eve, 1906, Reginald Fessenden used a synchronous rotary-spark transmitter for the first radio program broadcast, from Brant Rock, Massachusetts. Ships at sea heard a broadcast that included Fessenden playing O Holy Night on the violin and reading a passage from the Bible. The first radio news program was broadcast August 31, 1920 by station 8MK in Detroit, Michigan. The first regular entertainment broadcasts commenced in 1922 from the Marconi Research Centre at Writtle, near Chelmsford, England.

Developments in Early 20th Century

Aircraft used commercial AM radio stations for navigation. This continued until the early 1960s when VOR systems finally became widespread. In the early 1930s, single sideband and frequency modulation were invented by amateur radio operators. By the end of the decade, they were established commercial modes.

Radio was used to transmit pictures visible as television as early as the 1920s. Standard analog transmissions started in North America and Europe in the 1940s. In 1954, Regency introduced a pocket transistor radio, the TR-1, powered by a "standard 22.5 V Battery".

Developments in Latter half of the 20th Century

In 1960, Sony introduced their first transistorized radio, small enough to fit in a vest pocket, and able to be powered by a small battery. It was durable, because there were no tubes to burn out. Over the next 20 years, transistors replaced tubes almost completely except for very high-power uses.

In 1963 color television was commercially transmitted, and the first (radio) communication satellite, TELSTAR, was launched.

In the late 1960s, the U.S. long-distance telephone network began to convert to a digital network, employing digital radios for many of its links.

In the 1970s, LORAN became the premier radio navigation system. Soon, the U.S. Navy experimented with satellite navigation, culminating in the invention and launch of the GPS constellation in 1987.

In the early 1990s, amateur radio experimenters began to use personal computers with audio cards to process radio signals. In 1994, the U.S. Army and DARPA launched an aggressive, successful project to construct a software radio that could become a different radio on the fly by changing software.

Digital transmissions began to be applied to broadcasting in the late 1990s.

2

Uses of Radio

Many of radio's early uses were maritime, for sending telegraphic messages using Morse code between ships and land. The earliest users included the Japanese Navy scouting the Russian fleet during the Battle of Tsushima in 1905. One of the most memorable uses of marine telegraphy was during the sinking of the RMS Titanic in 1912, including communications between operators on the sinking ship and nearby vessels, and communications to shore stations listing the survivors.

Radio was used to pass on orders and communications between armies and navies on both sides in World War I; Germany used radio communications for diplomatic messages once its submarine cables were cut by the British. The United States passed on President Woodrow Wilson's Fourteen Points to Germany via radio during the war.

Broadcasting began to become feasible in the 1920s, with the widespread introduction of radio receivers, particularly in Europe and the United States. Besides broadcasting, point-to-point broadcasting, including telephone messages and relays of radio programs, became widespread in the 1920s and 1930s.

Another use of radio in the pre-war years was the development of detecting and locating aircraft and ships by the use of radar (RAdio Detection And Ranging).

Today, radio takes many forms, including wireless networks, mobile communications of all types, as well as radio broadcasting. Read more about radio's history.

Before the advent of television, commercial radio broadcasts included not only news and music, but dramas, comedies, variety shows, and many other forms of entertainment. Radio was unique among dramatic presentation that it used only sound.

There are a number of uses of radio:

Audio

AM broadcast radio sends music and voice in the Medium Frequency (MF—0.300 MHz to 3 MHz) radio spectrum. AM radio uses amplitude modulation, in which louder sounds at the microphone causes wider fluctuations in the transmitter power while the transmitter frequency remains unchanged. Transmissions are affected by static because lightning and other sources of radio add their radio waves to the ones from the transmitter.

FM broadcast radio sends music and voice, with higher fidelity than AM radio. In frequency modulation, louder sounds at the microphone cause the transmitter frequency to fluctuate farther, the transmitter power stays constant. FM is transmitted in the Very High Frequency (VHF—30 MHz to 300 MHz) radio spectrum. FM requires more radio frequency space than AM and there are more frequencies available at higher frequencies, so there can be more stations, each sending more information. Another effect is that shorter VHF radio waves act more like light, travelling in straight lines, hence the reception range is generally limited to about 50-100 miles. During unusual upper atmospheric conditions, FM signals are occasionally reflected back towards the Earth by the ionosphere, resulting in Long distance FM reception. FM receivers are subject to the capture effect, which causes the radio to only receive the strongest signal when multiple signals appear on the same frequency. FM receivers are relatively immune to lightning and spark interference.

FM Subcarrier services are secondary signals transmitted "piggyback" along with the main program. Special receivers are required to utilize these services. Analog channels may contain alternative programming, such as reading services for the blind, background music or stereo sound signals. In some extremely crowded metropolitan areas, the subchannel program might be an alternate foreign language radio program for various ethnic groups. Subcarriers can also transmit digital data, such as station identification, the current song's name, web addresses, or stock quotes. In some countries, FM radios automatically retune themselves to the same channel in a different district by using sub-bands.

Aviation voice radios use VHF AM. AM is used so that multiple stations on the same channel can be received. (Use of FM would result in stronger stations blocking out reception of weaker stations due to FM's capture effect). Aircraft fly high enough that their transmitters can be received hundreds of miles (kilometres) away, even though they are using VHF.

Marine voice radios can use AM in the shortwave High Frequency (HF—3 MHz to 30 MHz) radio spectrum for very long ranges or narrowband FM in the VHF spectrum for much shorter ranges.

Government, police, fire and commercial voice services use narrowband FM on special frequencies. Fidelity is sacrificed to use a smaller range of radio frequencies, usually five kHz of deviation, rather than the 75 kHz used by FM broadcasts and 25 kHz used by TV sound.

Civil and military HF (high frequency) voice services use shortwave radio to contact ships at sea, aircraft and isolated settlements. Most use single sideband voice (SSB), which uses less bandwidth than AM. On an AM radio SSB sounds like ducks quacking. Viewed as a graph of frequency versus power, an AM signal shows power where the frequencies of the voice add and subtract with the main radio frequency. SSB cuts the bandwidth in half by suppressing the carrier and (usually) lower sideband.

TETRA, Terrestrial Trunked Radio is a digital cell phone system for military, police and ambulances. Commercial services such as XM, WorldSpace and Sirius offer encrypted digital Satellite radio.

Telephony

Cell phones transmit to a local cell transmitter/receiver site, which connects to the public service telephone network through an optic fiber or microwave radio. When the phone leaves the cell radio's area, the central computer switches the phone to a new cell. Cell phones originally used FM, but now most use various digital encodings.

Satellite phones come in two types: INMARSAT and Iridium. Both types provide world-wide coverage. INMARSAT uses geosynchronous satellites, with aimed high-gain antennas on the vehicles. Iridium provides cell phones, with the cells being satellites in orbit.

Video

Television sends the picture as AM and the sound as FM, on the same radio signal. Digital television uses quadrature amplitude modulation. A Reed-Solomon error correction code adds redundant correction codes and allows reliable reception during moderate data loss. Although many current and future codecs can be sent in the MPEG-2 Transport stream container format, as of 2006 most systems use a standard-definition format almost identical to DVD: MPEG-2 video in Anamorphic widescreen and MPEG layer 2 (MP2) audio. High-definition television is possible simply by using a higher-resolution picture, but H.264/AVC is being considered as a replacement video codec in some regions for its improved compression. With the compression and improved modulation involved, a single "channel" can contain a high-definition program and several standard-definition programs.

Navigation

All satellite navigation systems use satellites with precision clocks. The satellite transmits its position, and the time of the transmission. The receiver listens to four satellites, and can figure its position as being on a line that is tangent to a spherical shell around each satellite, determined by the time-of-flight of the radio signals from the satellite. A computer in the receiver does the math. Loran systems also used time-of-flight radio signals, but from radio stations on the ground.

VOR systems (used by aircraft), have an antenna array that transmits two signals simultaneously. A directional signal rotates like a lighthouse at a fixed rate. When the directional signal is facing north, an omnidirectional signal pulses. By measuring the difference in phase of these two signals, an aircraft can determine its bearing from the station. An aircraft can get readings from two VORs, and locate its position at the intersection of the two beams.

Radio direction-finding is the oldest form of radio navigation. Before 1960 navigators used movable loop antennas to locate commercial AM stations near cities. In some cases they used marine radiolocation beacons, which share a range of frequencies just above AM radio with amateur radio operators.

Radar

Radar detects things at a distance by bouncing radio waves off them. The delay caused by the echo measures the distance. The direction of the beam determines the direction of the reflection. The polarization and frequency of the return can sense the type of surface.

Navigational radars scan a wide area two to four times per minute. They use very short waves that reflect from earth and stone. They are common on commercial ships and long-distance commercial aircraft. General purpose radars generally use navigational radar frequencies, but modulate and polarize the pulse so the receiver can determine the type of surface of the reflector. The best general-purpose radars distinguish the rain of heavy storms, as well as land and vehicles. Some can superimpose sonar data and map data from GPS position.

Search radars scan a wide area with pulses of short radio waves. They usually scan the area two to four times a minute. Sometimes search radars use the doppler effect to separate moving vehicles from clutter.

Targeting radars use the same principle as search radar but scan a much smaller area far more often, usually several times a second or more.

Weather radars resemble search radars, but use radio waves with circular polarization and a wavelength to reflect from water droplets. Some weather radar use the doppler to measure wind speeds.

Emergency Services

Emergency position-indicating rescue beacons (EPIRBs), emergency locating transmitters or personal locator beacons are small radio transmitters that satellites can use to locate a person or vehicle needing rescue. Their purpose is to help rescue people in the first day, when survival is most likely. There are several types, with widely-varying performance.

Digital Radio

The oldest form of digital broadcast was spark gap telegraphy, used by pioneers such as Marconi. By pressing the key, the operator could send messages in Morse code by energizing a rotating commutating spark gap. The rotating commutator produced a tone in the receiver, where a simple spark gap would produce a hiss, indistinguishable from static. Spark gap transmitters are now illegal, because their transmissions span several hundred megahertz. This is very wasteful of both radio frequencies and power.

The next advance was continuous wave telegraphy, or CW (Continuous Wave), in which a pure radio frequency, produced by a vacuum tube electronic oscillator was switched on and off by a key. A receiver with a local oscillator would "heterodyne" with the pure radio frequency, creating a whistle-like audio tone. CW uses less than 100 Hz of bandwidth. CW is still used, these days primarily by amateur radio operators (hams). Strictly, on-off keying of a carrier should be known as "Interrupted Continuous Wave" or ICW.

Radio teletypes usually operate on short-wave (HF) and are much loved by the military because they create written information without a skilled operator. They send a bit as one of two tones. Groups of five or seven bits become a character printed by a teletype. From about 1925 to 1975, radio teletype was how most commercial messages were sent to less developed countries. These are still used by the military and weather services.

Aircraft use a 1200 Baud radioteletype service over VHF to send their ID, altitude and position, and get gate and connecting-flight data.

Microwave dishes on satellites, telephone exchanges and TV stations usually use quadrature amplitude modulation (QAM). QAM sends data by changing both the phase and the amplitude of the radio signal. Engineers like QAM because it packs the most bits into a radio signal. Usually the bits are sent in "frames" that repeat. A special bit pattern is used to locate the beginning of a frame.

Systems that need reliability, or that share their frequency with other services, may use "corrected orthogonal frequency-division multiplexing" or COFDM. COFDM breaks a digital signal into as many as several hundred slower subchannels. The digital signal is often sent as QAM on the subchannels. Modern COFDM systems use a small computer to make and decode the signal with digital signal processing, which is more flexible and far less expensive than older systems that implemented separate electronic channels. COFDM resists fading and ghosting because the narrow-channel QAM signals can be sent slowly. An adaptive system, or one that sends error-correction codes can also resist interference, because most interference can affect only a few of the QAM channels. COFDM is used for WiFi, some cell phones, Digital Radio Mondiale, Eureka 147, and many other local area network, digital TV and radio standards.

Radio-frequency Energy for Heating

Radio-frequency energy generated for heating of objects is generally not intended to radiate outside of the generating equipment, to prevent interference with other radio signals. Microwave ovens use intense radio waves to heat food. Diathermy equipment is used in surgery for sealing of blood vessels. Induction furnaces are used for melting metal for casting.

Mechanical Force

Tractor beams: Radio waves exert small electrostatic and magnetic forces. These are enough to perform station-keeping in microgravity environments.

Conceptually, spacecraft propulsion: Radiation pressure from intense radio waves has been proposed as a propulsion method for an interstellar probe called Starwisp. Since the waves are long, the probe could be a very light metal mesh, and thus achieve higher accelerations than if it were a solar sail.

Other Uses of Radio

Amateur radio is a hobby in which enthusiasts purchase or build their own equipment and use radio for their own enjoyment. They may also provide an emergency and public-service radio service. This has been of great use, saving lives in many instances. Radio amateurs are able to use frequencies in a large number of narrow bands throughout the radio spectrum. They use all forms of encoding, including obsolete and experimental ones. Several forms of radio were pioneered by radio amateurs and later became commercially important, including FM, single-sideband AM, digital packet radio and satellite repeaters.

Personal radio services such as Citizens' Band Radio, Family Radio Service, Multi-Use Radio Service and others exist in North America to provide simple, (usually) short range communication for individuals and small groups, without the overhead of licensing. Similar services exist in other parts of the world.

Wireless energy transfer: A number of schemes have been proposed that transmit power using microwaves, and the technique has been demonstrated. These schemes include, for example, solar power stations in orbit beaming energy down to terrestrial users.

Radio remote control: Use of radio waves to transmit control data to a remote object as in some early forms of guided missile, some early TV remotes and a range of model boats, cars and aeroplanes. Large industrial remote-controlled equipment such as cranes and switching locomotives now usually use digital radio techniques to ensure safety and reliability.

Energy autarkic radio technology consists of a small radio transmitter powered by environmental energy (push of a button, temperature differences, light, vibrations, etc.).

3

Radio as a Mass Medium

Radio has its own strengths and weaknesses. Understanding the medium, which capitalizes mainly on sound, will act as a guide to using radio effectively for development and education.

1. *Radio, a medium for hearing.* The most striking attribute of radio is that it is an auditory medium. It has no visuals. It is blind. Listeners cannot see its messages. With radio, they can only hear and imagine objects, actions and ideas.

2. *Radio is a mass medium.* It addresses a many at the same time. With distance the contact becomes less personal than in face-toface communication. The chance of being misunderstood is great. Also, feedback is not immediate.

3. *Radio lacks permanence.* The audience may not read and re-read messages as in the print press. Radio is transient.

4. *Radio has no visuals.* There is no image and no text. The receivers cannot see the sender or broadcaster as they do on television or film. Radio's codes are purely auditory - speech, music, sounds, and silence. The occasion of being misunderstood, or of complete communication failure, is high. To use radio effectively much effort must be expended in order to compensate for the lack of visuals.

5. *Radio stimulates imagination.* The listeners of radio supply the visual data for themselves. They picture the messages

suggested by voices, words and sound effects. When one school was asked about television drama the response was "I prefer radio, the scenery is so much better."

6. *Radio is personal and intimate.* Real voices, insinuating personalities and emotions are passed on through radio impulses. Warmth, compassion, anger, pain, and laughter are conveyed more adequately in an audio medium. With accent, inflection, hesitation, pause, and a variety of emphasis and speed the voice report is able to convey far more than the printed speech. The fact that radio often reaches the listener during his/her situation of solitude and privacy adds to the intimate character of radio.

7. *Radio listeners do other things.* They can be plowing in the field, traveling, driving, washing clothes or mending fishing nets. One drawback of this is that the audience may be only half listening, and much of the message could be missed, ignored or misunderstood. The radio speaker cannot command full attention from a housemaker who is attending to her children going to school, or who may be chatting with a neighbor.

8. *Radio appeals to disadvantaged groups.* Being portable and inexpensive it is affordable to the common people, especially to farmers, fishermen and rural audiences. Those who have little access to newspapers can get news and information through radio. The less educated, such as those who have difficulty reading, are easily attracted to radio.

9. *Radio negates geographical and physical barriers.* Radio reaches the radio listener who could be anywhere, in the sea, on a mountain or on a bus. Radio can bring a commonality to people separated by geography, culture, learning or status.

10. *Radio gets messages to the listeners instantly.* The words spoken by an announcer in the radio studio are sent to

thousands of listeners at the speed of light. The speed and reach of radio should also apply to situations whereby the availability of piglets or rambutan seedlings in a nearby farm could be made known to the rest of the community. Such local items are too numerous and minor for big networks and newspapers. They are, however, vital to small communities and can be publicized far more cheaply and quickly through community radio.

11. *Radio is selective.* Program materials have been chosen previously. The radio presenter selects exactly what is to be received by his/ her listener. With radio the selection process takes place in the studio. The listener is presented with a single thread of material. Choice for the listener exists only in the mental switching off and switching on, such as when the news or program material fails to maintain the listener's interest. He/she might tune to another station.

12. *Radio has music.* Radio provides the enjoyment of listening to a guitar or to the ballad of a songbird. Music on radio can serve as a background or can be the focus of total absorption. Music relaxes, induces pleasure, nostalgia, excitement or curiosity.

13. *Radio can suffer from interference.* While the printed page is received in exactly the form in which it left the press, radio is always subject to interference. What leaves the studio is not necessarily what is heard in the possibly noisy environment of the listener. Intrusion of other station's signals, atmospheric noise, distortions of sound, a fading signal all add to the infidelity of message.

14. *Radio is an entertainment medium.* A majority of listeners accept radio as a means of entertainment rather than as a source of education. Therefore, when one looks to radio as a means to serve development and education, the design of enjoyable and stimulating programs is essential.

Heavily laden development programs fail to attract the desired number of listeners, which is waste of effort and the chance to change people's lives.

With the knowledge of the basic characteristics of the medium comes the realization of the possibility of how radio can be used effectively to affect the lives of individuals or society.

Role of Radio

1. *Radio for the Individual*

— Provides relaxation and entertainment. It moves people away from their problems and anxieties.

— Helps to solve problems by providing information and advice.

— Widens the horizons of people by stimulating interest in previously unknown topics.

— Promotes creativity.

— Contributes to self-knowledge and awareness, enabling the listeners to see themselves in relation to others.

— Guides social behavior by setting standards and offering role models.

— Provides topics of conversation through shared experience and hence facilitates personal contacts.

— Allow individuals to exercise choice, make decisions and act as responsible citizens.

— Inspires the individual and can move him/her into action.

2. *Radio for the Community*

— Speeds up the process of informing the community and therefore acts as a catalyst of change.

— Serves as a watchdog on power holders, affording active relationships between leaders and the citizens.

— Helps to approach consensus and to develop common objectives by providing debate and discussing issues.

—. Exposes options for community action.

— Enhances artistic and intellectual culture.

— Brings out and disseminates ideas promoting diversity and change.

— Reinforces values to help maintain social order through the status quo.

— Offers chance for individuals and groups to speak to each other, thus developing awareness of a common membership of community.

— Mobilizes both private and collective resources for personal or community needs.

The radio producer may aim to achieve program objectives along any of the impacts outlined above or by some other community and individual purpose. He/she should be able to state his/her program purpose clearly.

Selection of Broadcast Materials

The events and personalities that the station choose to put on air, including the amount of time that it devotes to them, will reflect the station's bias. If it broadcasts the entire proceedings of a beauty contest listeners get the impression that it condones, or gives social significance to, the event. If it puts a ten-minute interview on air with a gambling lord who doled out a P1,000 donation to a charity ball the station. puts aside the adverse impact of gambling. On the other hand, if the station gives more importance to those who strive to achieve than to less motivated personalities it can send an inspirational message to young people. Science contests, in lieu of pure movie gossip, can demonstrate the serious educational thrust of the station.

If it concentrates on playing American rock music and fails to give adequate time for local and community developed renditions, the station does not promote patronage of native talent and products. Similarly, if an event of one political party is covered, and not the other, the station can be seen as taking sides in an electoral contest. The station is expected to always strive for balance in presentation of material, particularly in cases of diversity of ideas and conflicts. While the perfect balance is unattainable the broadcaster must bear in mind that audiences can readily discern the bias and prejudices of a broadcaster or the station.

In general, the station should project a positive image by opting for materials that educate the listeners. Program material must present facts and depth. The presentation should be geared towards uplifting the community. Education, motivation, intellectual deliberation, opinion formation based on reason should be developed. Even as community broadcasters are urged to "join the building gang rather than the wrecking crew," malpractice and wrongdoing of leaders and public officials must be pointed out. These exposes, however, should be a product of meticulous research and establish unimpeachable data rather than conjecture or speculation.

Views and Opinions

Interpretation, analysis, editorials and opinions have to be well thought out. Better still, they must be the output of careful deliberation by a group of responsible people in the radio station who have access to adequate facts. The community radio council, or a special editorial board mandated by the CMC, might handle the station editorials on such issues as forest denudation, child rights, cooperativism, education on family relationships.

Personal attacks should give way to logical analysis and presentation of facts. The oft repeated phrase "walang personalan' [nothing personal] might well find its application as a policy for opinion slots. Opinions expressed by community members on tape, telephone or live interviews must always be divested of slanderous remarks or name-calling. Nothing defamatory or libelous must be allowed to go on the air.

Vox pops

The voice of the people (voz populi) is important in community radio. Views coming from a wide social spectrum depict the conscience of the citizenry. A mobile tape recorder that picks up speech, from the one sentence to three-minute interview, will develop the authenticity of public opinion. Again, the station must endeavor to achieve balance of views.

Vox pops can either be aired at random during whole program hours or aired in specific slots devoted solely to public opinion. They can also be accommodated in a public affairs, news or documentary program.

Documentary Programs

Considered as the highest form of radio programs, documentaries usually take more time, effort and perhaps money to prepare. Documentaries take an intense look at an issue and present the findings in as balanced and comprehensive a manner as possible. The feature usually starts from originally compiled information, voice clips and lowdowns gathered in normal news activities and interviews accomplished by the station. Other information, actualities and materials are sought to paint a thorough picture of a problem. The documentary can have a short dramatization of the situation, interviews, vox pops, voice clips, relevant music as well as live commentaries. While it is easy to tilt balance in documentary presentation the noble aim is to paint an impartial picture of a question. Integrity is put on line every time the station presents a documentary.

Side Remarks

Most of the strong and hard-hitting comments do not come during a commentary or editorial program. They are off-the-cuff remarks delivered, either wittingly or unwittingly, by the station personalities or guests.

In one instance a TV newscaster, who scorned the interview done by the station with a notorious couple, was asked to resign when she wryly commented, "why does television have to glorify thieves?" The author of this manuscript used to give out news and receive live field reports in a radio magazine program. At the end of one field report about a statement coming from the President the technician played one of the many voice clips done by a seven year old girl, "Tito Louie, isn't it a sin to tell lies?" Consequently a letter was received from the Information Minister pleading for the program not be too harsh on the President.

Some radio personalities are adept at employing these short quips. The impact could be truly stinging but unless done on purpose, and as part of the general picture painting, they must be used sparingly. The seemingly off-the-cuff remarks can be repulsive, amusing, and derisive or simply arise out of bad taste. People who use the station microphone should be advised to doubly watch their tongue. When the tongue slips it is sometimes worse than the foot.

Interviews and Panel Discussion

The very choice of interviewees and panelist often indicates the partiality or impartiality of the station. The length of the interview, together with the manner of questioning, reveals the leanings of the producer, host and/or the station. Leading questions reveal the interviewers positions. The way guests are addressed gives away the disposition of the program host.

4

All India Radio

All India Radio (AIR), officially known as Akashwani is the radio broadcaster of India and a division of Prasar Bharati (Broadcasting Corporation of India), an autonomous corporation of the Ministry of Information and Broadcasting, Government of India. It is the sister service of Prasar Bharati's Doordarshan, the national television broadcaster.

All India Radio is one of the largest radio networks in the world. The headquarters is at Akashwani Bhavan, on the Parliament Street next to the Indian parliament. Akashwani Bhavan houses the drama section, the FM section and the National service. The Doordarshan Kendra (Delhi) is also located on the 6th floor of Akashwani Bhavan.

Broadcasting house is an old building next to Akashwani Bhavan. The New Service Division of All India Radio under the Director General (New functions) from this building. Built during the British rule, it is a very popular location and easily recognised building in New Delhi.

History of AIR

Radio broadcasting began in India in 1927, with two privately-owned transmitters at Mumbai and Calcutta.

These were nationalised in 1930 and operated under the name Indian Broadcasting Service until 1936, when it was renamed All India Radio (AIR). Although officially renamed again to Akashwani in 1957, it is still popularly known as All India Radio

Coverage

AIR covers 99.37% of India's populace, the largest democracy in the world with over one billion inhabitants. AIR maintains approximately 200 broadcasting centres around the country and transmits in 24 different languages. In spite of recent penetration by other media such as Cable TV, AIR remains the most common means of gaining access to information and entertainment, as the radio receivers are relatively cheap and affordable.

AIR Services

AIR has many different services each catering to different regions/languages across India. One of the most famous services of the AIR is the Vividh Bharati Seva (roughly translating to "Multi-Indian service"). This service is the most commercial of all and is popular in Mumbai and other cities of India. This service offers a wide range of programmes including news, film music, comedy shows, etc. The Vividh Bharti service operates on different MW band frequencies for each city as shown below.

Some programs broadcast on the Vividh Bharti:

— Binaca geet mala (later renamed to Cibaca geet mala) - Featuring Hindi film songs.

— Hawa-mahal - Skit based on some novels/plays.

— Santogen ki mehfil - Jokes & humour

The following is a partial list of AIR services.

North Regional Service

— Agra 1530 kHz

— Allahabad 1026 kHz

— Delhi 'Indraprastha' 819 kHz

— Delhi 'Rajdhani' 666 kHz

— Delhi 'D' 1017 kHz

— Jaipur 'A' 1476 kHz

— Jalandhar 'A' 873 kHz

— Jammu 'A' 990 kHz

— Jodhpur 'A' 531 kHz

— Lucknow 'A' 747 kHz

— Srinagar 'A' 1116 kHz

— Varanasi 'A' 1242 kHz

East Regional Service

— Bhagalpur 1458 kHz

— Cuttack 'A' 972 kHz

— Darbhanga 1296 kHz

— Jamshedpur 1584 kHz

— Kolkata 'A' 657 kHz

— Patna 'A' 621 kHz

— Ranchi 'A' 549 kHz

North-east Regional Service

— Agartala 1269 kHz

4

All India Radio

All India Radio (AIR), officially known as Akashwani is the radio broadcaster of India and a division of Prasar Bharati (Broadcasting Corporation of India), an autonomous corporation of the Ministry of Information and Broadcasting, Government of India. It is the sister service of Prasar Bharati's Doordarshan, the national television broadcaster.

All India Radio is one of the largest radio networks in the world. The headquarters is at Akashwani Bhavan, on the Parliament Street next to the Indian parliament. Akashwani Bhavan houses the drama section, the FM section and the National service. The Doordarshan Kendra (Delhi) is also located on the 6th floor of Akashwani Bhavan.

Broadcasting house is an old building next to Akashwani Bhavan. The New Service Division of All India Radio under the Director General (New functions) from this building. Built during the British rule, it is a very popular location and easily recognised building in New Delhi.

History of AIR

Radio broadcasting began in India in 1927, with two privately-owned transmitters at Mumbai and Calcutta.

— Madurai 1269 kHz

— Ootakamund 1602 kHz

— Pondicherry 1215 kHz

— Port Blair 684 kHz

— Thiruvananthapuram 'A' 1161 kHz

— Tiruchirapalli 'A' 936 kHz

— Vijayawada 'A' 837 kHz

— Visakhapatnam 927 kHz

Vividh Bharati Service

— Chennai 'C' 783 kHz

— Cuttack 'B' 1314 kHz

— Delhi 'C' 1368 kHz

— Jalandhar 'C' 1350 kHz

— Kanpur 1449 kHz

— Kolkata 'C' 1323 kHz

— Lucknow 'C' 1278 kHz

— Mumbai 'C' 1188 kHz

— Panaji 'B' 1539 kHz

— Vijayawada 'B' 1503 kHz

— Varanasi 'B' 1602 kHz

— Varanasi FM' 100.6MHz

The Voice of Youth

The Yuv-vani service of AIR provides an enriching and novel radio-experience by encouraging youth participation and experimenting with varied script ideas. With shows like

"Mehfil", "In the groove" and "The Roving Microphone" which have been around for more than three decades, Yuv-vani still holds a firm ground of its own.

Some of the big names on the Indian media scene began their journey with Yuv-vani. Comments Praful Thakkar, a well known documentary maker - "Yuv-vani came as a breath of fresh air in our reckless college days. It was a great learning experience for me and it made me realize that radio is not all about goofy quotes and PJs."

Some of the other names that have been associated with Yuv-vani in the past include Celebrity game show host Roshan Abbas, VJ Gaurav Kapoor, DJ Kaushal Khanna, and DJ Pratham among others.

News-on-phone Service

All India Radio, after launching the news-on-phone service on 25th February 1998 from New Delhi, is running the service from Chennai, Mumbai, Hyderabad, Patna and Bangalore also. The service is accessible through STD, ISD and local telephone calls. The service is going to be started from 9 more cities — Ahmedabad, Guwahati, Imphal, Jaipur, Kolkata, Lucknow, Raipur, Simla and Thiruvanthapuram shortly.

5

FM Radio

FM radio is a broadcast technology invented by Edwin Howard Armstrong that uses frequency modulation to provide high-fidelity sound over broadcast radio.

Broadcast Bands

The original FM broadcast band in the USA in the early-1940s was on 42-50 MHz with 0.2 MHz channel spacing. This band was abandoned after World War II and is now allocated to a seldom-used two-way communications service.

The name "FM band" is misleading, since one can transmit FM on any frequency within the VHF range. All of these bands mentioned are in the VHF band which extends from 30MHz to 300MHz.

Throughout the world, 87.5-108 MHz (or some portion thereof, in the U.S. is 88.1-107.9 MHz) is used as a broadcast band, with one very notable exception: Japan, which uses its own unique 76-90 MHz band with 0.1 MHz channel spacing.

The frequency of an FM broadcast station (more strictly its assigned nominal center frequency) is usually an exact multiple of 100 kHz. In the Americas and Caribbean only odd multiples are used. In Italy, multiples of 50 kHz are used.

The bandwidth of an FM transmission is normally somewhat wider than these figures, and depends on whether stereo is used and the manner in which the peak deviation is regulated. In the UK, for example, broadcast licences specify that the nominal bandwidth of the transmission is 270 kHz.

In many countries the minimum spacing for stations intended to serve overlapping areas is 400 kHz.

In the former Soviet republics, and some Eastern Bloc nations, an additional older band from 65.9 to 74 MHz is also used. Assigned frequencies are multiples of 30 kHz. This older band, sometimes referred to as the OIRT band is slowly being phased out in many countries.

Technical Characteristics

Random noise has a 'triangular' spectral distribution in an FM system, with the effect that noise occurs predominantly at the highest frequencies within the baseband. This can be offset, to a limited extent, by boosting the high frequencies before transmission and reducing them by a corresponding amount in the receiver. Reducing the high frequencies in the receiver also reduces the high-frequency noise. These processes of boosting and then reducing certain frequencies are known as pre-emphasis and de-emphasis respectively.

The amount of pre-emphasis and de-emphasis used is defined by the time constant of a simple RC filter circuit. In most of the world a 50 μs time constant is used. In North America, 75 μs is used. This applies to both mono and stereo transmissions.

The amount of pre-emphasis that can be applied is limited by the fact that many forms of contemporary music contain more high-frequency energy than the musical styles which prevailed at the birth of FM broadcasting. They cannot be pre-emphasized as much because it would cause excessive deviation of the FM carrier. (Systems more modern than FM broadcasting tend to use either program-dependent variable pre-emphasis (e.g. J.17) or none at all.)

FM Stereo

The Zenith-GE pilot tone multiplex system was added to FM radio in the early 1960s to allow FM stereo. It is important that stereo broadcasts should be compatible with mono receivers. For this reason, the left (L) and right (R) channels are matrixed into sum (M) and difference (S) signals, i.e. $M=(L+R)/2$ and $S=(L-R)/2$. A mono receiver will just use the M signal. A stereo receiver will matrix the M and S signals to recover L and R: $L=M+S$ and $R=M-S$.

The M signal is transmitted as baseband audio in the range 30 Hz to 15 kHz. The S signal is amplitude-modulated onto a 38 kHz suppressed carrier to produce a double-sideband suppressed carrier (DSBSC) signal in the range 23 to 53 kHz. A 19 kHz pilot tone, at exactly half the 38 kHz subcarrier frequency and with a precisely defined phase relationship to it, is also generated. This is transmitted at 8-10% of overall modulation level and used by the receiver to regenerate the 38 kHz subcarrier with the correct phase.

The final multiplex signal from the stereo generator is the sum of the baseband audio (M), the pilot tone, and the DSBSC subcarrier (S). This multiplex, along with any other subcarriers, modulates the FM transmitter.

Converting the multiplex signal back to left and right is performed by a stereo decoder, which is built into stereo receivers. It is normal practice to apply pre-emphasis to the left and right channels before matrixing, and to apply de-emphasis at the receiver after matrixing.

Other Subcarrier Services

The subcarrier system has been further extended to add other services. Initially these were private analog audio channels which could be used internally or rented out. Radio reading services for the blind are also still common, and there were experiments with quadraphonic sound. If there is no stereo on a station, everything from 23kHz on up can be used for other services. The guard band around 19kHz (±4kHz) must still be maintained, so as not to trigger stereo decoders on receivers. If there is stereo, there will typically be a guard band between the upper limit of the DSBSC stereo signal (53 kHz) and the lower limit of any other subcarrier.

Digital services are now also available. A 57kHz subcarrier (phase locked to the third harmonic of the stereo pilot tone) is used to carry a low-bandwidth digital Radio Data System signal, providing extra features such as Alternate Frequency (AF) and Network (NN). This narrowband signal runs at only 1187.5 bits per second, thus is only suitable for text. A few proprietary systems are used for private communications.

The United States is the only country attempting to put digital radio onto FM rather than using EUREKA 147 like most other countries (including Canada), or ISDB like Japan. This in-band on-channel approach results in highly-compressed audio, and blocks any opportunity for new stations to broadcast. The proprietary iBiquity system, branded as "HD Radio", uses subcarriers and extends out somewhat into the sidebands. The hybrid digital (hence "HD") system can later take the bandwidth used by the current analog stereo system, and eventually go all-digital, though this would shut out every existing analog radio.

6

Radio Craft

To understand radio language it is useful to examine the raw materials of radio - words, sounds and music. They are the audible signs and symbols used to convey messages. It is also essential to look at the nature and functions of silence.

The Spoken Word

Verbal language is the primary code of radio. The spoken word is a representation of the objects and ideas that the listener must visualize, picture or imagine. There is a difference between words printed on a page and words on radio. Words on radio are always spoken, the voice offers an index of the person or the character that is speaking. For example, a smile in the voice of an announcer may automatically depict a congenial personality. It may also serve as an index of the type of program being presented or even of the radio station or network. What might a frown indicate?

Another point about the radio talk is that most of it is scripted. However, radio talks must not sound as though they are written and rehearsed. They should sound spontaneous. Everyday language, colloquialism, common expressions and embellishment phrases are encouraged. A prepared script must be delivered as if it were unstructured. When reading of a script becomes obvious the listener gets the impression that the presenter is simply conveying words, probably prepared by somebody else.

The news, however, is not upheld as impromptu. Today's audiences accept news reading from a script, although some news presenters try to provide a conversational tone both in the writing and in delivery of news.

Literary programs, when identified as such, may also be presented without having to be 'disguised' as spontaneous.

Much of radio talk must suppress its literary style in favor of the casual and the conversational. Spoken words must be simple, or concrete enough to be easily understood through the ear alone. Frequent repetition may be practiced if only to ensure those meanings are clearly received. Remember that the listener has no chance of going back to a missed point except on rare occasions when he/she has taped the program.

The Sound

Sound is commonly a manifestation of the presence of something. The sound of a bell ringing, a cow mooing, barking of dogs, the tractor engine, closing of a door all signify that something is happening. As a tool sounds are used deliberately to establish time, mood and setting. Sound can suggest occasions. A crowing sound frequently signifies not only a rooster but also daybreak.

In general, sounds are introduced in radio to add realism to an event or to enhance the mood or atmosphere of a scene. The varied sounds of footsteps in a radio play, hurried, slow and eerie, suspenseful, casual or in chase provoke an environment or set an emotional frame. When portraying a scene, such as in drama, it is not necessary to put in all the sounds that could be heard in the real world.

The producer prioritizes sounds for the listeners. He selects the more suggestive sound or foregrounds the most important one. The irrelevant sounds are either eliminated or reduced to a minimum.

Many of the sounds used in drama are created in the studio rather than actually recorded in the real world. The rustling of a bunch of recording tapes or of shredded papers signifies walking through undergrowth. The clapping of coconut shells conveys horse's hooves. To create the sound of fire, crumpling plastic sheets makes an easier and less dangerous exercise than recording a real conflagration. Finally, words often compliment a sound for greater effect. Most suggestive sounds would require the support of dialogue or narration.

The Music

On radio, music performs two functions. It invites aesthetic appreciation as well as signifies something outside itself. Music is a predominant output in radio programs. In the Philippines many FM stations offer little, or nothing, but music. The lyrics, melody, beat and rhythms are objects of pleasure for the listeners. Words and sound largely give reference to something outside themselves. Distinct from the meaning conveyed by lyrics, wordless music may serve listeners differently. Some music may convey emotion, while other melodies may indicate cultural and historical circumstances.

Much of melody does not contain the clear meaning that words offer. However, music is usually self sufficient as radio material. It can be fully appreciated even if the particular track has never been heard before. This absence of precise meaning in music makes it suitable for radio. It allows listeners to assimilate music in harmony with their respective thoughts and moods. This perhaps is one reason why music is popular on radio.

1. *Music as a Boundary and Program Frame*: It has been customary for producers to use snippets of music [at times specially composed short melodies] to denote a program's beginning or ending. Musical opening or closing stingers, for instance, marks segments of magazine or variety programs. The use of music, played during talk shows, is becoming a more frequent practice.

    As a framing mechanism, or as a denotation of sectional boundaries, the music sets the tone of programs or slots such as a children's show, drama, news, comedy, documentary or farm program.

2. *Music as a Link*: Like the closing and opening of curtains in between acts in a theatre play quick pieces of music are often played between the scenes of a radio drama or between segments of long programs. These snatches of music indicate the shifting of subject, time, location or setting.

3. *Music Sets Mood*: To serve as a clue to listeners, or to enhance feelings portrayed in a drama, appropriate mood music is played. Music is placed as background sound, usually sneaked in and out. Musical chords are used as a punctuator to highlight an action or statement.

4. *Music as Sound Effects*: To indicate parties, carnivals or a rural setting the corresponding music can aid in establishing a locale, a situation or an era. In order to mark scenes - battle, suspense, a saloon or a Spanish setting - the producer selects signifying music. Special music could be created in more sophisticated productions.

5. *Music Application Techniques*: Whether as signature, theme, bridge, background, stinger or sound effect musical pieces should be applied judiciously,

    — using music only appropriate to the mood and content of the production;

— avoiding excessive use of music for background sound
  or for establishing mood; and

— using craft in music fading in and out.

Some terms used in music application techniques.

— Fade in - starting music from nothing and then slowly
  bringing it up to a desired level.

— Fade out - bringing down the music from existing
  level to zero.

— Fade down - bringing down music from existing level
  to a lower optimum level.

— Fade under - bringing down the volume of music to
  a background level.

— Sustain - keeping a constant level of music over a
  certain period of time during the show.

— Cross fade - bringing down one piece of music
  simultaneously with the fading up of a second piece.

— Sneak in - introducing music slowly during dialogue
  or speech, practically unnoticed, to help enhance the
  mood of a scene. _ Sneak out - fading out of a piece
  of music, virtually unnoticed by listeners, when it is
  no longer relevant.

— Segue - playing of the succeeding music immediately
  after the last note of the previous music.

The Silence

As in the song, the sound of silence "can be heard". Silence
normally signifies that there is nothing happening.
Alternatively it can also be deliberately applied to indicate
that there is something happening, such as thinking. It can
also heighten the interest of the listeners in a certain section
of an action scene. " Ahh..This heavy stone could put you

out forever... Ahh... here... Take it!.... Uhhh......
[SILENCE]". A pause in the noise - sound, music and voice
- could be employed to heighten a dramatic scene or to
indicate a comical punch.

Radio Talk

Radio is simply people talking with people. The main
difference is that, in radio, the conversationalists are at a
distance, not seeing eye to eye. Hence, audio signal is the
only tool of conversation. It is not necessary to be a formal
communication graduate to be able to use radio and speak
to a whole community.

A good radio talk should be interesting and should
effectively drive home the message.

Here is a possible structure for an interesting two to
five- minute radio talk.

1. *Get the attention*: The first sentence is always the most
    critical. Do not prolong the take off. The runway of
    listening span is short. You may employ a striking fact,
    a loaded question, an intriguing statement or a dramatic
    situation.

2. *Point the direction*: This is the line that leads the opener
    to the body of the talk.

3. *The body of information*: Sustain the interest of the listeners
    by logical presentation of ideas and by presenting facts.
    This means that each part of the talk flows easily out of
    the preceding one and equally easily into the one that
    follows. Give specific situations and concrete examples.
    Your talk must stick together. You must always stay with
    the main idea. There should be no words or sentences
    that do not clarify the main idea. Your talk should be easy
    to understand and sentences easy to say.

4. *A strong ending*: Leave your listeners at the end with
    something that is important or thought provoking.

The Radio Script

The script is the written material that the announcer or a radio performer reads. The radio script may include technical instructions and inserts that have to go into the program. It may contain various directions for dialogue, sound effects, music, action and much more. The script is the written program that tells the presenter what to say and do, when and how to say it.

This does not mean that everything that we hear on radio is scripted. But then, as listeners, we do not know for sure. Unlike television, we do not know when someone is reading the lines on radio.

Knowing that there is a prepared script during a broadcast lessens the stress on the performers and participants in the program. Everyone has an idea of how the program should run. Each would know what to say and do.

Even in individually run programs, it is important to have a script as it:

— ensures smooth continuity of the program;

— helps in proper program timing;

— ensures accuracy of information;

— helps to present information in an organized manner.

Tips on Writing a Radio Talk

— Write, as you would speak. Be conversational.

— Don't generalize. Be concrete. Illustrate. Give examples.

— Provide a bold beginning, it keeps the listeners tuned.

— Make a strong impressive ending.

— Employ a logical progression of ideas in building up a picture or a story.

— Use simple words, ideas and sentences. Do not heap adjective upon adjective to twist the tongue.

— The listener cannot look back and forth in a talk. Repetition is the essence of radio presentation.

— You may forget grammar as long as you communicate clearly. Your ideas are your message, not your language.

— Be personal and informal. Use "I," "You," "Your." Talk to a friend.

— Write in the way that a good personal conversationalist would speak. Use your own experiences as examples.

— Be accurate and precise.

— Avoid technical terms foreign to the listener's ear such as destierro, statutes, habeas corpus, conflagrations, civil liability and concubinage

— Avoid too many figures and statistics.

— Be timely. Choose topics that are relevant to the needs and interest of the times. Write about events.

— Be clear with your instructions.

— Use familiar words and ideas.

— Do not sermonize. Listeners are looking for entertainment.

7

Radio Spots

Radio spots are made up of short catchy messages of anything from 15 to 30 seconds duration designed to deliver information, inspiration or instruction to the listeners. They are effective conveyors of quick messages. Usually well-prepared, although terse, these materials are interspersed like commercial advertisements in a program proper, between programs, as intermission for long-winded segments or in program breaks such as around the time station identification is given.

The Content

Themes can range from civic to social, political, religious, agricultural, health, environmental, livelihood to moral. Many national information and social mobilization campaigns have effectively been carried out riding mainly on the efficacy of radio spots, jingles and plugs.

Advantages

The following are the main advantages of short materials.

— Being short, radio spots can be easily accommodated, even in tight sequence guides.

— Announcers and broadcasters recognize that radio spots add spice to their programs.

— Radio spots are relatively inexpensive to produce.

— Radio spots drive home the message in a short time.

— Radio spots can be played over and over in one program or station.

— Radio spots can be recycled over years.

— Radio spots can be played in programs, which already have a captive audience. There is no need to worry about building an audience.

Guidelines

A good radio spot should offer extra entertainment value to an existing program as it conveys the intended message in a snap. In commercial, competitive situations the programs traffic officer normally rejects dull material. Audiences who typically seek excitement and entertainment spurn non-stimulating programs. It is therefore important that radio spots be charged with an interesting message and strong audience appeal.

The following are some guidelines when preparing spots, jingles, plugs and short materials.

1. Define the specific intended message(s) as well as the target group(s). Indicate the main and secondary messages. Clarify the principal audience as well as secondary, or even incidental, listeners. Remember that the spot cannot deal with discursive instructions principally because of the limitation of time and space. Verbosity and over embellishment are unaffordable in a 30 second, or even a one-minute, production. The effort should be used to directly shoot a terse message that may need to be repeatedly pummeled to the listeners.

Example:

a. Main message - Brown rice is more nutritious than polished white rice.

b. Secondary message - Much of the vitamins are lost in washing] rice.

Principal audience - farmers, rural home makers. Secondary audience - other home makers, other members of the rural family and rural improvement club members.

2. Make the radio spot really appealing so as to merit playing and replaying it in a popular program or radio station. Employ some attention catchers such as.

a. A startling revelation: Did you know that madre kakaw leaves could be used to drive away the pests eating your vegetables?

b. Striking information: Did you know you may harvest your rice one week earlier by direct seeding?

c. An intriguing question: Who are really better - the old farmers or the young ones?

d. A highly dramatic point: I love you, Thalia. Yes...but my child with Mercedes has to carry my name!

e. A stimulating dialogue or discussion.

f. A lively voice that grabs listeners' attention.

g. An odd or curious fact: Did you know that if all the eggs produced in a day in Bantayan Island were lined up, the long queue would reach the City of Cebu?

h. A personality endorsement: Listen to Miss Ara Mina on the benefits of breast-feeding.

i. A human-interest report: Did you know that the infant in the womb of the mother can already appreciate music and laughter in the outside world?

j. A pun: GATT is what we've got. Few benefits, burden to a lot.

k. A curious sound effect such as the sound of the child laughing inside the mother's womb.

In addition,

— Avoid making the plot too complicated. There is not much room for complex story lines.

— Stay away from awkward dialogue, petty plots and trivial scenes, they will only bore the audience.

— Keep a lively pace, both through snappy delivery of lines and quick progress of ideas. You cannot afford to crawl and drag in one minute.

— Focus on one dominant message. Do not submerge the central theme under peripheral and incidental points.

— Examine the spot for the unintended and latent dysfunctions or hidden messages.

— Use strong endings such as:

  — a punctuating statement;

  — a thought-provoking question;

  — a strong declaration;

  — pleasant or amusing repartee;

  — a comical note;

  — a resolution of the conflict;

  — an open but provocative ending;

  — a clear reminder.

— Repeat key lines several times, or as often as necessary and possible.

— Take the cue from commercial advertisements that repeat their slogan or the brand three to six times, if only to heighten recall value.

— Make the tag line distinct from the principal message. It should not interfere, muddle, complicate or becloud the main issue. Do not be tempted to overload the end

obtrusively with institutional credits. The acknowle-
dgements could backfire on these institutions. A more
subtle approach might be considered rather than the
apparent propaganda-like manner of putting tag lines.
The tail should not wag the dog!

— Base the format to be used on practical considerations:

- Which line shall be most effective in delivery of the
  message?

- What logistical requirements can be met?

- Can we afford the fee for a star-personality
  endorsement?

- Do we have transportation, money and staff to get a
  testimonial from a farmer in a place 500 kilometers
  away?

- Are there competent musical talents-composer,
  arranger, musicians, band, etc -available in the station?

- Beware, some literary pieces may deserve literary
  awards.

However, they are not necessarily effective message carriers.
At the end of the production, check result message against
the intended message. Pre-test the final appeal with some
intended receivers.

Various Formats of Radio Spots

1. Mini-drama

- Dialogue must be clear, exciting and natural.

- Delivery of lines should be lively and realistic.

- The plot must be simple.

- The story should zero in on, and drive home, the
  principal message.

— Transition should be swift and smooth.

— Resolution should come in a reasonable and logical manner rather than forced through.

2. Straight Announcement

— This format is the easiest and least costly to prepare.

— The script must be exciting and moving.

— The producer must select the most effective voice to deliver the script.

— There must be some flexibility and variation in the mode of delivery. Avoid monotony.

— While you employ ways to make the script stimulating there is no need to be flimsy and unnatural in both the script writing and delivery. Triviality could turn off listeners.

— A solid punch line should clinch the message to:

— conclude a discussion

— resolve an issue

— stimulate the audience to think hard

— summarize points

— open up a line of thought

— deliver a specific instruction

3. Endorsement by Authorities and Personalities

For the message and information to carry the highest credibility and preclude any controversy it should originate from the most recognized experts - from the "horse's mouth", so to speak. A doctor or specialist should issue health tips. Agricultural information should preferably come from a farmer or an agriculturist. Other personalities such as celebrities, sports figures, political leaders or respectable persons in the community may have credibility but their respective areas of work do not indicate professional or vocational expertise. A movie celebrity or a basketball star will lack credibility endorsing an agricultural practice or a technological practice if he/she is not directly involved in it.

Testimonial: This is also an endorsement, usually from somebody who has actually tried a product, idea, practiced a method or a regular denizen who might have seen how something that is being promoted actually worked. A testimonial brings down the programme material to the level of regular people.

Collage, Montage and Vox Pops: These are quick snatches of people's voices that are arranged to demonstrate the range of views and feelings of the citizenry. A differentiation among the terms could be made in the following manner.

— Vox pop (vox populi) - voice of a regular member of society expressing an opinion from his/her personal point of view.

— Collage - an assembly of unrelated voices focusing on an issue.

— Montage - a series of assorted voices of people, played one after the other with the design to portray one theme or story.

4. Dialogue

Use two voice qualities that are distinctly identifiable rather than mistakable - man and woman, old and young, gruff and pleasant, big and small, high pitch and low pitch, etc. Common every-day language that flows in a conversational manner should characterize the dialogue in order for it to sound natural. The dialogue must excite and stimulate the audience.

5. *Musical Jingle*

It does not always require a professional musician to make a good jingle. Any one who has some fascination for music may come up with a big hit with little expense. The musical jingles that became popular are those that have the following characteristics.

— Simplicity of message, melody and lyrics.

— Clarity of the wording and idea.

— Unity of the message.

— Repetition of a main line.

— Outstanding melodic line that lingers in the minds of listeners.

Do not succumb to the temptation of loading too many ideas into one minute, much less 30-seconds. It is more practical to repeat a central idea that you consider would become a byword, or an anchor melody for remembering some details of the message. Do not discount the possibility that old popular melodies with adopted lyrics can work wonders. You need not create entirely new melodies for every jingle you make. Old melodies could also be adopted.

Do check with recording companies if a particular popular song could be adopted for a developmental jingle without violating intellectual property rights before venturing to use it. Instrumentation must not be so heavy as to drown the lyrics. Bright and lilting instrumental sounds may be selected, if only to add brilliance to the sound of the jingle.

One professional jingle maker, a senior producer of a music recording company, says he normally adopts his melody from a familiar tune. He makes some modifications on old pop songs to give the melody the lead of easy recognition. After all, he says, some 50 to 80 percent of all compositions are virtual adaptations of certain other musical patterns.

6.Question and Answer

This form of dialogue should excite the listeners by way of thought provoking questions and interesting answers.

7. Puzzles and Quizzes

When the listener is placed in a situation where he gropes for answers to questions and puzzles he is captivated. As in other formats, the questions must be stimulating and relevant. Trifling queries, hackneyed and corny questions, will only sound cheap and petty. They will drive the listeners away. Only new ideas and interesting questions will arouse the listeners.

Magazine Program

The name, and perhaps the concept of radio magazine, is borrowed from the printed version. It features a variety of topics and formats that are presented regularly. However, the magazine is often designed with a specific audience in mind. It is usually aired as a regular series of programmed editions - daily, weekly, or several times a week. A good magazine uses a wide range of applicable program forms - dialogue, field reports, special features, interviews, music, puzzles, vox pops, moral messages, jokes, news, practical tips, etc. The most potent reason for tuning to a particular program is that the listener liked what he heard previously. Therefore the program must be of similar mould, not too much of change. Needless to say there must be consistency in the program texture, both at the intellectual level and in the emotional appeal of the material.

The magazine program must present fresh and updated content. It must present frequent surprise features. The program that has predictable content is likely to bore listeners.

The Title

As in any radio program the title should be catchy. The name of the program should preferably reflect the presentation's mood and content.

Signature Tune

Identity music is designed to permeate the whole show. The present trend uses the signature tune as "bed" - played as background, transition and filler of gaps during the program. As such it serves as an additional program identity. Hence, the signature music must convey something of the program style and content such as light hearted, cultural, serious, rural or science-orientated.

The Host or Presenter

The host, or hosts, regulates the tone of the program by approach and style. Unless the host has attained superstar status there is good reason to have two presenters working in a lively dialogue style. It makes for a dynamic presentation.

Should the host be a good broadcaster or an expert on the subject matter? This is one decision the producer may have to make. Indeed, the ideal is to find both in the same person. Diversely the expert can be trained into a broadcaster and vice versa to some limited extent. An alternative is to use both as co-hosts. The person who knows his material is generally preferable. Credibility is crucial. The following are virtues that would add to the "listenability" of the program:

— friendly and outgoing sound

— companionable

— informal

— briskly business-like

— knowledgeable and authoritative.

Linking Style

Once again the way in which items are introduced, the type of humor used, joviality and enthusiasm must remain constant. The presentation should ensure that the various sections and formats blend together.

Keeping the interest high, the dynamic pace going and the vibrant quality of the program sustained is the task of the host. Such qualities are also to be the object of every segment production.

Program Content

The subject matter offered in every section should be new, relevant and interesting. The type of useful information will naturally depend on the particular needs of the target groups. What interests you may be a guide. But first ask yourself how different are you from your listeners.

Section lengths must be trimmed to bite sizes of stimulating scraps and chunks. Reject any item that is too long, too dull, above the listeners' heads or remote from their experience. Throw away items of unsatisfactory technical quality - even if you went 500 kilometers to make the interview.

Long segments of speech, especially by one voice, should be avoided. Different voices, locations, actuality and the use of music bridges and stingers will produce an overall effect of brightness and variety. These music stingers and segment intros need not be trivial.

Studio Production

— Rehearse the scripted narration for pace, pronunciation, emphasis, and style.

— All tapes, segment intros, music, interviews should be well timed.

— Provide the technician with a copy of the script, or at least a sequence guide. Confer with him/her on cue points and on flow of material. In and out cues must be clear with the technician.

— When recording or doing the program live give warning of approaching cues to the technician. Alert the studio operator or engineer of coming up segments, ending or starting of new material.

— Recognize the limitations of the machine and the personnel who will be handling the engineering side of the production.

Radio Voice Performance

Voice that little sound produced by vibrations in the throat and mouth triggered by small amounts of wind passing through the upper respiratory system, can move a whole army. It can also prevent armies from marching. By learning to use and control the voice, "armies" can be "created" and "dissipated". How do you communicate on radio so that you will influence the lives of people in your community? This pursuit is not easy, but when you discover how to use your voice properly you will be on your way. The word 'announcer' is used primarily to describe any one of the men and women who convey information via the electronic media. The term includes several categories of radio performers - deejay, newscaster, emcee, sports caster, host, narrator and commentator. An important and fascinating radio performing personality, not usually included in the announcing group, is the drama talent.

Qualities of Radio Performers

The first responsibility of the men and women behind the mike is to communicate in an intelligible way. Hence, the radio performer needs to develop and refine his/her speaking skills - articulation, enunciation, pronunciation, variety, intonation and naturalness. Increasingly, education in the communication field has become an important factor. While a strong case can be made for a formal education, education alone is not a guarantee of employment, much less of success. Other inherent qualities serving as capital are the talent of the performer, basic speaking qualities, intelligence and natural rapport with the audience. Regardless, all the inborn and acquired qualities of a beginner announcer, or talent, could be enhanced through practice, study and conscientious effort to improve.

Experience may come in all shapes and forms. The expectation is that experience cultivates the endowed abilities of a person and moulds his/her personality. Confidence, adeptness and maturity are, of course, acquired through years of actual work on the air. One can never stop working at improving.

Voice Quality

No one will dispute that a naturally rich and lushly textured voice is an initial asset to an aspiring performer. A deep voice alone does not shape an announcer or a talent. Take an industry survey. Not all the top radio personalities possess the deep golden voice. What most of them posses is the ability to talk in a clear, concise and personable style. After all, that is what communication is all about. The substance and choice of material for the speech is another issue that will not be discussed in this module.

Every person can cultivate his/her voice to a level that is pleasing and appealing to listeners. There are ways to enhance voice quality, to strengthen a weak or thin voice. For example, correct breathing helps greatly. Simply allow the lungs to replenish themselves with air during pauses. Do not gasp or force air into the lungs. Lack of oxygen when speaking can make the voice weak.

Poor breathing may be attributed to a number of things such as bad posture. Slouching, slumping or sitting too rigidly twists and contorts the lungs and the diaphragm. When the body is bent over it is difficult to take in air freely.

Relaxing the Voice

A relaxed voice sounds best. A nervous or agitated voice loses its depth, range and texture. Radio performers must learn to relax before they go on air.

Rotating the upper body and the head for several minutes can relieve tightness in the muscles related to the production of the voice, specifically those in the neck or shoulders.

Casually flexing the arms and shoulder muscles, letting the jaw hang open and shaking the arms may loosen up muscles. Deep breathing exercises and humming can work to loosen up the muscles around the voice box.

Some broadcasters meditate before airtime to achieve a relaxed state. A short walk in the fresh air, if possible, may help.

Articulation

Easy and clear expression is another key to improve voice quality. Proper articulation and enunciation add substance to the voice. The tongue, lips and jaw must effectively form words. Unclear speech generally stems from deficient use of the mouth and jaw muscles. All the resonation chambers - mouth, throat, nostrils and chest - must be active and balanced. Mumbling and slurring of words makes for incomprehensible speech, often the defect of many broadcasters. Practice is the only guarantee that will improve articulation and enunciation. Taping one's voice and listening to it may reveal defects and can certainly speed up the process of development.

Inflection

Using the blind medium, a radio talent or announcer improves his performance by varying tone and pitch. Moving voice pitch from low to high, or vice versa, better conveys color and emotion. Whether doing sports casting, a drama personification or a deejay stint the voice performer must be able to alter an otherwise monotonous delivery. Do not exaggerate so as to sound affected and pretentious! There is no alternative to being natural.

Nervousness

Microphone fear is not an unusual phenomenon, especially for newcomers. Most of the fear is self-imposed. Fear is self-defeating if not checked and it is only the broadcast performer who can defuse his/her apprehension. Indeed, experience does eventually develop confidence but there are things that the inexperienced broadcast performer can do to overcome microphone anxiety. A broadcaster who is prepared to deliver his/her piece should automatically feel secure. He/she is not only confident of the content of script [if he/she prepared it] he/she has also spent time rehearsing. Concentrating on the content of the material rather than the performance can help vanquish fear.

Accents

Radio management normally seeks announcers and performers who are free of regional accents, unless there is the intention to portray provincial or ethnic identities. Nonetheless, more than a few performers have succeeded in carrying their peculiar home accent to a successful career in the competitive broadcasting world. In community radio it is even an advantage.

Pronunciation

The problem of inaccurately pronouncing words often stems from the:

— poor articulation of word parts

— lack of familiarity with a word or name.

Hence, avoid a lazy mouth and slurring of words. Effective articulation contributes to good pronunciation.

Since announcers are often models of good speech, on air they have the responsibility to demonstrate good language - correct grammar and correct pronunciation. Furthermore, listeners take pronunciation as an index of wisdom and familiarity with facts. When encountering strange and unfamiliar words, don't guess, check the dictionary or consult a knowledgeable person. Names of people and places are often pitfalls.

Ad-libbing

To adlib with authority and ease the voice performer must have an agile mind. Effective adlibbing is anchored on knowledge of subject matter. There are numerable situations demanding that the reporter, the announcer, deejay and the talk show host possess skills in delivering spontaneous speech.

A thorough appreciation of the situation, and insight regarding the topic being extemporized, helps the announcer from getting caught without anything to say. Therefore, research and preparation help the announcer to gather a wealth of knowledge from which to derive sensible, though unscripted, speech.

Even in an impromptu situation the skilful ad-libber immediately tries to make a structure of his/her speech in his/her mind. A good beginning and strong ending can be achieved if the habit of organizing thoughts is ingrained in the radio voice performer. As in everything else, practice can enhance spontaneity. Tape yourself describing an object or a situation.

Effercive Radio Announcing

The announcer should create a favorable impression with the audience. He/she should have a balanced personality, be extrovert to the extent that he/she speaks with assurance and conviction. He/she should have an interest in people and appreciate what makes listeners think, act and say the things they do. He/she should enjoy meeting people from all walks of life. He/she should enjoy reading and be capable of appreciating and interpreting good writing.

Today's radio announcer is a salesman, performer, teacher and a good citizen. He/she advertises, educates, informs and entertains. He/she influences buying habits and tastes. He/she affects the social, cultural, and political life of the community.

The good announcer is creative enough to come up with fresh ideas each day. He/she is serious enough to discuss civic problems, and humorous enough to greet every morning with a smile, a good joke and a happy song.

The capable announcer is more than a voice. He/she is a good citizen, sitting in a key spot with a realistic approach to identifying with community life and taking part in a large number of charity drives and worthwhile projects.

If one seriously intends to exploit potential to the hilt, the announcer must establish a program of practice. The frequency and length of practice depends on how many habits need changing. How often should a beginner practice? The more frequently the better. However, speech practice should not be a half-hearted, absent-minded ritual. Without a critical person evaluating one's speech, pointing to the undesirable points and those that need to be improved, the practice will lead to nothing other than to establish the habit of repeating mistakes. He/she should seek an objective ear, or better still - ears, to listen and provide critical evaluation.

Analyzing the speech of others is recommended. It is important that the performer wanting to improve his trade hears and scrutinizes varieties of speech, good and bad. He/she needs to make comparisons to identify what is good about one voice and bad about another.

8

Tips for Effective Radio Reporting

Radio can be a lot of things: It can be a news report. It can be a commentary. It can be a conversation. It can be an audio postcard. Your story can be a combination of all this and more. Using voices and sounds to tell a story are great ways to get your views/points across to an audience. Here are some ways to report using audio.

— *Keep an audio journal:* Use the tape recorder as an electronic diary. Relax and try to forget about the microphone. Speak the way you do normally. Imagine that you're just talking to a friend. Being natural takes practice.

— *Do interviews:* Talk to your family, your friends, your bus driver, the fireman down the street. Get people to tell you their stories.

— *Story Ideas:* Just about anything can make a good radio story. A profile on where you live, your school, your family history, how teens in your school feel about their community and their futures. A special occasion - Christmas and Christmas traditions unique to your community, New Years Eve, Drama in your school. It can be about an issue that affects you.

— *Sample Story Formats:*

   — *soundscapes* - a creative mix of sound and voice, mixed digitally, about an event or issue, usually 4 to 5 min in length.

— *mini-docs* - a highly focused mix of script and voice/interview clips, with a sound bed, usually 4 to 6 minutes in length.

— *commentaries* - the taped performance of a written (and edited) script - not about a macro issue - but about a personal issue/experience, usually 3 min in length.

— *streeters* - a mix of voices/interview clips (one after the other) about an event or issue, about 3 to 4 minutes in length. usually the same question is posed to all interviewed.

— *discussions* - a taped group discussion hosted by a New Voicer on a topic chosen by the group, usually edited down from 20 minutes of freewheeling talk to about 5 to 6 minutes of broadcast-ready tape.

— *Be curious*: Think like a reporter. The best thing about carrying around a tape recorder is that it gives you permission to ask people about themselves. Sometimes you find yourself talking to people – even friends and family – about things you would never talk about without a microphone. Being a reporter is a license to be curious.

— *Paint a picture with your voice:* Be a play-by-play announcer. Tell us where you are, who you're talking to, the date, the time, what's happening. Be the listeners' eyes and ears.

— *Show, don't tell*: Be creative and pay attention to words, sound and language. Good tour guides do more than just talk, they show. There are tricks for "showing" things on the radio. You can actually point to objects, for example: "over there on the sidewalk is a big blue dog." Even though the listener can't see the dog, a space is created in our imagination for where the blue dog should be. You can often use the microphone the same way you would a movie camera: panning, cutting, zooming in for a close-up. All of these things help create a picture inside our heads. It may sound funny, but radio is a very visual medium. You have to give listeners something to "look" at... with their imagination instead of their eyes.

— *Use the small details to tell the big stories:* Look for the little things that surprise you. Here's an example: Mrs. Jones is forty-five years old, a doctor, has a family and a dog. But even more interesting — and revealing — is the fact that Mrs. Jones sets every single clock in her house five minutes fast, and that she collects bus transfers from her commute to work and keeps them all in a shoe box in the closet. You can learn a lot about people from a few unexpected details.

— *Be there:* Let things happen in front of your tape recorder. Record in the moment, instead of telling us about it later. The best documentaries are the ones that let the audience participate and experience things as they happen. There are two types of tape: verb tape (action) and adjective tape (description). Adjective tape is good, but verb tape is more powerful because it pulls the listener inside your story. More verbs. Less adjectives. Be prepared, don't leave home without it If you want things to "happen" in your story, you have to carry your tape recorder with you as much as possible. You should be prepared to be in the right place at the right time. You never know when you will stumble onto something that will be the best part of your story. Being lucky requires a lot of work.

— *Always strive for one "memorable moment":* Every story should have at least one little part that you just completely love: a great clip of tape, a good scene, a funny anecdote, an unexpected detail. It's the thing you run back and tell your friends about. Often the "memorable moment" is something that catches you by surprise.

— *Record everything*: Long pauses are okay. Umms are okay. Saying stupid and embarrassing things is okay. Often the stuff you think is weird, worthless, or that you initially want to edit out, will end up being the best and most surprising parts of the story.

Technical Tips

— *Get comfortable with the equipment*: Play around with the recording device (minidisc recorder, DAT machine, tape recorder) on your own until you are very familiar with all the buttons and knobs. It's important to do this before you begin; if you're relaxed with the recorder and the microphone, the people you're interviewing will be too.

— *Get organized*: Always make sure you have enough minidiscs, DATs or cassettes and an extra set of batteries. Don't leave long cables hanging out, or you'll have to spend time untangling everything. Get a shoulder bag to hold everything. The more prepared you are, the more you can concentrate on the important things.

— *Do a test*: Always do a test before you begin. Record a few seconds, then play it back to make sure the sound is good.

— *Label your tapes and disks*: Always label everything before you start. When you're in the field it's easy to forget and tape over something you've just recorded. (It happens.) And after you're done recording, pop out the safety tabs to make sure you don't erase over anything.

— *Always wear your headphones*: Recording without headphones is like a photographer taking pictures without looking through the viewfinder. Headphones help you focus on exactly what you're recording. If something sounds weird, stop and check it out.

— *Beware of the pause button*: When recording, make sure the tape is rolling and that you're not in pause mode. Don't use the pause button. It's a very tricky little button it can make you think you are recording when you're not.

— *Keep the microphone close*: The most important thing of all: keep the microphone close to the sound source (your mouth or the mouth of the person you're interviewing). About 5-6 inches is good, the length of your outstretched hand. If it's any farther away you will still be able to hear what people say, but the recording will lose its power and intimacy. It's also best to keep the microphone a little bit below the mouth to avoid the "popping P" sound.

— *Collect good sounds*: Every time you record, collect all the specific sounds you can think of: dogs barking, doors slamming, the radio being turned on, the sound of your blender, or even your mom snoring. Be creative. You will use these sounds later when you produce the story.

— *Record everything*: Long pauses are okay. Umms are okay. Saying stupid and embarrassing things is okay. Often the stuff you think is weird, worthless, or that you initially want to edit out, will end up being the best and most surprising parts of the story.

Interview Tips

A good interview depends on more than just a list of questions.

— *Make your approach polite and respectful*: Explain what you're doing. Be confident. Assume your subject will want to talk to you. The way people respond depends on how you approach them. The trick is to make people realize that your project is both fun and important. Also let people know that everything can and will be edited.

— *Make the interview situation comfortable before you start*: Move chairs around, get close so you don't have to reach. For example: sit at the corner of a table, not across, so you can hold the microphone close and your arm won't grow weak.

— *Record interviews in the quietest place possible*: Be careful of TVs, stereos, traffic noise, wind, anything that will be distracting from the interview. Even refrigerators can make an annoying sound that you might not notice until you get home and listen to the tape. Sometimes you want the sound of the environment. But it's best to gather that separately, and record all the important interviews in a quiet place. Anytime you are in a loud room or noisy environment, remember to collect a few minutes of that sound on its own ‹ what is called a "sound bed" or ambiance. If you have to record an interview in a loud place, it can help to bring the microphone even closer (2-3 inches) to the speaker's mouth.

— *Keep the microphone close*: It bears repeating here: just as when you are recording yourself, the most important thing is to keep the microphone close to the speaker's mouth (5-6 inches). If you want to record your questions too, you'll have to move the microphone back and forth.

— *Always hold the microphone*: Don't let the interviewee take the microphone. It's better if you keep control of the equipment.

— *Put people at ease*: Talk about the weather. Joke about the microphone. It's a good idea to begin recording a few minutes before you actually start the interview. That helps you avoid the uncomfortably dramatic moment: "Okay, now we will begin recording." Just chat about anything while you begin rolling tape. Before they realize it, you've started the interview.

— *Maintain eye contact*: Keep the microphone below the line of sight. Talk to people just as you would normally. In groups, don't let everyone talk at once If you are interviewing a few people at once, have them gather around close to the microphone.

— *Try to focus on one or two people*: Less is more. You're better off zeroing in on the characters you think are the best.

—   *Watch out for uh-huhs*: Be aware of natural conversational responses like uh-huhs or laughter. Try to use quiet responses: a concerned nod, questioning eyes, the silent laugh.

—   *Don't be afraid of pauses and silences*: Resist the temptation to jump in. Let the person think. Often the best comments come after a short, uncomfortable silence when the person you are interviewing feels the need to fill the void and add something better.

—   *Let people talk in full sentences*: Avoid questions that can be answered with a simple yes or no. Instead of, "Are you a doctor?" ask, "Tell me how you became a doctor." Remember that you want people to tell you stories.

—   *Get people to 'do' things*: In addition to the sit-down interview, have people show you around; record a tour of their house, their photo album or their car engine. It's more fun to get people moving around and talking about what they're doing, rather than just sitting in a chair. It helps to relax people before and during an interview. It's also a way to get good tape.

—   *Listening is the key*: A good interview is like a conversation. Prepare questions, but don't just follow a list. The most important thing is to listen and have your questions come naturally. If your questions are rehearsed and hollow, the answers will be too. If you are curious and your questions are spontaneous and honest, you will get a good interview.

—   *Interviewing is a two-way street:* Conducting a good interview depends, in part, on asking the right questions. But it is also important to establish a relationship with the person you are interviewing. Sometimes it is appropriate to share some information about yourself in an interview. Remember that it's a conversation. What's more, for it to be an honest conversation, people must feel that you care about what they say, and will honor and respect their words and stories.

— *The foolproof question:* Here is one simple question that always works: "How do you see things differently since (blank) happened?" If you're talking to your mailman about the time he was chased for 2 blocks by a neighborhood dog, ask how he feels every time he goes by that house.

— *Take notes:* Remember specific details. Take notes immediately after the interview, while it's still fresh in your mind. You can also use the tape recorder like a dictating machine.

— *Relax and forget about the microphone:* One thing that's always amazing: in the beginning of an interview people are usually stiff and self-conscious, but after a while, they forget all about the tape recorder and start to be themselves.

— *The last secret to a great interview:* There is one simple rule for getting people to talk openly and honestly: you have to be genuinely curious about the world around you.

The Gear

— *Tape Recorder:* For diary projects, using Marantz PMD 222 cassette recorder will be nkce. Cassette machines are good because they are simple, durable, relatively cheap and have long battery life. Using the automatic level control setting for people who are not familiar with the equipment is highly recommendable. The best cassette field recorder is the Sony TCD5). It's more expensive, but will last longer than you will.

— *DAT Recorder:* DAT Recorder DAT recorders offer better sound quality but are more expensive and fragile. If you want to use DAT, the best low-end model is the Sony PCM-M1. Beware of the mini-connectors on these machines Ða little pull and the microphone comes unplugged.

—   *Minidisc Recorder*: There are many different versions on the market. They are a good economical alternative to DAT. Costs tange from $150 to $1,500, depending on quality. Check out Transom's equipment page for more information on what minidisc to buy.

—   *Microphones*: A decent microphone is very important. Whethet you use a professional recorder or a low-end consumer model, always plug in an external microphone rather than rely on the machine's built-in microphone. Beyer M58 or Electro Voice RE50 are the microphones we use. Directional (shotgun) microphones are also very helpful in certain situations, when you have to record from farther away.

9
Radio Interviews

Radio's main advantage over newspapers is that the audience can hear what people say in their own words and voice. Broadcast interviews and quotes carry an authority which quotes in the newspapers can never match. An interview is aimed at drawing out information, ideas or emotion from an expert, a personality or a regular person through asking questions. An interview is not a discussion. Therefore, the best advice given to an interviewer is to not be drawn into answering questions that the interviewee may put to him/her.

The interviewer is not there to argue, agree or disagree. He/she is there to ask questions! An interview is expected to be a spontaneous event. Any hint of it being rehearsed or scripted spoils the program material. There are three parties to the interview, the interviewer asking questions, the interviewee answering those questions and the listeners listening to the whole process. The most important party - the listener - is absent from the act.

Importance of Interview

A good interview:

— adds variety and interest to the program or the station

— adds credibility to the broadcast

— adds authenticity to a presentation

— makes for easy listening

— adds human interest

— allows members of the audience to participate

— brings experts, news sources and personalities into direct contact with other members of society.

Components of a Good Interview

Whether it is with a scientist, man-on-the-street, an outstanding farmer or a movie personality the following are virtues of a good interview.

— The purpose is clear. The interviewer is guided by the specific information he aims to get from the interviewee.

— Preparation and research is well done, no matter how short the time allowed. Tapes and fully charged batteries are on hand. Enough of the basic information has been obtained regarding the topic and the interviewee.

— Questions are focused on the objectives. They are direct and short, simple and intelligible as well as stimulating.

— The discussion develops logically from beginning to end.

— The audience is involved. Subject matter is relevant to the needs of the listeners. Questions elicit what the average person likes to know.

— The interviewer conducts the interview impartially. He/ she does not make judgments and does not express his/ her personal opinion

— The interviewer controls the pace, topic development, duration and the mood of the interview.

— The interview sounds spontaneous and conversational.

— The interview is interesting and must sound so. It should hold the audience from beginning to end.

Dig into the Background

Gather sufficient background on the subject matter of the interview. Listeners have little tolerance for shallowness and ignorance on the part of the interviewer.

You may not be given time to gather background on subject matter, especially for a short preparation interview such as an "ambush interview." Like the soldier's ammunition, you must forever need to carry much of the information in your head.

The interviewer must keep up to date about stories involving the station and the community. Reading and listening continually is unavoidable for real broadcasters.

Prepare the Questions

You must spend time preparing questions before interviewing. Jot down questions and arrange them in logical order (though you may not follow the same order in the actual interview). Often the mind becomes clearer when contents are spilled on to paper. Even if notes are not referred to this can be a worthwhile exercise. Beware of deviating from the designated topic to put other topics that might interest you, or a like-minded minority, but would be irrelevant to the majority. Keep to the point. Good questions naturally bring out good answers. With research and preparation the interviewer develops the knack of thinking ahead to the answer he/she is likely to receive before asking the questions.

Get Your Facts Right

There is nothing more embarrassing or more likely to undermine the broadcasters reputation, and that of his or her station, than an ignorant and ill-informed line of questioning.

Reporter: Director Holgado, how do you deal with the cholera epidemic that has broken out here in Olutanga?

Interviewee: Well, two cases of typhoid hardly constitute an epidemic. By the way, I am actually the assistant director and my name is Dr. Cortez. Dr. Holgado has been reassigned elsewhere.

Check Arrangements

Be sure that an appointment has been made. Confirm the time and place.

Check your portable recorder. You must be familiar with operating the particular machinery in use. There must be enough battery if required. If you should use the AC electricity, is there electricity and appropriate outlets in the place of interview? Does the microphone work? Do you have a blank tape? If necessary, carry spare tapes and batteries. A thorough equipment check should only take two minutes. It can save you hours, and your face.

Personal Presentation

How you look and conduct yourself can make or break the radio station. Your clothes and manner will introduce you to a first time interviewee. His/her first impression of you will affect the whole interview.

The way you sit, how you cross your legs and arms, reveals how you feel. If your interviewee is sitting legs crossed and arms folded you know that he/she is on the defensive and needs to be relaxed. Beware of putting up barriers. Even if you intend your interview to be adversarial, be friendly. To use the lingo of sport, the best punches are delivered when one's opponent's guard is down.

The Pre-Interview Chat

The short conversation before the interview establishes the rapport between the participants. Here the interviewer sounds out the course he/she proposes for the interview.

A congenial greeting, a firm handshake and a good deal of eye contact are conducive to good rapport. With the initial greeting you make an impression of who you are and the credibility of the radio station. If the interviewee is tense and nervous he/she needs to be put at ease. A complimentary phrase, a joke or a quip can effectively dissipate the fright of first time interviewees.

Rehearsing

Avoid rehearsing an interview, if necessary simply discuss it generally with your subject. Repeats of interviews are just like trying to rehearse a meal, the taste of the food could no longer be savored. Even a nervous interviewee performs better when the adrenalin is flowing. Never allow your interviewee to read from a script. Reassure him/her that he/she will perform better without reading from scripts or from notes.

Using Notes

The preparation and writing of questions is useful in planning the interview. The problems when using them during the interview are:

— eye contact is lost.

— When the interviewer is concentrating on the questions, he/ she is unable to listen to the interviewee.

— Fixed questions make for an inflexible interview. If you intend to use notes, use them sparingly. One good practice is to make brief notes or headings of important points only.

Ask Questions that Will Get Answers

Questions should be carefully structured to produce good, useful quotes rather than one-word comments or monosyllabic grunts.

— Who - calls for a name in response.

— What - asks for a description.

— When - pins down the timing of event.

— Where - locates it.

— Why - seeks an interpretation or explanation.

— How - solicits an opinion or an interpretation.

Avoid Questions that Yield Yes/No

A Yes or No answer is often unusable. It is useful only if it will establish a fact that will open the way for a new line of questioning or when it is the outstanding issue on hand. "Did you endorse the use the planting of Bt corn?"

Avoid Questions that call for Monologues

"Will you tell me what the position is regarding environmental problems in this country?" With this question you can leave your tape recorder running and come back an hour later when the tape is finished! You must pin your question to one clearly defined point. "What do you consider is the most urgent environmental problem of this town?"

Proper scope of your question is important. Too open a question leads to long speeches. Make it too narrow and your interview becomes halting. Flowing dialogue can be achieved with an interactive question eliciting an answer of appropriate length.

Clear Questions

Clear, simple and straightforward questions make for intelligible listening. Stick to one point at a time! The threads of issues should be clearly untangled.

Progress from Point to Point

To achieve logical flow each question should relate to the previous point. When the interviewer needs to refer to a previous point this should be done neatly and followed through by another question that advances the argument. Each question should naturally arise from the previous answer. If the two are only distantly related the interviewer should use a bridge.

Avoid Double Questions

One question should be asked at a time otherwise the interviewee might ignore one question and choose to answer the other. Even the most willing of subjects may forget half of the questions.

Relevance to Audience Needs

The interview must concern itself with the lives of people. An interview is neither merely a mental exercise nor plain art. It must address the needs of the community or society.

Immediately move away from abstract ideas. Confront day-to-day realities. If the question is about poverty do not talk about living standards, ask about the food that the people eat, get a description of their homes. Examples should be concrete and real. If you ask if the rate of inflation is real the concept should be brought down to wages, salaries and the price of specific food.

Mixing Statements with Questions

Occasionally, giving background information is called for before arriving at the question. The question and information should be kept separate for the sake of clarity. Then the question at the end should be brief. " Now that the Cowboy team has seven wins their coach claims that they will be this year's champion. Does your Rambo team have any chance?" Avoid statements posing as questions.

Avoid Sounding Ignorant

Always check your facts before you launch into an interview. Clear up details during the pre-chat.

Get basic information from all possible sources when you are not familiar with a situation. Beware when you rely merely on your interviewee for backgrounders, he/she can manipulate the interview to his/her advantage.

10
Community Radio

Community radio is a type of radio service that caters to the interests of a certain area, broadcasting material that is popular to a local audience but is overlooked by more powerful broadcast groups. The term has somewhat different meanings in the United Kingdom, the United States, Canada, and Australia. In the UK, it originated in the many illegal pirate radio stations that came about from the influx of Afro-Caribbean migrants in cities such as London, Birmingham, Bristol, and Manchester in the 1970s. Therefore, "community radio" remains synonymous with "pirate radio" for many people there. In America, community radio is more commonly non-profit and non-commercial, often using licenced class D FM band transmitters, although pirate radio outlets have been operated in many places. Canadian and Australian community stations operate somewhat similarly to their American counterparts.

Vision of Community Radio Outlets

Modern-day community radio stations often serve their listeners by offering a variety of music selections that are not necessarily catered for by larger corporate radio stations. Community radio outlets may also carry news and information programming geared toward the local area, particularly immigrant or minority groups that are poorly served by other media outlets. Unfortunately, when these broadcasters are illegal pirate radio outlets, they sometimes refuse to respect other legal radio stations and other entities, such as emergency services, and interfere with their transmissions. This can give community stations and conscientious pirate stations an unwarranted disreputable image. Pirate radio stations can apply for a broadcasting licence but they will usually need to go off air for a time to present a legal case. Community stations and pirate stations (where they are tolerated) can be valuable assets for a region. Community radio stations are aligned with communities rather than corporations.

History of Community Radio

Although there are many competing claims, it is widely accepted that the world's first community radio stations emerged in Bolivia during a tin miners' strike around 1947. Their trade union decided to use some of the emergency strike fund to pay for 27 local radio stations, offering union members and their families access to the airwaves and opportunities for social benefits – now a familiar formula. It is a measure of the power of the medium that over the next forty years these stations (and others in Latin America) faced regular persecution, arrests of activists and seizure of equipment by authorities.

Meanwhile in California, the Pacifica Foundation set up the USA's first 'listener-sponsored' radio station in 1950 – a variation on community radio that is still the most common model in North America today. From these beginnings, the demand for community radio began to take root around the world. Amid the political radicalism of the 1960s and 70s, community radio activists began lobbying for access to the airwaves across the developed world, both through legal lobbying and less-than-legal broadcasting.

Australia – with its small, dispersed population and little in the way of local commercial or public broadcasting in many areas – began licensing community stations in 1972, and now boasts one of the healthiest community media sectors in the world. In Africa and Asia progress was slower, although stations are now widespread in Southern Africa, Vietnam, India, the Philippines and beyond.

Although the nature of community radio varies considerably from country to country and station to station, some elements are consistent almost everywhere. Community radio anywhere in the world is committed to:

— Community development rather than profit;

— Providing access to the airwaves to underrepresented voices;

— Being based at grassroots level and serving a distinct local community;

— Being established and run primarily by volunteers and activists rather than paid staff

The role of pirate broadcasters such as Radio Caroline and Radio Luxembourg in pushing the development of mainstream radio has been well documented. In short, they provided the blueprint (not to mention many of the broadcasters) for BBC Radio 1 and many of the commercial stations we still hear today. These commercially-minded ventures have little to do with community radio as we know it.

But much less has been written about smaller, local pirate stations operating in urban areas and around campuses since the 1960s. It was these stations – driven by a love of radio and a perceived need for community broadcasting – that are the true ascendants of modern community radio. As time passed and wisdom accumulated, many activists began to see the advantages to be gained from working alongside rather than in opposition to the legal broadcasting apparatus.

In Britain the drive towards legal recognition was led by the Community Radio Association (now the Community Media Association), formed in 1983 to campaign for a third tier of broadcasting alongside the BBC and commercial stations. The CRA included many veterans of unlicensed stations, plus academics, community activists and other experienced campaigners.

Over the past two decades, the sector has lobbied successive governments and powerbrokers, patiently chipping away at the obstacles and objections. The (then) regulators at The Radio Authority helpfully identified spare pockets of frequencies which could perhaps be used for the purpose.

The culmination of these negotiations was contained in The Communications Act 2003 and then the Community Radio Order 2004, which established the final legal framework for full-time, long-term community radio licences in the UK. Throughout this process, the British communityradio sector, in negotiation with state regulators, has come to a broad consensus about what community radio should actually be. At its simplest, it has two crucial features:

— It is not run for financial profit;

— It is made by a community, for the benefit of that community.

If a station is being run for profit, or it is being imposed upon a community from outside, then it is not a community radio station. Community radio should also serve two principal functions:

— *Access:* an outlet for cultural, political and artistic voices and opinions which are excluded elsewhere;

— *Development:* social, cultural and educational gain for the community as a whole and for its individual members.

If a radio station is not offering access to voices which are under-represented elsewhere, and if a station is not of practical benefit to its community, it is not a community radio station. It should also be emphasised that a community radio station as we understand it operates within the law and alongside the authorities. Unlicensed pirate stations can offer access to the marginalised, and can under certain circumstances offer social gain to their community. But it is a sad truth that a radio station cannot ever be sustainable when seizure of equipment and arrest are a daily risk. So to any unlicensed broadcasters reading this, we strongly advise getting yourself straight. The rewards are limitless.

Models of Community Radio

Philosophically we can see two distinct approaches to community radio, though the models are not necessarily mutually exclusive. One stresses service or community model - focused on what the station can do for the community. The other stresses involvement and participation.

Within the service model localism is often prized, as community radio, as a third tier, can provide content focused on a more local or particular community than larger operations. Sometimes, though, the provision of syndicated content that is not already available within the station's service area, is seen as a desirable form of service. Within the United States, for example, many stations syndicate content from groups such as Radio, such as Democracy Now, on the basis that it provides a form of content not otherwise available.

Within the access or participatory model, the participation of community members in producing content is seen as a good in itself. While this model does not necessarily exclude a service approach, there is a tension between the two, as outlined, for example, in Jon Bekken's Community Radio at the Crossroads.

Characteristics of Community Radio

A community radio station is one that is operated in the community, for the community, about the community and by the community. The community can be territorial or geographical - a township, village, district or island. It can also be a group of people with common interests, who are not necessarily living in one defined territory. Consequently, community radio can be managed or controlled by one group, by combined groups, or of people such as women, children, farmers, fisher folk, ethnic groups, or senior citizens.

What distinguishes community radio from other media is the high level of people's participation, both in management and program production aspects. Furthermore, individual community members and local institutions are the principal sources of support for its operation.

Following are the characteristics of community radio:

— It serves a recognizable community.

— It encourages participatory democracy.

— It offers the opportunity to any member of the community to initiate communication and participate in program making, management and ownership of the station.

— It uses technology appropriate to the economic capability of the people, not that which leads to dependence on external sources.

— It is motivated by community well being, not commercial considerations.

— It promotes and improves problem solving.

Principles of Community Radio Operation

a) Access to the facility is the primary step towards the full democratization of the communication system. People have access not only to the media products but also to the media facilities. The feedback channel is always open and full interaction between the producers and receivers of messages is maintained.

b) Participation in the production and management of media is the logical step after access. Citizen's participation in radio is allowed at all levels - from planning to implementation and evaluation of the project. It involves the citizens in the decision-making process, including making decisions about the contents, duration and program schedule. The citizens, or their representatives, also have a voice in the management and financing of radio program projects.

c) Self-management of the communication facility follows participation. Once the community members gain necessary experience and assimilate the required skills there is no reason for preventing them from managing and owning the radio station.

d) Community mandate is the inevitable result of the process of democratizing the communication system. Community mandate encompasses not only management but also ownership of the radio.

e) Accountability is exercised. There is no sense in having the opportunity to operate, control and manage the station when accountability is not in the hands of the managers and broadcasters.

Community radio gives community members access to information because it gives them access to the means of communication. The most relevant information - educational and developmental - is disseminated and exchanged. Important local issues are aired. A free market place of ideas and opinions is opened up and people are given the opportunity to express themselves socially, politically and culturally. Community radio helps to put the community members in charge of their own affairs.

Distinct Features of Community Radio

Facilities

A community radio often uses the basic production and transmission equipment appropriate for the size, needs and capability of the community. Usual transmission equipment is comprised of a low-power FM transmitter of 20 to 100 watts. The production facility can range from a simple tape recorder or a karaoke playback machine to a simple studio that consists of an audio-mixer, tape decks, CD player and microphones.

In some facilities a simple loudspeaker or the community audio tower system (CATS) is used, either independently or coupled with a transmitter. Technically speaking, the community audio tower system is not radio. However, even with its apparent advantages and disadvantages the CATS serves a purpose similar to that of community radio. Regardless, the community prepares regular programs.

Sources of Support

Much, if not all, of the resources needed for operating the community radio come from individuals, institutions and organizations within the community. Private individuals are motivated to contribute to the station. Various fund raising schemes such as raffles draws, benefit dances, selling of FM receiver set are held. Institutional advertisements or sponsorships or outright donations are accepted. Host institutions such as schools, foundations, cooperatives, local government units and religious organizations may provide backstop support. Resource generation and appropriate fund raising schemes are planned and implemented by the station management.

Management

The management of a community radio station is entrusted to the Community Radio Council (CRC). The CRC is a multi-sectoral body, which obtains its mandate from the community to run the station. CRC is trained for the purpose for managing the station. It usually has seven to 25 members who are representatives from the most important sectors for the community such as farmers, fishermen, women, youth, laborers, ethnic communities, educators, and religious denominations. The members are initially selected from among wellrespected community leaders on the basis of their moral integrity, probity and community involvement. Eventually the council has a right to co-opt new members or replace those who retire. The functions of the council include, among other things, deliberating on the direction and polices of the station, and making major decisions for the situation.

Program Makers

A core of selected community members who have the time, ability and enthusiasm are chosen to prepare regular programs. Like the members of the management council, the program makers are from various sectors of the community. The program makers undergo training on preparing programs of various formats such as radio talk, interview, magazine, music, news, drama, documentary, or plugs.

The initial training normally lasts from two weeks to one month and is conducted by professionals and people from the academe. The production of community-oriented participatory programs is emphasized during the training.

The program makers are volunteers from the community. Although most of them do not receive honoraria, they undertake the day-to-day operation of the station. They serve as producers, announcers, hosts, scriptwriters, news gatherers, technicians and administrative personnel. Under the leadership of the designated senior manager, they prepare programs, operate the equipment, and handle the administrative responsibilities of the station.

Programs

Community radio's program format is similar to that of a mainstream radio including news, drama, talk shows, interviews and magazine. However, in community radio programs, there is a heavy emphasis on local contents. For instance a program will feature the availability of seedlings from local farmers and the price of vegetables in the market along with public service items. News content focuses on events coming from the municipality, villages and local organizations. Discussions centers on issues of local concern such as ordinances, bridges that have to be completed, or the setting up of a factory in the village. Broad participation by community members is encouraged. There is a dominance of local language, color and personality in the manner in which programs are presented.

Not only the regular production group produces programs. Cultural and neighborhood programs are prepared with a wider involvement from villagers who may not have formal training in production.

Broadcast Hours

The broadcasters and the management council determine the broadcast hours for a community radio on the basis of the following:

— capability and number of trained personnel;

— availability of electricity or power;

— technical feasibility;

— needs of the community/audience;

— availability of resources necessary for operation;

— competition with other radio stations.

With such considerations, community radio normally comes up with shorter broadcasting hours than commercial or government or public radio.

Stimulating Community Participation

Community residents can be motivated to participate in program making by inviting them to neighborhood and village level production workshops. Peasants, rural women and unschooled people can be trained in the rudiments of broadcasting.

By bringing production to the rural areas, radio is demystified for the people of the community. Many forms of cultural programs and village activities may be adopted and accommodated in radio programming. After all, radio is simply people talking with people.

Activities in Setting-up a Community Radio

Organizing. A core of responsible leaders, initiators and workers who are convinced of the benefits of community radio has to be organized. Research / Evaluation. Baseline research will determine the socioeconomic situation of the community at the start of the community radio project. During early operations a periodic assessment of progress and monitoring has to be done. Evaluative studies are also called for in the later stages of operation.

Training. Three groups of people need to acquire basic skills - the core of managers, program makers and technicians.

Documentation. With a new communication set up it will be in the interests of prospective evaluators, simulators, and adopters to record, on print, film, paper or video the progress of the community radio. Installation of equipment. There will be a need to purchase equipment, construct a studio and put-up a tower. Qualified electronic engineers and/or technicians are to perform these tasks.

Legitimizing Community Radio

Requirements for legalizing the operation of radio stations vary from country to country. Initiators must check with the communicationregulating agency of their respective state. The agency should provide a checklist of requirements for setting up low power radio. In the Philippines, there are two main instruments to be secured from government, which are (1) a congressional [parliament] franchise; and (2) a license from the National Telecommunication Commission (NTC). Low power stations [20 watts and below] that are set up for education and training are not required to get a franchise, only a license that will serve as a permit to buy, install and operate radio. In this case the license is renewed every year but ideally the community radio should have the license valid at least for three to four years without the fear of having to close after a short license period.

Sustainability of Community Radio

Contrary to popular assumption regarding the operation of a commercial station, community radio is not an expensive operation to maintain for the following reasons:

— The operating cost is very low, mostly related to electrical consumption, spare parts, maintenance and office supplies.

— Volunteers, who receive, if any, minimal honorarium, staff the station.

— Management is trained in how to raise money from local, national and international sources for example through donations other fundraising activities.

— Since a community radio serves the interests of the community, people easily assume responsibilities in the operation of the station.

Community Radio Movement

Community radio is fast becoming a sound system of communication all over the world. In most regions and continents, Europe, North America, South America, Africa and Australia there are hundreds, or thousands, of community radios. In Asia there are barely two dozen known community radios that are located in the Philippines, Nepal, Sri Lanka and East Timor. There are so few community radios in Asia because of the domination of governments in the use of radio. There is, however, a growing acceptance of the concept of community radio in many countries of the region.

Equipment

The simplest community radio set up can consist of a low-power transmitter harnessed with an antenna, a tape recorder and a microphone. A motorcycle battery provides the power source. Its total weight may be much less than 10 kilograms. When affordable and necessary, a more technical set up should consist of the transmission equipment, antenna, tower and a decent production studio. This will allow more possibilities for production and mixing of voice, music and sound effect. Listed below is a cost estimate of a basic equipment for community radio.

In addition to the above there may be a need to purchase small items, e.g. extension cords, electrical outlets, etc. A two-way communication system would be ideal for more dynamic newsgathering and reporting. Instead of the above-mentioned analog equipment it is possible to configure the entire production set-up using computers and USB supported recording equipment.

Transmitter

The transmitter is the core piece of equipment in a community radio. The transmitter makes it possible for programs to be sent to distant places. A low-power transmitter can be designed between 5 and 300 watts serving distances of up to an approximate 30 kilometers radius. The customary transmitter available, and often suitable for a town level community, is a 20-watt FM [frequency modulation] transmitter. It can be used as the sole transmission equipment and can also serve as an exciter. Another piece of technology called a linear amplifier, or a power booster, may be attached to the 20-watt transmitter. The power booster could be available, or fabricated, with multiples of 50, 100, 200, 250, 300, and 500 or even 1,000-watts. Electronics engineers claim that the booster is easier to build, hence cheaper, than a transmitter.

FM transmission is often preferred to AM (amplitude modulation) for its features. It is

— Less costly to acquire.

— More available in the market.

— Has better signal quality.

— Requires a less complicated antenna system.

— Consumes less electricity; and

— Has more available frequencies in the band.

The main disadvantage of the FM transmitter is that the signal travels in more or less line-of-sight fashion. FM is most suited to flat terrain where there are no mountain obstructions and tall buildings, or where an elevated site could be identified for putting up the antenna.

Alternatively, an AM transmitter could be used with one distinct advantage. It works better where the terrain is hilly and mountainous. However, it needs a more sophisticated and costly antenna system and uses more electricity.

It must be pointed out that in most countries transmitters may be bought and possessed only upon securing a license from the telecommunicationregulating agency of the government. Depending on suppliers, the price of a 20-watt transmitter can be anywhere from US $400 to $2000. Unfortunately in most developing countries there are no local transmitter manufacturers. Most low-power transmitters are imported from Europe, China, Canada, Australia or the United States.

Signal Reach

The distance that the signal of a FM transmitter can reach is dependent on the following factors:

— Power of the transmitter

— Efficiency of the transmitter

— Height of the antenna

— Terrain of the community

— Atmospheric conditions.

A higher wattage transmitter will give a correspondingly wider coverage. However, the reach is not an exact numerical coefficient of the power. If the 20-watt transmitter hoisted on a 23-meter antenna could be heard with a Class A signal up to 10 kilometers on a flat terrain, the 100 watt transmitter could be expected to provide that same quality signal up to about 15 - 20 kilometers.

Understandably, the capacity of the receiver and its antenna could be factored in approximating strength and quality of reception. Where reception is rather weak, listeners could be advised to attach a metal wire to the antenna that extends to a pole above the roof possibly clear of structures and trees. A more sophisticated receiving antenna for FM radio may also be fabricated for better results. As much as 40% signal reception could be achieved with extended receiver antennas. 3. Mono or Stereo?

Most of the FM transmitter models available these days are stereo. If only for the advantage of more extended reach, a competent technician could disable the stereo function of a transmitter. By deleting the stereo chip, a signal could be strengthened by 20 to 35 percent. It is contended that rural people who crave for information do not mind if they get a mono signal. Stereo sound is more preferred in music broadcasting.

Transmission Antenna

Various antenna makes and designs could be fabricated, the most common of which is the folded single dipole. To increase signal propagation a two-bay or a four-bay antenna could be harnessed.

Antenna Tower

The height of the FM transmission antenna is an important factor that determines maximum signal reach. FM waves travel in nearly line-ofsight fashion. "If you can see it, you can hear it," says an experienced technician. Hills, ridges and building barriers can be overcome by raising the antenna up to approximately 20 to 30 meters. The higher the antenna the better and farther the signal can reach.

An antenna mast can be made of two-inch galvanized iron water pipe joined at the ends, erected and held firmly by guy wires. Triangular steps are also fitted on the side of the pipes to serve climbers. The base of the tower can be reinforced concrete, one square meter into the ground. The tower can also be erected above a strong roof where the mast needs to be fastened even more securely.

The water pipes, which are usually 20-foot sections in length, are arranged in descending diameters. The diameter of the lowest section can be three inches, followed by two inches and 1.5 inches. Bigger pipes are required for a more solid tower, appropriate for typhoon belt areas. Heavier pipes are more costly and will require some effort in erecting. Guy wires should be strong enough not only to hold the sway and weight of the antenna but also to withstand climbers. The guy wires must be secured strongly to the ground with iron pipes impaled about one and a half meters to the ground perpendicular to the direction of the guy wires. Guy wires are stretched in four isosceles directions. In some cases more sophisticated and expensive tower designs are used.

A lightning arrester is always recommended to avert any expensive tower damage on the transmitter during stormy weather situations. The major causes of breakdown for transmitters are unmatched antenna, faulty connections and lightning strikes, which ruin the expensive power module integrated circuit, called BGY 33, of the main transmitter output. The antenna mast should be grounded properly. If the mast is installed on top of a roof a half inch stranded copper wire can be welded to the mast and connected down to an iron bar that is driven into the earth. The iron bar should reach the wet part of the soil in order for the surge of high voltage electricity to be absorbed by the ground. The thick cable that runs from the transmitter to the antenna is usually a co-axial cable. An RG-11 or RG 58 cable is the most commonly used. Its cost is about US$2 per metre. Higher power transmitters of over 400 watts call for a heliax cable that offers the least power loss, but is more expensive than the co-axial cable. Heliax cable could cost about US$24 per metre.

The cable between the transmitter and the antenna must not be longer than 20 metres. With transmission lines longer than 60 feet, much of the transmitter power could be dissipated within the cable.

Location

The program production studio may be set-up in any existing house or room where there is enough space for the equipment and the operators to work. An optimum area for the announcer's booth is 30 square meters, technician's cubicle is 20 square meters, but smaller rooms are possible. In urgent need, the station could be provisionally operated in a cart, on a tricycle or even atop a walking horse.

In a more traditional set-up, a separate building that will house the station may be constructed. The station should preferably have an announcer's booth and a technician's cubicle as well as a receiving and working area.

The following criteria are recommended when choosing a studio site:

i.   Closeness to center of population

ii.   Accessibility to the participants

iii.   Accessibility to the community members

iv.   Low or no rental fee

v.   Neutrality from vested interests

vi.   Security from pilferers and vandals

vii.   Availability of power source

viii.   Freedom from uncontrollable noise [particularly when the studio is not enclosed tightly for air conditioning and noise proofing]

ix.   Favorable technical conditions:

    a. There is an elevated location of transmitter.

    b. It is unobstructed by tall buildings.

    c. It is away from high voltage power lines.

The studio should be centrally located in the community where there is a tall building to hoist the antenna. A higher elevation for the studio location would be an advantage. Where it is necessary to hoist the antenna higher, the studio may be located up to several hundred meters away from the antenna. As mentioned earlier, the co-axial cable linking the transmitter to the antenna should not exceed 20 meters. A preferred set up would be for a program line [a pair of insulated wires connecting the studio to the transmitter] to be extended to the location of the transmitter and studio. Telephone drops wires, or even electric wires can be used as program line. The wire may be propped up on existing electric posts, or bamboo poles, throughout the length of the line. The length of the program line should preferably not be longer than one kilometer.

Building an Inexpensive Studio

The most important part of a studio is the announcer's booth, which houses the production equipment such as tape recorders, turntables, tape decks, audio mixer, amplifier, microphones, or speakers. This is where the announcer conducts his/her live broadcast. In some cases, the technician may control the equipment and the announcer has only the microphone to control. However, most announcers prefer to operate the turntables and tape recorders.

The announcer's booth should optimally have a minimum space of three metres by four metres and should be properly enclosed. The main features of a professional announcer's booth are that it is sound proof and it meets simple acoustical requirements.

It would also be a good idea to have a staff working area that can also serve as a receiving room.

Studio Acoustics

The acoustical balance of the studio room can be achieved by fitting some sections of the wall and ceiling with soft materials such as egg trays, styropor, drapes, coconut coir, curtains, cardboard or mats. The objective is to avoid too much bouncing of sound from the wall to the microphone. Sound reverberation makes for a "cathedral effect". Alternatively, too much of the soft materials can create an open field effect.

To limit noise from infiltrating the production room all passages should be sealed airtight with rubber lining if possible. Double walling is recommended, particularly if the partition is made of thin boards such as ¼ inch plywood. The usual passage of extraneous sound is through the gap between the panel and the doorframes, as well as the gap between the door panel and the floor. Some rubber fittings can be made to seal off these sound passages.

A small, silent-type air-conditioning unit may be installed inside the big studio. To avoid the hum from being picked up by the microphone the unit should preferably be installed in the technician's room or the working area. The cold air is then blown to the announcer's booth through an airduct with a silent exhaust fan.

If the studio is directly below galvanized iron roofing, there must be an intact ceiling to avoid too much heat during sunny days and to prevent the sound of raindrops being picked up by the microphone. Holes on a wooden floor should also be plugged.

The usual announcer's booth has a glass panel [possibly double] between it and the working area. This glass panel is necessary to facilitate communication between the announcer and the staff in the adjacent room. Hand signals, prompters, "idiot boards" and other means of non-oral communication are commonly passed between the announcer and the technician. The size of the glass panel can be one meter by 1.3 meters or larger. Again, this glass paneling must be tightly fitted to the frame to prevent external sound from being picked up by the sensitive microphone in the announcer's booth. It would be advisable for the assigned master carpenter or architect to visit local radio stations and to observe their respective acoustical treatment methods.

Production Equipment Layout

The pieces of equipment inside the studio are anchored on the audio console mixer, that processes, balances, amplifies and mixes any of the inputs and sends it to the transmitter, as well as to the monitoring speakers. The broadcast equipment such as turntables, tape player/recorders, cassette tape players, compact disc players and microphones should be laid out neatly where the announcer can easily reach the knobs, switches and faders.

Wiring and Installation of Equipment

Wires that connect the studio equipment to the audio console mixer should not be too long or short, and hence must be cut at proper lengths. Extraneous long wires are not only expensive but can also cause difficulties in a cramped studio space. Extra long wires can also cause humming sounds. Laid out wires must be laced or properly bundled together. Program lines that connect studio to transmitter, should not run close to electric power lines.

Dummy Load

It is a resistive element used as a substitute for the antenna element. The dummy load is useful in a situation where a proper antenna could not be connected, such as in a transmitter testing session. By connecting the transmitter output to a dummy load, any problems with antenna, transmission line and output can be isolated and identified.

The transmitter should preferably be housed in one building with the studio. The technician and the announcer should occasionally check the transmitter to find out whether it is working. Its audio level and power meter indicate this. Should there be a need to locate the antenna in quite a distance from the studio, it is necessary that the transmitter be placed close to the antenna. This split operation would require a longer program line from the studio to the transmitter.

The telephone drop line/cable can be used to facilitate the conduct of studio sounds to the transmitter. It is durable, resistant to weather elements, and a good sound conductor. It is so designed for transmission of sound. If the telephone drop line is not available electrical wires may be used instead. However, these may have to be replaced more often as electrical wires easily develop cracks on the rubber insulators when exposed to heat and rain. Electrical wires with double insulation would be preferred for reason of durability. These electrical lines used as program lines should not exceed 500 meters. With longer distances noise or impedance of sound may manifest.

Microphone lines or standard studio audio lines are ideal sound conductors. However, they are more expensive and need to be laid out in a conduit to protect them from damage. They are not designed for outdoor installation.

Off-Studio Broadcast

In the absence of an outside broadcast van, program lines could be extended from the studio down to a coverage area such as the church, market place, gymnasium or the town plaza.

The program line will serve as link between the outside coverage points down to the studio. The telephone drop line is recommended for this purpose. Other electrical conductors such as flat cord or ordinary lamp cord could be used as cable. It should be noted that many of these types of cords are not designed for changing weather conditions, therefore expect to replace them when they show signs of brittleness such as cracking and when inner conductor is exposed. It is suggested that the program line must not exceed 1,000 meters.

While a microphone may be simply attached to the line at the coverage area, a remote microphone mixer is necessary, especially when several microphones and inputs are required. The remote mixer [sometimes called an auxiliary microphone mixer] can be bought for approximately US$150. The one that is powered by a battery instead of the alternating current is preferred so that it can still be used in case of blownout. Also look for mixers that are provided by individual output and input control knobs. Auxiliary mixers can be used to put on air recorded voice clips, interviews, music, sound tracks, and other material outside the live proceedings. During remote broadcasting, cables must be taped to the floor surface firmly to avoid accidental tripping and pulling that can cause disruption of on-air program or recording. Avoid running loose lines in passageways. Only the volume control knobs of switches to the microphones and inputs being used should be open. Turn off all others to minimize catching extraneous noise.

Remote broadcasts are usually exposed to various forms of audio interference such as mechanical, electrical or crowd noise. It is always wise to carry grounding materials. Copper wires may be used to ground the mixer to a water pipe or to any metal buried in the ground.

Community Radio Council

The community radio shall:

— serve as an avenue for the free flow of beneficial information aimed at uplifting the plight of the various sectors of the community. The station shall open up possibilities for everyone, especially regular citizens, to express themselves socially, culturally, politically and spiritually, thus preparing each and every member of the community to participate in decision-making;

— strive to help create a self-reliant interactive community and seek its own development, fully harnessing locally available resources;

— be the catalyst for social, political, moral and cultural development and promote harmony among all community members and sectors.

Objectives

a) It will be the general objectives of the community radio to:

— give voice to the people who normally have no access to the mass media nor opportunity to express their views on community development;

— seize every chance to use the radio station in a constructive way ensuring fullest respect for, and adherence to, basic democratic processes and journalistic ethics.

b) Through its regular operations the community radio shall seek to:

— provide a development forum for the community;

— encourage participatory community development;

— promote active involvement of underprivileged groups such as women and young people;

— intensify the sharing of information within the community;

— encourage innovation in community development;

— increase the free flow of accurate and balanced information to, and within, the community;

— provide a forum for local cultural expression; and

— improve people's access to information in local languages.

c) Furthermore, the station was established with the understanding that:

— it shall in no way give advantage or disadvantage to a political party or candidate, political platform or purely partisan interest;

— its newscasts and information programs shall be edited for strictly factual and objective presentation; and that

— in the case of error or shortcoming the community radio shall rectify the said error, and issue corrective statements immediately.

Composition of the Community Radio Council (CRC)

The community radio council (CRC) is a group of leaders representing a cross-section of the community. Its task is to make decisions and formulate policies with respect to the operation of the community radio. The CRC composition is based on representation by the principal sectors in the community such as the following:

— business groups

— church sectors

— civic organizations, notably NGOs

— education sector

— ethnic groups, if any

— farmers

— fishermen

— labor groups, including professionals and employees

— local /national government

— senior citizens

— transportation groups

— volunteer staff member of the community radio

— women

— youth

A minimum number of political factions represented in the CRC should be three or four, if any need to be represented.

The council members should preferably be selected, or nominated, by the sectors concerned.

The members must have demonstrated a genuine concern in uplifting the plight of the sector and the community at large. Should a sector be so divided that no outstanding person appears to be a deserving representative, the other members of the community media council may determine the criteria and considerations necessary to decide who should be eligible to sit on the CRC. Selective representation by influential groups such as politicians or businessmen should be strictly ruled out. The station manager and volunteer staff are eligible to be members of the CRC. Should it happen that no member of the staff is a member of the CRC by virtue of their representation of a sector enumerated above, the staff may elect a representative to the CRC.

Observers

It is possible that a sector such as farmers, fishermen, youth and the ethnic communities would nominate more than one representative for the purpose of taking a more active part in the deliberations of the council. During the time of voting, however, it may be decided that each sector should have only one vote. Voting privileges should have been decided beforehand.

Annual Review

The CRC shall review its composition at every annual meeting, to ensure that it adequately reflects the principal sectors of the community, including newly emergent sectors.

Selection Criteria

A wide representation of key leaders in the community should make the decision as to which sectors should be represented in the CRC. The community representatives should be in a good position to determine who is best suited to represent the various sectors shown above. Certain criteria should be laid down in order to avoid confusion.

To be a member of the CRC, a person must:

— have proven integrity;

— be able to participate effectively and soundly in a democratic deliberation of community matters;

— have demonstrated a high level of interest in the wellbeing of the community;

— espouse the cause of his/her sector but be willing to subjugate sectoral interest in favor of the greater community;

— possess leadership qualities; and

— be willing to participate in workshops/seminars on the operation of the community radio and related issues.

Functions

The CRC, representing the whole community, shall collectively make decisions and formulate policies with respect to the community radio. The CRC shall decide and resolve the major issues regarding the community radio and serve as its steering committee. Among the specific acts that shall reserved to the CRC as a collegial body, are the following.

1   Initiate, develop and approve the radio station's code of conduct.

2   Approve the job descriptions of the station manager, deputy station manager, the cashier and any other volunteer staff member as may be deemed necessary.

3   Appoint the station manager, deputy station manager, and cashier.

4   Appoint an external auditor.

5   Exercise the authority to review the decisions of the station manager to ensure that they are consistent with the goals and objectives of the station.

6   Decide on possible honoraria, salaries/ fees and allowances for the members of staff or management of the community radio.

7   Decide on what kind of fund-raising schemes, announcements, sponsorships and other income generating revenue should be allowed.

8   Confirm and review the fees for announcements, sponsorship arrangements, public awareness spots by individuals, local businesses, development agencies, government/non-government organizations, etc.

9   Decide on following matters:

    — broadcast hours

    — types of programs to be aired

    — weather to air political programs or not and approve the related guidelines, based on objectives of the station

    — type of religious program to be aired

    — programs to be accommodated

    — programs to be cancelled

— program airtime.

10   Deliberate and make a decision regarding any other major issue that is presented by community members, the staff, and the station management.

The CRC should ensure that the program schedule is in line with the mission statement and objectives of the station, taking into account the needs of audiences and ensuring that the community radio is responsive to the needs.

The CRC should further

1.   Decide how often it will meet, and how and when the meeting invitations should be delivered. Meetings can be weekly, fortnightly, monthly, bi-monthly or quarterly. All decisions should be recorded in minutes for reference of the staff/community and for documentary purposes;

2.   Siscuss its own term of office, systems of decorum, honoraria [if any], and other matters relating to the CRC that it may truly represent the community in its decision-making functions.

The CRC should adopt measures to avoid making its deliberations an arena for political bickering.

Right to Sign

In situations where the CRC is taken as a mere deliberative body, not an organization, it is recommended that the operation of the radio station be placed in the hands of a duly registered co-operative, foundation or association. Without an existing organization or agency that is officially responsible for the operation of the station the CRC shall act as an organization by itself. For practical and legal purposes it may consider acquiring a juridical personality.

Until the CRC has been duly registered it should nominate the chairperson and the station manager to make transactions, enter into contracts, engage in business and receive grants on behalf of the community radio. It should also decide on the mechanism of receiving local announcements and payments for them, as well as the related financial reports.

Terms and Conditions

The term of office of the individual members of the CRC is one year. However the term may be renewed/extended based on recommendation of the sector and the acceptance of the CRC.

The CRC shall have the option to replace those members with unsatisfactory performance, including the chairperson or vicechairperson. The CRC should request for an alternative representative from the sector concerned.

A member shall be replaced if he/she is absent from more than half of the meetings organized in six months. Should the sector fail to send another acceptable representative, it forfeits its chance to participate in deliberations.

The CRC as a body may terminate, suspend or refuse to accept an individual member for any misconduct that it deems to be prejudicial to the deliberations of the council. Habitual tardiness, absenteeism, nonobservance of proper decorum, coming to the meeting under the influence of liquor and drugs, along with other recognized forms of misbehavior, shall be grounds for sanction by the council.

Official invitation letters indicating the period of time for which office is to be held should be sent to each member of the CRC.

Election of officials

The chairperson of the CRC shall be subject to yearly election, renewable for three years. Any member in good standing can be nominated and elected to the chair. While observers and resource persons can be invited to the meetings of the CRC, voting rights shall be limited to the membership of the council.

The council can decide whether election shall be by secret ballot or by viva voce.

The CRC shall also elect a vice-chairperson, cashier and secretary, subject to election every year.

Relations with Volunteer Staff

The station manager, and/or in his/her absence the deputy station manager, should attend the CRC meetings. The chairperson, station manager and/ or deputy station manager should hold regular [weekly or bi-weekly] meetings with the volunteer staff to discuss editorial policy on important community matters, new program schedules and formats and inform them of decisions of the CRC. Feedback should be collected from reporters to ensure their views, experience and contact with the community are adequately reflected in the policy decisions.

The preceding suggestions may be adopted, improved, modified or altered by the community leaders. They can also be taken as either the terms of reference or the constitution of the CRC. Each member of the CRC must sign the constitution to make it a binding document.

Community Radio around the World

Australia

In Australia, community radio is structured similarly to the United States, where stations operate as non-profit organisations, generally funded through sponsorship and listener subscriptions. One of the most successful Australian community radio stations is Melbourne's 3RRR. Like commercial radio stations, community stations need to apply to Australian Communications and Media Authority (ACMA) for a license to broadcast.

Contributing factors to the creation of community radio in Australia include the frustration felt by Vietnam War protestors at the mainstream media, classical music aficionados counteracting government inaction on the introduction of FM broadcasting and universities who wanted to explore the educational potential of radio.

Existing to support and represent community stations nationally is the Community Broadcasting Association of Australia (CBAA), which provides advice, assistance and also a satellite network so that stations can share content. A comprehensive list of Australian community broadcasters, and other information is available from CBOnline which also hosts a history of the Australian sector, "Diversity On The Airwaves".

Canada

Community radio stations in Canada are also similar in format to American community stations. Most commonly, Canadian community radio stations target commercially underserved minority language communities such as Franco-Ontarians, Acadians or the First Nations, although some small communities also have English language community stations. Community radio stations are most commonly operated by cooperatives.

In larger cities, community-oriented programming more commonly airs on campus radio stations. Some cities do, however, have community radio stations as well. Most community stations in Canada are members of the National Campus and Community Radio Association, or NCRA.

The province with the largest number of community radio stations in Canada is Saskatchewan. The majority of those stations are affiliated with Missinipi Broadcasting Corporation, an aboriginal public radio network.

India

In India, the campaign to legitimise community radio has been going on since almost the past decade. The Supreme Court of India ruled in judgement of 1995 that "airwaves are public property" came as an inspiration to groups across the country, but so far only educational (campus) radio stations have been allowed, under somewhat stringent conditions. First Indian Campus Community Radio. Anna FM is India's first campus community radio which is run by Education and MultiMedia Research Centre (EM²RC) and all programmes are produced by the students of Media Sciences Anna University.

Ireland

Ireland has had self-described community radio stations since the late 1970s, though it was not until 1995 that the first 11 licensed stations came on air as part of a pilot project run by the Independent Radio and Television Commission. Early stations were represented by the National Association of Community-Radio Broadcasters, which in 1988 published a guide to setting up new stations. More recently licensed stations have formed CRAOL as a representative group.

United Kingdom

"Community radio" has recently been taken up by the radio industry regulator Ofcom as the name for the new 'third tier' of the UK radio industry. The idea for this new level of radio broadcasting was piloted by the Radio Authority (now Ofcom) in 2002 with the licensing of 15 "Access radio" stations. The one-year licenses were extended in 2003 for a further year, and in 2004 a consultation was issued by Ofcom on the creation of community radio. The first full licences for Community Radio stations in the UK were issued in 2005. Community radio stations are usually limited to broadcast areas smaller than commercial or BBC local stations, usually within 5 kilometres (km) of their transmitter. They focus on a specific community or on a range of listeners inside their small broadcast area. Their job is to benefit communities rather than make a profit.

In order to get a community radio licence, applicants must demonstrate that the proposed station will meet the needs of a specified target community, together with required "social gain" objectives set out in the application. A target community can be defined either by geography or by reference to a particular sub-community in an area, otherwise known as a "community of interest". A geographic community can be any defined local area, particularly those which would not sustain a fully commercial broadcaster. A community of interest can be any identifiable local community; existing Community stations are aimed at groups as diverse as the elderly, religious groups such as Christian and Muslim, lifestyle groups such as gay and transgender and cultural/ recreational groups such as artists.

Community stations are not permitted to raise more than 50% of operating costs through on-air advertising and/ or sponsorship; the remainder of operating income must be met through other sources. This can include public funding via grants, donor income, lottery funding or charities. Alternative methods of broadcasting include short-period licences, known as Restricted Service Licences, allowing community groups and special events to run local area low power stations for up to 28 days, and webcasting.

The Access Radio Pilot: The Access Radio Pilot, initiated by the UK Radio Authority, was designed to test the demand for community radio and to see whether such small-scale radio broadcasting projects were feasible. Some of the projects targeted a particular community of interest, ranging from religious and minority groups to children and older people, others such as Manchester's ALL FM and WythenshaweFM targeted geographical communities.

Access Stations included:

— Resonance FM - in London, run by the London Musicians Collective.

— Sound Radio - serving a range of groups in Hackney in London.

— BCB 96.7 - serving Bradford's diverse communities, with a mix of ethnic programming, specialist music and sport.

— Desi Radio - in London, serving the Punjabi community.

— ALL FM 96.9 - serving the communities of Ardwick, Longsight & Levenshulme in Manchester.

—]WythenshaweFM - serving the large housing estate of that name in Manchester.

— Cross Rhythms City Radio - Stoke-on-Trent

The Ofcom Community Radio Consultation: The Ofcom community radio consultation was issued on 17 February 2004. The consultation gave a brief outline of the Access radio projects, and made some proposals as to how the new sector would be managed. Included in the consultation were a series of questions which interested parties were invited to suggest comments on. These included whether community radio stations should have a cap of 50% of their income coming from advertising, and the order and method by which licenses should be applied for.

The closing date for contributions was 20 April 2004, and since this date all of the contributions have been published on the Ofcom website. Following the success of the pilot scheme, applications for full licences were invited in 2004 and the first full licences awarded in 2005.

United States

American community radio stations are often staffed by volunteers and air a wide variety of programming. They are generally smaller than public radio outlets. Community radio stations are distinct from public radio in that most of their programming is locally produced by non-professional DJs and producers, where public radio tends to rely on more syndicated programming. Community stations often try to reduce their dependence on financial contributions from corporations in comparison with other public broadcasters. Some examples of community stations are WAIF in Cincinnati, Ohio, KGNU in Boulder, Colorado, KSPC in Claremont, California, KDVS in Davis, California, KBOO in Portland, Oregon, WDBX in Carbondale, Illinois, WLUW and WZRD in Chicago, Illinois, WERU in Blue Hill, Maine, WMNF in Tampa, Florida, WORT in Madison, Wisconsin and Coast Community Radio (KMUN-Astoria and KTCB-Tillamook) in Oregon. These stations are licensed by the Federal Communications Commission. Many community stations are licensed as full-power FM stations, while others - especially newer community stations - are licensed under low-power broadcasting rules.

The National Federation of Community Broadcasters formed in 1970 as an umbrella organization for community-oriented, non-commercial radio stations. The NFCB publishes handbooks for stations and lobbies on behalf of community radio at the federal level. The Grassroots Radio Coalition is a very loose coalition of stations that formed as a reaction against increasing commercialization of public radio and lack of support for volunteer-based stations (including in the NFCB). Some stations are part of both groups.

11

Radio in Development Communication

Development communication is a rather broad area in which one finds many approaches and various ideologies. Beyond the differences in ideologies and methodological approaches, however, we may underscore that the lessons from experience in this field have demonstrated the importance of emphasizing interactive and participatory processes, rather than the production and dissemination of information separate from the community processes.

Although the term is sometimes used to indicate the overall contribution of communication to the development of society (communications in the service of development), or sometimes to highlight the use of the media to deal with development themes (media products), it generally refers to the planned use of strategies and processes of communication aimed at achieving development. It is at the level of this "aiming at achieving development" that the differences abound: extend participation to decision-making and strengthen community institutions; compensate for gaps in terms of attitude and information; produce a consensus among the participants in a development initiative; promote social justice and democracy; etc.

The concept of development communication arose within the framework of the contribution that communication and the media made to development in the countries of the Third World. In the 1950s and 1960s, the

United Nations Educational, Scientific and Cultural Organization (Unesco) and US AID (the American Aid Agency) sponsored numerous projects utilizing the media for communication, information, or educational purposes, with a view to facilitating development. Other major United Nations agencies, like the Food and Agriculture Organization (FAO), the United Nations Development Programme (UNDP), and the United Nations Children's Fund (UNICEF) also got into the act, and subsequently promoted communication within the framework of development project implementation.

As for the expression "development communication," according to the Clearinghouse for Development Communication, it was apparently first used in the Philippines in the 1970s by Professor Nora Quebral to designate the processes for transmitting and communicating new knowledge related to rural environments. The fields of knowledge were then extended to all those likely to help improve the living conditions of the disadvantaged people.

What we have here, in fact, is more of an approach than a discipline. As far as its definitions are concerned, they usually consist of general statements. Thus, it is referred to as a combination of information and evaluation processes, as well as a combination of actions likely to solicit and motivate local participation in its own development, or in any series of planned communication activities aimed at individual and social change, or in the application of communication with a view to promoting socioeconomic development — that is, a type of planned social change, etc.

There are also some definitions that give a more restrictive meaning to the way communication supports a development activity or a development project. We can then talk of development communication as a social process aimed at producing a common understanding or a consensus among the participants in a development initiative. The expression "development support communication" is in fact more correct, and designates, quite accurately, an effective methodology that has proved itself. Finally, there are definitions that emphasize access by the population to the communication process with a view to promoting social justice and democracy. These various definitions — to mention only a few — demonstrate the extent of this field of intervention.

Whatever the case may be, one will find, at the heart of this concept, the need for an exchange of information to contribute toward the resolution of a development problem and improve the quality of life of a specific target group, as well as to implement needs analysis and evaluation mechanisms within the communication process.

Trends in Development Communications

Development communications are organized efforts to use communications processes and media to bring social and economic improvements, generally in developing countries. The field emerged in the late 1950's amid high hopes that radio and television could be put to use in the world's most disadvantaged countries to bring about dramatic progress. Early communications theorists like Wilbur Schramm and Daniel Lerner based their high expectations upon the apparent success of World War II propaganda, to which academia and Hollywood had contributed.

With World War II came dozens of new, very poor, countries, left by their former colonial overseers with little infrastructure, education, or political stability. It was widely accepted that mass media could bring education, essential skills, social unity, and a desire to "modernize." Walt Rostow theorized that societies progress through specific stages of development on their way to modernity, what he termed "the age of high mass consumption." Lerner suggested that exposure to Western media would create "empathy" for modern culture, and a desire to move from traditional to modern ways. Early development communications, especially that sponsored by the U.S. government, was also seen as a means of "winning hearts and minds" over to a capitalist way of life.

These early approaches made a number of erroneous assumptions, and have been largely forsaken in contemporary approaches to development. Obstacles to development were naively seen as rooted in developing countries, not as products of international relationships. Modernization was presumed to equate to Westernization, and to be a necessary prerequisite to meeting human needs. Development was seen as a top-down process, whereby centralized mass media could bring about widespread change. Producers of development media often failed to ask if the audience can receive the message (television penetration in developing countries is minimal and radio penetration in the early days of development communication was light), understand the message (a problem in countries with dozens of languages and dialects), act upon the message (with the necessary tools or other forms of structural support), and want to act upon the message. And because it was based upon a propaganda model, development communications efforts were often seen as propaganda and distrusted.

Projects embodying these philosophies have enjoyed little success. In the 1970s and 1980s, a new paradigm of development communication emerged which better recognized the process of deliberate underdevelopment as a function of colonialism, the great diversity of the cultures involved, the differences between elite versus popular goals for social change, the considerable political and ideological constraints to change, and the endless varieties of ways different cultures communicate.

But in some instances mass media technologies, including television, have been "magic multipliers" of development benefits. Educational television has been used effectively to supplement the work of teachers in classrooms in the teaching of literacy and other skills, but only in well designed programs which are integrated with other educational efforts. Consumer video equipment and VCRs have been used to supplement communications efforts in some small projects.

Some developing countries have demonstrated success in using satellite television to provide useful information to portions of their populations out of reach of terrestrial broadcasting. In 1975 and 1976, an experimental satellite communications project called SITE (Satellite Instructional Television Experiment) was used to bring informational television programs to rural India. Some changes in beliefs and behaviors did occur, but there is little indication that satellite television was the best means to that end. The project did lead to Indian development of its own satellite network. China has also embarked on a ambitious program of satellite use for development, claiming substantial success in rural education. When television has succeeded as an educational tool in developing countries, it is only when very specific viewing conditions are met. For example, programs are best viewed in small groups with a teacher to introduce them and to lead a discussion afterwards.

A variety of types of organizations work with local governments to develop communications projects. The United Nations provides multi-lateral aid to governments. Non-profit non-governmental organizations (NGO) conduct development projects worldwide using U.N., government, or private funding. And government agencies, such as the U.S. Agency for International Development (USAID) provide assistance to developing countries, but with political strings attached. There are three common types of development campaigns: Persuasion, changing what people do; Education, changing social values; and Informing, empowering people to change by increasing knowledge. This third approach is now perceived as the most useful.

Instead of attempting to modernize people, contemporary efforts attempt to reduce inequality by targeting the poorest segments of society, involving people in their own development, giving them independence from central authority, and employing "small" and "appropriate" technologies. The emphasis has shifted from economic growth to meeting basic needs.

In this new view of development, communication becomes an important catalyst for change, but not its cause. Local folk media, for example, is employed to reduces media's bias toward literacy and provide information in a traditional, familiar form. Development journalism provides people with information on change in their society, and works at the local level to advocate change. Where mass media is now employed in developing societies, community newspapers and radio prove far more accessible and useful than television. The rapid spread of entertainment television in the developing world is proving to be more a disruption to traditional social structures than an agent of progress. One emerging genre of television does show promise for contributing to development. The telenovela, pioneered in Brazil, has demonstrated some success in disseminating "pro-social" messages. Such programs are now being evaluated in many countries for their effectiveness in contributing to population control, health education, and other development goals.

Experiences of the past forty years has demonstrated the crucial importance of communication in the field of development. Within this perspective of development communication, two trends developed successively: an approach that favoured large-scale actions and relied on the mass media, and an approach that promoted grassroots communication (also called community communication), promoting small-scale projects and relying especially on the light media (videos, posters, slide presentation, etc.). These trends, which still coexist today to various degrees within the field of development communication, are linked to the evolution of the development and communication models that have marked development efforts up to now.

The trend toward mass communication initially marked the first two decades during which the media were utilized in the field of development. It espoused the idea that it was enough to disseminate the knowledge and the technologies of the North to ensure that they were adopted. Once adopted, they would achieve the development of the South. This first vision of development is referred to as the paradigm of "modernization." These initial experiences, centred mainly around the mass media, relied both on a communication model based on persuasion and information transmission, and on a development model based on increasing economic activity and changes in values and attitudes.

The intervention paradigm of these two decades, which is found in two publications that had a decisive impact on the orientations adopted at that time — The Passing of Traditional Society by Daniel Lerner and Mass Media and National Development by Wilbur Schramm — consists of a very simple communication model that can be described in stimulus-response terms, based both on the logic of persuasion and on a development model linking the latter to increased productivity.

One of the models resulting from this paradigm that had a major influence on communication practices in the area of educational development is the innovation dissemination model. This model, resulting from an extension of agricultural practices exported to the developing countries, involves the transmission of information to farmers by a resource person and was formulated in theory by Everett Rogers in 1962. This theory rested on three main elements: the target population of the innovation, the innovation to be transmitted, and the sources and communication channels.

This model has been criticized by several people for its reductionism. It did not take into account the different types of target populations (e.g., prosperous farmers who own land and are open to new techniques versus other farmers who are illiterate, poor, and exploited). It also failed to take into account the impact of the economic and political structures on the capacity to adopt innovations. The same charge of blindness where social, political and economic factors are concerned also applies to innovations that require a process of diffusion. Finally, communication channels and sources were generally used within the framework of vertical, top-to-bottom communication. There was never any mention of horizontal communication between the groups in the communities affected by the problem that the innovation was meant to resolve, or of vertical, bottom-to-top communication, which would have made it possible to bring the people's problems to the attention of the decision-makers and the experts.

Since then, the development model as well as the communication models have evolved considerably. The vast amount of experience in the use of the media for educational or informative purposes in the development process has led to the development of new orientations and new practices. At the same time, several criticisms have been raised with regard to the first development models and to the functionalist vision of the development communication model.

A new model emphasizing the endogenous character of development has made it possible to define development as a global process, for which societies are responsible. In this new perspective, development is not something that can come from the outside. It is a participatory process of social change within a given society. This model has also made it possible to extend the concept of development to nonmaterial notions by bringing into the equation notions of social equality, liberty, revenue distribution, grassroots participation in development, etc.

The conceptions everyone had of the role of communication in development have changed radically. In the first development model, the communication paradigm consisted of transmitting the technology necessary for the growth of productivity. In the second, it consists of stimulating the potential for change within a community. The concept of grassroots participation in the development process has become a key concept.

The first result of these changes in vision on day-to-day practice was the need to move from a relatively simple vision of a one-way transmission of technical information, to the promotion of bi- or multilateral systems based on grassroots participation. At the same time as this change in communication and development models was taking place, two development paradigms were developing which helped to orient communication interventions.

On one hand, several people were questioning the modernization model because they saw that communication did not lead to development, and observed that in fact, the countries of the South appeared to be sliding further and further into poverty, low salaries, and poor living conditions. This criticism, which was developed above all in Latin America, emphasized the link between this situation and the situation of economic dependence on the industrialized North: the development of the countries in the North was conditional on the underdevelopment of the countries of the Third World, and the "centre" developed at the expense of the "periphery."

This situation is referred to as the paradigm of "dependence." According to this paradigm, obstacles to development come first and foremost from external, not internal, obstacles: that is to say, the international economic system. Consequently, the mass media cannot act as agents of change, since they transmit the western message, and the capitalist and conservative ideology. This paradigm, which is still in existence today, was also criticized because it put too much emphasis on the contradictions at the international level and not enough on the contradictions at the local and the national level. The resulting discussions and recommendations regarding the "new information order" related to this paradigm.

Its extension at the national level emphasized the relationship between communication and politicization. One of the models resulting from this paradigm, which exercised in the past, and today still exercises a determining influence on the development communication practices, is the consciousness model developed by Paolo Freire (1973). Freire, and several other communicators after him, identified communication as a process that is inseparable from the social and political processes necessary for development.

Freire insisted on the fact that the mere transfer of knowledge by an authority source to a passive receiver did nothing to help promote growth in the latter as a human being with an independent and critical conscience capable of influencing and changing society. According to him, for development communication to be effective, it had to be linked not only to the process of acquiring technical knowledge and skills, but also to the awareness-raising, politicization and organization processes.

In his model, which he explains in The Education of the Oppressed, development communication can be considered as a tool that the grassroots can use to take control. This tool can be used for the following purposes: becoming aware of the various facets of the real development problems in their region; organizing in order to react collectively and effectively to these problems; bringing to light the conflicts that divide the various interest groups; becoming politicized — learning to provide alternatives to problem situations and finding solutions to various problems; and becoming "technicized" — obtaining the necessary tools to put to concrete use the solutions provided by the community.

This model and its applications have also been subject to criticism. It was stated, among other things, that politicization through the community media may constitute an adequate approach in countries that tolerate recourse to political action; but in most developing countries, this political action would lead to the overthrow of the governing, "have" élite without providing the means for changing conditions, and the confrontations that follow would commonly lead to repression and regression of democratic rights. Thus, rather than a direct politicization approach, many prefer an approach based on education, where the objective is not to cause a confrontation but to provide the tools necessary for organization.

A third paradigm orienting the formulation of development communication models and interventions is one that is generally called the paradigm of another development. This paradigm emphasizes not only material development but also the development of values and cultures. Where development communication interventions are concerned, it emphasizes the small media operating in networks and the use of grassroots communication approaches. According to this paradigm, grassroots participation reinforces the chances that communities will adopt activities appropriate for them.

The concept of interactivity, with the light media as its operational instrument, makes possible the endogenous acquisition of knowledge and skills within the framework of a search for solutions and the communication process. This is referred to as a recourse to a methodology of community media, whose principal elements are:

— identification of needs by means of direct contacts with the groups;

— concretization: examination of the problem identified by the groups in the light of local conditions;

— selection of priority problems by the groups;

— formulation of a durable methodology for seeking solutions;

— identification of the amount of information required and access to this information;

— action: execution by the groups of the projects they have designed;

— expansion towards the outside to make known the points of view of the groups to other groups or to the authorities; and

— liaison with the communication system to make known their action.

Other models combine different concepts. This is true, for example, of the practices for supporting communication in development projects, which combined the community approach and recourse to the small media with practices that can often be linked to a model for disseminating the innovations. This approach emphasizes the planning of communication activities as a support to a development project. Its aim is to produce a common understanding or a consensus among all the participants in a development initiative. It emphasizes the facilitation of exchanges of points of view among the various people involved in the development project and aims at taking into account the grassroots perceptions in the planning of the project and mobilizing them in the development activities set out in the project. The methodology results from educational technology and is characterized by the integration of needs analysis and evaluation mechanisms in the communication process.

Other practices are based on the community approach and the grassroots awareness-raising model. The same is true of the alternative for democratic development communication, which emphasizes grassroots access to the communication process for the purpose of promoting social justice and democracy. In certain cases, this is translated by an emphasis on participation by the most disadvantaged in the communication process (access to small media at the local level), and in other cases, by actions promoting cultural expression and the search for ways of taking control of the mass media.

Finally, notably in the case of the fight against AIDS and the promotion of condom use, approaches resulting from social marketing, having recourse at the same time to research techniques adapted to small groups, and to communities and the large-scale use of the mass media. We are also witnessing the renaissance of projects utilizing the mass media — for example, interactive school radio projects in Latin America and Africa, and the promotion of a television for development. To these approaches we will also have to add all the practices related to basic education, informal education, distance learning, literacy, and post-literacy activities that have their own methodologies and community-level communication and media communication approaches.

The field of development communication is vast and its divisions are numerous. The different paradigms that have marked its evolution are still active to various degrees, and the models that are attached to them are as different as the ideologies and the orientations that inspired them. In spite of the diversity of approaches and orientations, however, there is a consensus today on the need for grassroots participation in development and on the essential role that communication plays in promoting development.

Radio for Development Communication

Radio for development is a well established sector, which is increasingly reassigned under the banner of information and communication technologies for development (ICT4D), and as such is often included in the broader debates about the role and impact of ICTs for development.

Within development communication radio has featured as a tool in most of the methodologies and paradigms. As a broad sweep if development communications is divided into two main paradigms - the dominant 'delivery' mode and the more participatory mode - we can see radio as a significant feature in all the areas. Historically development communication has been conceptualised as either within the dominant paradigm of message/information delivery, where effective communication is received with understanding; or within the critical/participatory paradigm of context and process, whereby communication is viewed as a route to increase participation in development, empowerment and increased articulation of social relations among people.

Many commentators see health communication in the past 10 years as having lead the development of communication because it has been the site of innovations in methodologies. The use of social marketing and 'edutainment' for example has been significant, and there has been a trend for increased 'cross-over' methodologies employed whereby a campaign may include both diffusion and participation. And there is an increasing awareness within major NGOs and agencies that messaging has failed and that more participatory dialogical communication strategies are needed. While health communication is increasingly seen as the area of innovation within these different paradigms 'radio in health communication' in often on the cutting edge of this innovation.

Within a mass media focus radio has been used widely in public health awareness raising, and significantly in HIV and AIDS awareness raising, both in developed and developing countries. There are many case studies of effective awareness raising campaigns, with a growing body of evidence about behaviour change and broader impact. The Soul City evaluations are an often sited reference in this area, as they track the impact of radio (and TV) programming produced by Soul City in South Africa, but there are many other examples. The Communication Initiative website has a 'radio window' that includes numerous studies. The work of governments, NGOs and UN agencies has ensured that radio is central in large-scale public health campaigns.

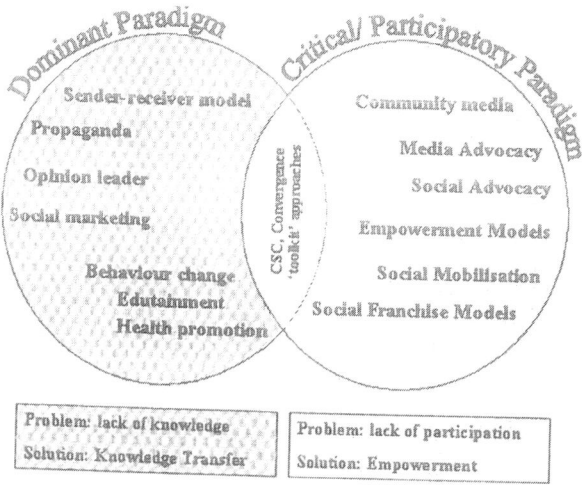

Figure 1. Paradigms of development communications

Within a community/participatory focus radio has been developing strongly in Latin America and Africa, and emerging in South Asia. The work of organisations such as AMARC (Association of Community Radio) has put community radio on the map, and 'community radio' is broadly acknowledged in development communication to be a powerful route for both reaching local communities and for local communities to actually voice their own concerns and views, and for them to reach out to others. The voice of community radio is being amplified through innovative uses of convergent technology. Radio and the internet is a powerful combination, and many community radios are also broadcasting online, participating in networks and global broadcast events.

Community radio also presents donors and NGOs with an enticing arena for delivering pre-produced or pre-conceptualized programming. This presents a strong tension within the field - some support agencies and organisations are strong proponents of delivering high quality products, while others believe the focus of money and effort should be on directly building the capacity of local broadcasters themselves, in order for them to then produce content that is locally relevant and to develop a local media infrastructure and talent pool that is sustainable. Within these two positions there is also a plethora of projects and organisations that are aiming to both develop community radio content and capacity, but providing trainings, fellowships, competitions for programming, distributing fact sheets, scripts and 'locomotive inserts' of short programming that can be placed in a local programme as an engine for further discussion.

When thinking about radio in development the challenges, lessons learnt and pros and cons of the medium need to be examined. This is the case for radio in development generally, as well as specifically in looking at top-down approaches and bottom-up approaches.

A helpful grid in thinking about radio in development might be:

	Radio in Development - Generally	Radio in Top-Down approaches	Radio in Bottom-Up approaches
Pros	Language usage		
	Reach - beyond literacy		
	Reach - beyond geography		
	Reach - beyond social limits		
	Access to women and children		
Cons	Blanket approaches - what impact?		
	Problem of context		
	Problem of evaluation		

The importance of 'resourcing' the media in health is also a vital one. Media in developing countries require both training and resources in the form of content development, authoritive and trustworthy information sources, confidence and experience in health reporting and potentially strong support from peers around the world via networks of media who share a concern and focus on health, and who want to share experiences and content. Many organisations are active in the area of 'media support' for health, particularly training of journalists, but there is a level of duplication in many instances and a need for more comprehensive knowledge sharing and coordination among support agencies. There is also a new question - should we be rethinking radio interventions in the light of the new technologies and ways of communicating that are emerging? Are there new opportunities to reach people and hear people via the convergence of radio with mobile, the web, PAD, and other technologies?

Radio in health communication is a vibrant and dynamic field, and one that has signs of lasting many years as radio retains a pre-eminence in media in developing countries as well as experiencing a 'renaissance' in the developed world over the past ten years. Health communication will continue to innovate with radio in seeking to impact on behaviour change, delivery of key health information and broad health education. The role of appropriate resources however is vitally important; training, information and networking are a potential route for building a strong and effective media, whether on a national or local scale.

Role of Amateur Radio

The world is now divided into two. One part is affluent in information, the other poor in information. At present time the nation that does not have any way or knowledge to acquire information through information &communication

technologies is poor. Presently there has also been severe change in the definition of 'Literacy'. The citizen able to use or having access to Internet, computer, telephone, radio & other technologies, is a digitally literate citizen.

And the one's unfamiliar to use or not having access to these are digitally illiterate. This new dimension of illiteracy has added up to our society in this age of information & communication technologies. In the third world, specially in Bangladesh there has emerged a regrettable distance rather than the expected proximity. And this pitiable distance is called Digital Divide. Information & Communication Technology consists of facility to communicate, Information resource & authority to communicate. Presently in Bangladesh for every thousand people there are only 1.5 computers, 4 telephone connections & 7 televisions. That means from the above instance we can see digital divide is not only limited between the first & third world but have spread between the cities & villages, between men & women of Bangladesh. In recent times the rapid flourishing of ICTs is playing a significant positive role in poverty alleviation. The increased possibility of acquiring & sharing information resulting from the expansion of Information & Communication Technology creates positive atmosphere for poverty reduction.

So, today the biggest challenge stands before us is how we will use Information & Communication Technologies as the greatest tool of poverty reduction in Bangladesh. How the poor people will use Information & Communication Technologies to empower themselves, how they can use to bring about positive change of their condition & position & how can their access to the knowledge society be increased. Above all how to establish Information & Communication Technology as a human & public right rather than opportunity. A preeminent medium of Information & Communication Technology is amateur or ham radio. Amateur radio is a science related Hobby.

People having this hobby are called Ham or Amateur Radio Holder. Hams communicate with other Hams all over the world through radio transceiver after getting license from the Government. The Hams have opportunities to attain plenty of skills in the attractive world of Information & Communication Technologies.

Hams play a major role in national disasters, emergency medical treatment & other public services. Specially in situations when the general communication systems like telephone, mobile, satellites are devastated hams instantly come to action by setting up alternative communication & serve people as volunteers. A ham is devoted to be tolerant, honest, friendly & patriot.

The authority of amateur radio can play a big role as part of ICTs in a developing country like Bangladesh. Because,

a)   A workforce skilled in electronics or technology can grow up without any extra investment though the expansion of amateur radio.

b)   The skill of amateur radio holders in electronics & modern communication system can be used in nationally important aspects including poverty reduction.

c)   The amateur radio holders can provide such important public services that are not possible by the government bodies in such a short time.

d)   The individual skill, knowledge & experience of the amateur radio operator's helps to make the nation confident & self-dependent & present the country to the world with respect.

Bangladesh Government approved the introduction of amateur radio service for the first time in 1992. Ministry of Post & Telecommunication of Bangladesh works as the focal ministry for amateur radio through the T & T Board. The T & T Board used to provide license for General grade, or

High Frequency through a one level examination. At present the number of license receiver is around 60 - 70. But in Japan a total of Thirteen lakh, Fifty thousand One hundred & Twenty seven & in Australia Twenty two thousand nine hundred & sixty five, in India Fifteen thousand amateur radio operators are operating now. The T & T board stopped taking the exam to acquire amateur radio license for last three years without any pre declaration.

'Bangladesh Amateur Radio League' was established on 20th May 1979 as a amateur radio related organization. This organization became member of International Amateur Radio Union in 1992. Besides, in 1993 the Foundation for Amateur Radio Services (FAIRS) Bangladesh branch was established. These two organizations worked as amateur radio organizations in Bangladesh from 1993 to year 2000. But afterwards due to change of leadership & other reason, Bangladesh Amateur Radio League became an ineffective & now defunct organization. The person whose name is in the web site as general secretary has been staying in America for long. This is quite unwanted to us. Bangladesh is absent in the world amateur related forums only because of it's ineffective organizations. But still some people are trying to stay with it. As a result Bangladesh's representation in amateur radio programs has collapsed home & abroad. BARL is failing to play any effective role to preserve the interest of amateur holders & clear the roadblocks in the way of amateur radio growth.

BNNRC was established on year 2000. Since then BNNRC started nationwide campaign for the spreading of amateur radio. For this awareness about amateur radio increased nationwide specially among the civil society along the coastal belt.

BNNRC started continuous advocacy since Bangladesh Telecommunication Regulatory Commission was established on 2oo1. As a result amateur radio exam was first held under BTRC on January 2004 & for the first time Morse code was withdrawn in Bangladesh. Keeping the exam in front BNNRC started nationwide campaign. A total of 300 applied for the exam & 237 of them took part in it. A total of 76 passed the exam overcoming all barriers.

Amateur radio can play a positive role in development communication of Bangladesh. Specially alternative communication can be built up between the coastal zone such as the 16 districts & the capital city. Already amateur radio network between Dhaka- Chittagong, Dhaka-Coxsbazar, and Dhaka - Barishal & Dhaka - Bhola has been established & working successfully. Moreover, recently experts identified Bangladesh as an earthquake prone area. They said, Bangladesh is situated on the harmful tectonic plates of Indian sub continent. An earthquake of 6-rector scale can turn cities like Dhaka/Chittagong or Shylhet into piles of debris. Besides devastating buildings earthquake also harms the service structures. For instance, conflagration from bursting the gas pipes etc. Water, electricity & telecommunication systems are severely damaged during earthquake. So communication systems other than amateur radio can't be initialized instantly.

Bangladesh's major weakness in taking cyclone precautions & carry post cyclone activities is malfunction of telecommunication system. Besides, the tendency of cold wave, heat wave, boat capsizing & water surge is increasing everyday. Amateur radio can stand beside public as an Information & Communication service.

Barriers of the Growth of Amateur Radio

a)   Amateur radio is not yet popularized nationwide for lack of mass awareness regarding amateur radio operation.

   Recommendation: To campaign regularly with the initiative of BTRC, Ministry of Science & ICT, various university, educational institute & to take initiative to establish at least one amateur radio club station in every district.

b) To introduce one level examination system & arranging examination every six month.

   Recommendation: To take examination every 6 months with the initiative of BTRC & to re introduces one level examination. To give general grade license to the examinees passed in last January instead of novice license. BNNRC has already submitted an application to the honorable chairman.

c) 71% direct & indirect tax on the import of amateur radio set

   Recommendation: As amateur radio is accepted as part of ICTs & moreover, according to paragraph 3.2.7 of Bangladesh Government's Information & Communication Policy it has been said that "Use of Information & Communication technology & information services has to be brought under the purchase ability of mass people". Furthermore, as it is not used in any commercial activity & amateur radio holders contribute to establish life line communication for public interest, so all the direct & indirect taxes on amateur radio should be reduced & brought to 5% like India. Initiative from the Ministry of Science & ICTs is expected in this regard.

d) About the new application form purchase rate & processing fee set by BTRC. Presently BTRC has set 500 taka as purchase rate of all kinds of form & 5000 taka as processing fees.

   Recommendation: As amateur radio is never used in commercial purposes & it contributes to establish lifeline communication for public interest & it is a hobby of common citizen so all the fees of application form & processing fees should be withdrawn.

Participatory Development Communication

It is now increasingly recognized that people's active

participation is an essential component of sustainable development. Any intervention with the intent of achieving a real and sustainable improvement in the living conditions of people is doomed to failure unless the intended beneficiaries are actively involved in the process. Unless people participate in all phases of an intervention, from problem identification to research and implementation of solutions, the likelihood that sustainable change will occur is slim. Development communication is at the very heart of this challenge: it is the process by which people become leading actors in their own development. Communication enables people to go from being recipients of external development interventions to generators of their own development.

The point of departure for development communication is not the dissemination of an innovation or of a new idea that is full of promise, but the grassroots expression of its needs. It follows that the communication models based exclusively on models of information transmission removed from community processes clearly are doomed to failure.

Participation, by putting the emphasis on the needs and the viewpoints of the individuals and groups, becomes the key concept of development communication. Recourse to a systemic methodology and the implementation of horizontal processes — in which the people are directly associated with the communication process and are thus more likely to formulate their problems themselves, become aware of new possibilities, and take their knowledge and their viewpoints into consideration in the communication process — constitute the major elements of its methodology. The implementation processes are essentially interactive and participatory at all levels, and coincide with the fundamental mission of IDRC — Empowerment through Knowledge: "Empowerment is often seen as something one can do to another person. This is not so. People are empowered by an environment that gives them the freedom to express themselves".

Where the orientations to be pursued are concerned, a major line is the communication support of the concept of "new development," as presented by the Dag Hammarskjöld Foundation (Development Dialogue magazine) and several authors and researchers who emphasize decentralization, access to communication, and participation. Among the characteristics of the "new development," we find:

— action based on needs, including nonmaterial needs like social equality, democracy, etc.;

— endogenous and autonomous nature (change based on a community definition of community resources);

— protection of the environment (rational use of potential within the limitations of the local ecosystem);

— efforts to achieve structural transformation of social relations, economic activities and power structures; and

— exercise and promotion of participatory democracy at all levels of society.

Several researchers also emphasize the reinforcement of institutional and individual skills, ways of approaching decision-makers, and grassroots communication. Thus, recently, Beltran proposed the following notes for "an agenda for the 20th century":

— combine the best of the development support communication activities with alternative means of communication (technical skills with political perception);

— aim increasingly to reinforce institutions rather than mount short-term operations;

— persuade the large communication schools to include development communication in their curricula;

— support research into communication aimed at democratic development;

— support the small communities, the NGOs, the small community and union organizations;

— place emphasis on communication aimed at health, hygiene, nutrition and the grassroots;

— insist that political planners and leaders use communication to reach development objectives;

— encourage basic communication training at all levels; and

— reinforce institutional regional communication.

The fact remains that to be durable, development must take into account human factors and make it possible for the communities in question to decide for themselves what objectives they want to aim for and what means they want to use. Development communication is the tool that makes this process possible. As a corollary, the directions to be pursued are predicated on knowing the needs of the target group and their channels of communication, stimulating the processes of community participation and decision-making, reinforcing the action of agents of change, and influencing the development of institutional and national policies.

In this perspective of durable development communication, what remains to be done is to identify the lines of research to be used. Historically, where research themes are concerned, attention has always been paid to the effects of the mass media. This focus has corresponded to a modernization paradigm and the utilization of the media to create a global environment for development and the transmission of ideas, knowledge, and new attitudes.

It is interesting to note that this trend is now coming back, with interactive school radio, television for development, and the utilization of the mass media in the fight against AIDS. Satellite television devoted to education and development is also the order of the day. Subsequently, in the 1970s, people turned to the role of communication in supporting development activities and specific projects (family planning, oral rehydration, basic health care, agriculture, etc.). Attention then turned to the potential of small media and community media: participatory videos, audio cassette forums, and traditional media (theatre, puppet shows, stories, etc.). People also placed more emphasis on the contribution of communication to the promotion of democratic and social rights, which led to the development of community radio and communication agencies in the South dedicated to these aspects.

During these past few years, interest has focused on various areas like the impact of new communication technologies (satellite, telephone, E-mail, etc.), appreciation of the knowledge held by First Nations, implementation of communication units within government structures for the purpose of analyzing needs, training of personnel, and production of training materials. Each of these areas has its respective importance and still contributes to stimulating and supporting development communication interventions.

Recognizing the importance of development communication, IDRC has started to develop a research program in that field. This program aims to support people's participation in their development by enabling groups and communities to diagnose the problems they face, make well-informed decisions, mobilize for action, and assume responsibility for their own development. We choose to use the term "participatory development communication" to draw attention to this emphasis on two-way communication processes, and to distance ourselves from one-way communication approaches that involve disseminating messages, transmitting information, or persuading people to change their behaviour.

The program wants to give preference to horizontal approaches that involve encouraging dialogue centred on problem analysis and a search for solutions, as well as bottom-up approaches that aim to raise the awareness of decision-makers. These approaches are based on a process of community communication. By allowing for participation in development, participatory development communication becomes a tool for emancipating people and communities. In terms of its overall thrust, the program takes an interactive and participatory approach and stresses the interrelationships that exist in practice among the main lines of action. This concept is called as "CIME": Communication at the grassroots level, the exchange of Information, two-way Media, and nonformal Education.

CIME

Grassroots Communication

The program focuses on communication at the grassroots level in particular. Experience over the past 50 years has clearly demonstrated that if communication is really to help involve people in identifying a development problem, understanding its causes, proposing solutions, and organizing themselves to take appropriate action, it must start at the community level. It must also promote "horizontal" interchange among people rather than some kind of "vertical" transmission from an expert to his audience.

Exchange of Information

The program also attempts to link information to the process of communication. Information is of no use by itself, without a community communication process that allows people to grasp it and make it their own. We must also make use of proper channels of communication that will encourage the circulation and sharing of information flowing from the information source to the community, or from the community to the various levels in the decision-making process, or among groups and communities themselves.

Two-way Media

Under this aspect, the program tries to promote use of various media within systems of interactive or two-way communication that can be appropriated by groups or communities, and that are based not on the transmission of information or hortatory messages, but on facilitating the exchange of ideas. In any given context, the use of these systems must be linked to a process of community communication that will define the parameters under which they are designed or introduced, the conditions for setting them up, and the ways in which they can be evaluated.

Nonformal Education

Finally, the program takes into account the fact that nonformal educational processes are closely linked to grassroots communication processes. Information by itself is not enough to produce the kinds of behavioral and attitudinal changes that development requires. This means that development communication has to do with the processes of knowledge sharing that allow individuals and groups to organize themselves and to make sense of the information, knowledge, and attitudes that flow through the communication process.

By stressing the interrelationships between grassroots communication, exchange of information, the two-way use of media, and the process of nonformal education, the program supports participatory development communication as a process for facilitating interaction targeted on a specific category of users and specific development problems, for the purpose of producing social change. In terms of research, therefore, the program encourages the kind of work that will help groups and communities identify and implement solutions to their own problems of development.

Defining the role of participatory communication as a tool for nonformal grassroots education, as put forward by one of the discussion groups at the meeting, requires a sound understanding of the concepts of grassroots education and participatory communication. First, it must be recognized that the concept of grassroots education is closely linked to that of basic education.

Basic education was defined by the World Conference on Education for All (held in Jomtien, Thailand in March 1990) as education that seeks to respond to the basic needs for learning. It refers to providing basic formal education, nonformal education and literacy skills. The approach includes two key components: i) basic learning tools — reading, arithmetic, writing, and development of analytical skills; and ii) content — the knowledge, attitudes, aptitudes, and values required in daily life. Basic education may be acquired through formal channels (schools), nonformal ones (outside educational structures), or informal ones (through exposure to the environment and the family).

The concept of nonformal education refers to organized and structured educational activities designed for the benefit of a specific target group, which take place outside the official educational system. Nonformal education seeks to make contact with people who do not normally have access to educational and training structures. It deals generally with subjects related to key activities, such as agriculture, health, community development, etc.

Participatory development communication, on the other hand, recognizes the importance of feedback and dialogue in the communication process. It encourages individuals and groups to voice their perceptions of reality and to act on these realities. As a process based on dialogue, participatory communication, supported by group media, mass media, or interpersonal interactions, may come to respond to the needs of nonformal, grassroots, or basic education. It may also lead to a rethinking of what is meant by nonformal education, as a result of action based on exchanges of knowledge, rather than linear transmission of content.

Several key questions still require further attention and discussion. Research efforts need to focus on: clarifying the boundary between nonformal basic education and nonformal grassroots education; means to encourage participation in nonformal education, particularly by women and young girls; ways to identify and respond to development communication needs in key development sectors; means to assist communities in developing and implementing programs that fulfill their needs; how to integrate traditional forms of learning and knowledge into current practices; etc.

It is also important to consider the contribution of participatory development communication in fulfilling the needs of women and young girls in the area of nonformal grassroots education. In the most basic terms, and at the risk of generalization, African women are normally responsible for the majority of daily activities: domestic labour, food production, transformation and storage, animal husbandry, supply of drinking water and fuels, etc. We must add to this caring for children, and assisting their husbands in agricultural production and small-scale, commercial activities to earn extra income. In this context, the needs to which participatory development communication may respond are numerous.

There is certainly a fundamental need to transform this situation and to change social roles. Women also need to raise their self-esteem and self-confidence and, as a result, change their image of their role in society. At the same time, they must assume a larger role in public life. Women also need communication support for nonformal education activities and increased participation in community development.

In terms of learning experiences, there are several sociocultural and socioeconomic barriers that restrict women's access to education. Often, access to education is largely reserved for boys; the education of girls is seen as a luxury, not a fundamental need. Sometimes school attendance is seen as presenting opportunities for danger (safety, unwanted pregnancies, etc.), when the school is located far from the village. Sometimes, as well, it is seen as a poor investment of the family's money, when girls with schooling do not find a job and leave their community. Sometimes, again, women's education is seen as a threat to traditional community values and culture, since education promotes alien values, and so on.

How, then, can participatory communication support educational efforts for women and help them overcome these cultural barriers? The ways are many, including: locating nonformal educational projects within communities; taking women's working hours into account; promoting models that demonstrate the advantages of educating girls and women; establishing incentives; developing types of learning that are relevant to the needs of communities; and taking local knowledge into account.

Finally, focusing the program on women and young girls does not only mean identifying their needs and attempting to respond to them. There is also a need to identify their potential for acting as social communicators within their communities, and to seek to overcome the major obstacles that could hold them back. Women will be able to play a significant role in the community communication process only if these constraints are removed.

12
Public Broadcasting System

Public broadcasting, also known as public service broadcasting or PSB, where radio, television, and potentially other electronic media outlets receive funding from the public, has traditionally been the dominant form of broadcasting around the world. The broadcasters' funds can come directly from individuals through donations or fees, or indirectly as state subsidies that originated in taxes or other national funding sources. Some public broadcasters supplement this with contributions from corporations, which may be granted a limited amount of advertising time in return. However, when advertisements occur on public broadcasting outlets, they are usually much shorter and less attention-grabbing than on commercial broadcasting stations. Commercial broadcasting now occurs in many countries around the world, and the number of countries with only public broadcasting has declined substantially.

One of the best known public broadcasters is the British Broadcasting Corporation, based in the United Kingdom, whose mission is to "inform, educate and entertain". In the United States, public broadcasting is more decentralized and is not government operated, but does receive some government support. The majority of funding comes from community support to hundreds of public radio and public television stations, each of which is an individual entity licensed to one of several different non-profit organizations, municipal or state governments, or universities. These organizations often produce their own programs, but largely depend upon national producers and program distributors such as National Public Radio (NPR), Public Broadcasting Service (PBS), Public Radio International (PRI), and American Public Media. U.S. government support is filtered through a separate organization, the Corporation for Public Broadcasting (CPB).

There is no standard definition of what public broadcasting is exactly, although a number of official bodies have attempted to pick out the key characteristics. Public service broadcasters generally transmit programming that aims to improve society by informing viewers. In contrast, the aim of commercial outlets is to provide popular shows that attract an audience—therefore leading to higher prices when advertising is sold. For this reason, the ideals of public broadcasting are often incompatible with commercial goals. Of course, public broadcasters also strive to entertain their viewers, but they can still come across as being overly paternalistic in nature.

The Broadcasting Research Unit lists the following as major goals or characteristics of a public broadcaster:

— *Geographic universality* — that the stations' broadcasts are available nationwide. However, in the case of PBS in the United States and the CBC/Radio-Canada in Canada, the "nationwide" criterion is satisfied by either member stations (as is the case with PBS) or, as is the case with most public broadcasting systems around the world (including Canada's CBC/Radio-Canada), the system owning transmitters to broadcast nationwide.

— *Catering for all interests and tastes* — as exemplified by the BBC's range of minority channels (BBC2, BBC Radio 3, and various digital services), but also by the commercial Channel 4.

— *Catering for minorities* — much as above, but with racial and sexual minorities etc.

— *Concern for national identity and community* — this essentially means that the stations should in the most part commission programmes from within the country, which may be more expensive than importing shows from abroad.

— *Detachment from vested interests and government* — in other words, programming should be impartial, and the stations should not pander to the desires of advertisers or government. In practice however, such impartiality is questionable, even with the BBC. Even when a station is removed from corporate and government interests, there may be a sense that it panders to a particular social group.

— *One broadcasting system to be directly funded by the corpus of users* — the licence fee in the case of the BBC, member stations asking for donations in the case of the US's · PBS/· NPR.

— *Competition in good programming rather than numbers* — quality is the prime concern with a true public service broadcaster. Of course, in practice, ratings wars are rarely concerned with quality, although that may depend on how you define the word "quality".

— *Guidelines to liberate programme makers and not restrict them* — in the UK, guidelines, and not laws, govern what a programme maker can and cannot do, although these guidelines can be backed up by hefty penalties.

Some of these definition points may not be acceptable everywhere. For example in the United States public radio may see part of its mission to bring in foreign shows, e.g. shows from the CBC/Radio-Canada or the BBC. In the modern world, the mass media is tremendously competitive, and as such, it can be difficult for a public service broadcaster to survive amongst commercial interests, especially with the increased number of channels that digital broadcasting provides.

Modern public broadcasting is typically a mixed commercial model. For example, the CBC has always relied on a subsidy from general revenues of the government, and more recently, in the case of the CBC television, advertising revenues, making them competitive with commercial broadcasting. Some argue that this dilutes their mandate as truly public broadcasters, who have no commercial bias to distort their presentation of the news. In most countries in Western Europe, state broadcasters are similarly funded through a mix of advertising and public money, either through a licence fee or directly from the government.

Advantages and Disadvantages

A key advantage of public broadcasting is that it can rely on stable management and policies to attract and develop journalistic talent. This tends to make public broadcasters worldwide particularly trusted for reporting news. Even in the United States, where there is far more competition for top news anchors, journalists, hosts and commentators, some of its public broadcasts, such as The Newshour with Jim Lehrer, are widely respected and can attract important people to comment on the issues of the day. Those guests can in turn count on a commitment to balance, and perhaps also more educated questions, which assured them they would not be turned into a public spectacle for the sake of ratings (always a risk in any TV or radio programme.)

Another key advantage of public broadcasting is that a cultural policy (an industrial policy and investment policy for culture) is relatively easy to implement. For instance, the Canadian government commitment to official bilingualism creates stable work at the CBC for translators, journalists who work in French in English regions of Canada, encourages production of cross-cultural material. Some, such as Quebec separatists, argue that this is also a policy of cultural imperialism and assimilation. However, this is a criticism of the policy, rather than of the cultural methodology. In the UK, the BBC has also taken a strong stance in favor of multiculturalism and diversity: many of its on-screen commentators and hosts are of different ethnic origins.

For those who oppose cultural policy on principle, the above arguments are actually arguments against public broadcasting. However, even opponents of government cultural policy (who may state their objection as disagreement with 'culture being shoved down their throat'), rarely object to being exposed to the "cultural policies" of commercial broadcasting: pop culture, law presented as if it were truth, militarism and identification with 'our boys' etc., all manner of culture bias, and consumerism in the form of advertising itself. In public broadcasting, these things can be centrally controlled and limited, or at least openly discussed. Some will say lack of a cultural policy is a policy in itself: commercialism.

An interesting example of this balancing role is the use of the word "terrorism". While commercial broadcasters often use the word as if it were a category one could observe directly, public broadcasters are forced by their very mandate to justify their use of the word — the BBC at one point claimed it would label no one a "terrorist" as they considered it a political term. Throughout the IRA crises, the BBC steadfastly referred to "the IRA", "Republican forces" or to "militants". They avoided the term "terrorist" and even "extremist".

One viewpoint is that some public broadcasting, and also some pirate broadcasting, provides a necessary counterweight to the commercial media. Advocates of deliberative democracy, which requires much 'air-time' and 'feedback' and access to public figures to work, usually consider public broadcasting to be an absolute necessity to the maintenance of a complex modern technological democracy.

Whether one likes it or not, in many nations, public broadcasting is all there is. Where commercial media is allowed at all, it may be seen merely as an avenue for the presentation of commercial products that few in the population can afford and as a cultural policy of foreign 'invasion'. Public broadcasting sometimes serves simply to put voices or languages on the air that may otherwise be completely ignored, and sometimes due to a lack of voice, obliterated. To the degree that rumours and hatred can be dispelled by diligent public broadcasting, it can be seen as a public good. Where it is used to amplify hatred and fear, as dictators have used it, it can even be an instrument to foment genocide.

Accordingly, public broadcasting must probably be managed as carefully as any nation manages its police or military forces. The ability of electronic media to mobilise and motivate the public to a common cause is profound, and its abuse is probably as serious as abuses of force.

Public Broadcasting around the World

Australia

In Australia, the Australian Broadcasting Corporation (ABC) is funded entirely through an Australian Government grant-in-aid, which has made it vulnerable to cuts in government spending. The multicultural Special Broadcasting Service (SBS), Australia's other public broadcaster, now accepts limited sponsorship and advertising.

In addition, there are a number of community television stations (most operating as Channel 31 despite being unrelated across different states) and radio stations that survive almost entirely on donations and corporate sponsorship. They are organised similarly to PBS and NPR stations in the US, however are much less powerful; largely due to competition from the ABC and SBS. They also take on the role that public access stations have in the US.

Canada

In Canada, the main public broadcaster is the national CBC, which operates two television networks (CBC Television and SRC), four radio networks (CBC Radio One, CBC Radio Two, La Première Chaîne and Espace musique) and two 24-hour news channels (CBC Newsworld and RDI) in both of Canada's official languages.

In addition, several provinces operate public broadcasters; these are not CBC subentities, but distinct networks in their own right. These include TVOntario, which operates two networks (English TVO and French-language TFO), Télé-Québec, SCN in Saskatchewan, public radio station CKUA in Alberta, and Knowledge Network in British Columbia. Some of the provincial broadcasters operate through conventional transmitters, while others are cable-only channels. Alberta also has a semi-public television network, ACCESS, which is licensed to provide some public service programming but is owned and operated by a commercial broadcaster. The network, formerly a public broadcaster operated by the provincial government, was sold to CHUM Limited in 1995. CJRT-FM in Toronto also operated as a public government-owned radio station for many years; while no longer funded by the provincial government, it still solicits most of its budget from listener and corporate donations and is permitted to air only a very small amount of commercial advertising.

Some local community stations also operate non-commercially with funding from corporate and individual donors. In addition, cable companies are required to produce a local community channel in each licensed market. Such channels have traditionally aired community talk shows, city council meetings and other locally oriented programming, although it is becoming increasingly common for them to adopt the format and branding of a local news channel. Canada also has a large number of campus radio and community radio stations.

Europe

The model, established in the 1920s, of the British Broadcasting Corporation – an organization widely trusted, even by citizens of the Axis Powers during World War II – was widely emulated throughout the former British Empire and later Commonwealth: the Canadian Broadcasting Corporation and Australian Broadcasting Corporation are simple applications of that model. In Scandinavia, too, the public broadcasters Sveriges Radio and Sveriges Television in Sweden, NRK in Norway, YLE in Finland, and Danmarks Radio in Denmark are basically an application of the model used in Britain, funded by television licence fees and carrying no advertising. So is the Flemish broadcaster VRT, at least as far as its television channels are concerned; for its radio services it depends on a mix of advertising income and government grants.

In theory, public broadcasting is not beholden to advertisers, political parties, or the government of the day — nor, some critics say, is it particularly responsive to its viewers. In the Netherlands a different system is used. There, member-based public-broadcasting associations are allocated time to broadcast their programmes on the publicly owned television and radio channels in proportion to their membership numbers. This system is intended to reflect the diversity of all the groups composing the nation.

Latin America

Latin America has never had a history of European style public service radio or television except for Chile's

Televisión Nacional, an open channel which serves the entire country (including Easter Island and Antarctica bases). Televisión Nacional, popularly known as channel 7 because of its Santiago frequency, is governed by a seven-member board appointed by the Chilean Senate. It is meant to be independent of political pressures, although accusations of bias have been made, especially during election campaigns.

State broadcasters tend to be either very weak and under-funded (as the Argentinian ATC), or to be clearly under the control of the party in power. Starting from these singularities, commercial broadcasting quickly and effectively conquered its audiences, leaving public and state broadcasting a token role. In some countries, such as Ecuador, where broadcasting was originally legally defined as a commercial venture, a public broadcaster was never born.

New Zealand

In New Zealand, the former public broadcaster BCNZ (formerly NZBC) was broken up into separate state-owned corporations, Television New Zealand (TVNZ) and Radio New Zealand (RNZ). While RNZ remains commercial-free, TVNZ has been heavily commercialised, leading to accusations of 'dumbing down'.

Japan

In Japan, the main public broadcaster is the national NHK, sometimes informally referred to as Radio Tokyo by English speakers. The broadcaster was set up in 1926 and was modelled on BBC Ltd, the precursor to the British public service broadcaster BBC created in 1927. Much like the BBC, NHK is funded by a "receiving fee" by every Japanese household, with no commercial advertising and the maintenance of a position of strict political impartiality. NHK runs two national terrestrial TV stations (NHK General and NHK Educational) and three satellite only services (NHK BS-1, BS-2 and the hi-definition NHK Hi-Vision services). NHK also runs 3 national radio services and a number of international radio and television services, akin to the BBC World Service. NHK has also been an innovator in television, developing the world's first high definition television technology in 1964 and launching high definition services in Japan in 1981.

United States

Public broadcasting in the United States is as old as broadcasting itself. Most early public stations were operated by state colleges and universities, and were often run as part of the schools' cooperative extension services. Stations in this era were internally funded, and did not rely on listener contributions to operate; some accepted advertising. Networks such as Iowa, South Dakota, and Wisconsin Public Radio began in this way. The concept of a "non-commercial, educational" station per se does not show up in U.S. law until the 1940s, when the FM band was moved to its present location; the part of the band between 87.9 and 91.9 MHz is reserved for such stations. Educational television, the forerunner of modern U.S. public television, evolved in big cities in the 1950s; in rural areas, it was not uncommon for colleges to operate commercial stations instead.

In the United States the Public Broadcasting Service (PBS) television network operates on a largely viewer-supported basis, with commercial sponsors of specific programs. Over time, sponsorship announcements have slowly transformed into something resembling regular TV advertisements, though they are usually shorter and have a more muted tone than what is seen on commercial TV, and many organizations still only receive a short thanks for their contributions. Most communities also have public access services on local cable television stations, which are sometimes supported in part through donations.

The first publicly funded radio network in the United States was the Pacifica Radio Network, founded by pacifist Lew Hill in 1946. Pacifica now operates six stations in Berkeley, Los Angeles, Houston, Washington DC, and New York City, and distributes syndicated programming via satellite to affiliates.

The second public radio network, NPR, was created in 1970, following the passage of the Public Broadcasting Act of 1967 which established the Corporation for Public Broadcasting. This network (generally exclusive of Pacifica) is commonly referred to as 'Public Radio. Independent local public radio stations buy their programming from distributors such as National Public Radio (NPR); Public Radio International (PRI); American Public Media (APM), and Pacifica, most often distributed through the Public Radio Satellite Service (PRSS). Public radio stations in the US tend to broadcast a mixture of news and talk radio programming along with some music. Some of the larger operations split off these formats into separate stations or networks. Public music stations are probably best known for playing classical music, although other formats have been used, including the emerging "eclectic" music format that is rather freeform in nature (common among college radio stations, though a well-known eclectic NPR member station is KCRW in California). There are also public college radio stations using an FCC Class D license. XM Satellite Radio provides a station of public radio programs licensed from all three content providers.

Local stations derive most of the funding for their operations through regular pledge drives and corporate sponsorship. The local stations then contract with program distributors and also provide some programming themselves. NPR produces some of its own programming such as Morning Edition; Weekend Edition; and All Things

Considered. PBS and PRI do not create their own content. NPR also receives some direct funding from private donors, foundations, and from the Corporation for Public Broadcasting.

Public Broadcasting Service

The Public Broadcasting Service (PBS) is a non-profit public broadcasting television service with 349 member TV stations in the United States. Its headquarters are in Alexandria, Virginia. PBS was founded in 1969, at which time it took over many of the functions of its predecessor, National Educational Television (NET). PBS commenced broadcasting in October 1970. PBS is not a broadcast network in the sense in which that term is usually used in the United States. Unlike the commercial television broadcast model of American networks such as NBC, CBS, ABC and Fox, in which affiliates give up portions of their local advertising airtime in exchange for network programming, PBS member stations pay substantial fees for the shows acquired and distributed by the national organization.

This relationship means that PBS member stations have greater latitude in local scheduling than their commercial counterparts. Scheduling of PBS-distributed series may vary wildly from market to market. This can be a source of tension as stations seek to preserve their localism and PBS strives to market a consistent national lineup. However, PBS has a policy of "common carriage" requiring most stations to clear the national prime time programs on a common schedule, so that they can be more effectively marketed on a national basis.

Unlike its radio counterpart, National Public Radio, PBS has no central program production arm or news department. All of the programming carried by PBS, whether news, documentary, or entertainment, is created by (or in most cases produced under contract with) individual member stations. WGBH is one of the largest producers of educational programming; news programs are produced by WETA-TV and WPBT, and the Charlie Rose interview show and Nature come from WNET. Once a program is distributed to PBS, the network (and not the member station that supplied it) retains all rights for rebroadcasts; the suppliers do maintain the right to sell the program in non-broadcast media such as DVDs, books, and licensed merchandise.

PBS stations are commonly operated by non-profit organizations or universities in their community of license. In some states, PBS stations throughout the entire state may be organized into a single regional "subnetwork" (ex. Alabama Public Television). Unlike the CBC-SRC state broadcaster in Canada, PBS does not own any of the stations that broadcast its programming. This is partly due to the origins of the PBS stations themselves, and partly due to historical license issues.

In the modern broadcast marketplace, this organizational structure is considered outmoded by some media critics. A common restructuring proposal is to reorganize the network so that each state would have one PBS affiliate which broadcast state-wide. However, this proposal is controversial, as it would reduce local community input into PBS programming, especially considering PBS stations are particularly more community-oriented than their commercial counterparts.

Programming

PBS's evening schedule emphasizes fine arts (Great Performances), drama (Mystery! and Masterpiece Theatre), science (Nova and Scientific American Frontiers), public affairs (Frontline, The Newshour with Jim Lehrer) and independent films (P.O.V. and Independent Lens).

PBS has distributed a number of highly regarded children's shows such as Sesame Street, The Electric Company, Villa Alegre, Zoom!, 3-2-1 Contact, The Letter People, Barney & Friends, Shining Time Station, Thomas & Friends, Ghostwriter, Reading Rainbow, Breakfast with Andy and Mister Rogers' Neighborhood. Popular animated series have included Clifford the Big Red Dog, Arthur, Liberty's Kids and The Magic School Bus. The service has also imported British kids' series including Teletubbies and Boohbah. Some of these programs have since migrated to commercial television, including Ghostwriter and The Magic School Bus.

However, PBS is not the only distributor of public television programming to the member stations. Other distributors have emerged from the roots of the old companies that had loosely held regional public television stations in the 1960s. Boston-based American Public Television (former names include Eastern Educational Network and American Program Service) is second only to PBS for distributing programs to U.S. non-commercial stations. Another distributor is NETA (formerly SECA), whose properties have included The Shapies and Jerry Yarnell School of Fine Art. In addition, the member stations themselves also produce a variety of local shows, some of which subsequently receive national distribution through PBS or the other distributors.

PBS stations are known for rebroadcasting British television dramas and comedies (acquired from the BBC and other sources) — these shows are generally seen on Saturday evenings, generally regarded as the least-watched evening of the week due to viewers doing outside activities such as going to a movie, a concert, or other functions; so much of the exposure (or lack thereof) of American audiences to British television (particularly comedies) comes through PBS it has been joked that PBS means "Primarily British Series." However, a significant amount of sharing takes place. The BBC and other media outlets in the region such as Channel 4 often cooperate with PBS stations, producing material that is shown on both sides of the Atlantic. Also, though less frequently, Canadian and Australian, among other international, programming appears on PBS stations (such as The Red Green Show, currently distributed by syndicator Executive Program Services); the public-broadcasting syndicators are more likely to offer this programming to the U.S. public stations.

Stations that produce a significant amount of PBS network programming include:

— WGBH-TV 2/19/43/44 Boston, MA

— WNET 13/61 Newark, New Jersey/ New York, New York

— WETA-TV 26/27 Washington, DC

— KCET 28/59 Los Angeles, CA

— WQED 13/38 Pittsburgh, PA

— WPBT 2/18 Miami, FL/ Ft. Lauderdale, FL

— KQED 9/30 San Francisco, CA

— WHYY 12 Wilmington, Delaware/ Philadelphia, PA

— WTTW 11 Chicago, IL

— WFYI 20 Indianapolis, IN

— KLRU 18 Austin, TX

— KPBS 11/15 San Diego, CA

— Oklahoma Educational Television Authority

— Kentucky Educational Television (KET) is the largest member broadcaster in the country (geographically) with 16 stations servicing all of Kentucky, and parts of Arkansas, Illinois, Indiana, Missouri, Ohio, Tennessee and West Virginia.

Criticism and Controversy

PBS has been the subject of some controversy. It is subject to repeated attempts to reduce federal funding. On June 8, 2006, the Los Angeles Times reported that a key House committee had "approved a $115 million reduction in the budget for the Corporation for Public Broadcasting, that could force the elimination of some popular PBS and NPR programs." This would reduce the Corporation's budget by 23%, to $380 million, for 2007. A similar budget cut was attempted in 2005, but was defeated by intense lobbying from the PBS stations and the Democrats.

PBS was founded to provide diversity in programming at a time when all television was broadcast (as opposed to today's cable or satellite transmission methods) and most communities received only three or four signals. Today many households subscribe to cable TV or have satellite dishes that receive tens or hundreds of signals, including varied educational and children's programs. But according to public television proponents, the service be intended to provide universal access, particularly to poor and rural viewers. They also say that many cable and satellite productions are of lower quality, including children's programs.

Most stations solicit individual donations by methods including pledge drives or telethons which can disrupt regularly scheduled programming. Although many viewers find it useful to raise funds, others think this is a source of annoyance since they replace the normal programs with specials aimed at a wider audience, while some find the commercial stations' ads even more annoying.

The Public Broadcasting Act of 1967 required a "strict adherence to objectivity and balance in all programs or series of programs of a controversial nature." It also prohibited the federal government from interfering or controlling what is broadcast. This set up an obvious tension where the government that created the CPB would not be able to do anything about a perceived failure to meet its obligation for objectivity and balance without interfering in some way.

At a more basic and problematic level is how and who should determine what constitutes objectivity and balance when there are massive disagreements over what that would be. There seems to be no consensus or even attempts at forming a consensus to resolve this dilemma.

Some conservatives perceive it to have a liberal bias and criticize its tax-based revenue and have periodically but unsuccessfully attempted to discontinue funding of CPB. Although state and federal sources account for a minority percentage of public television funding, the system remains vulnerable to political pressure. Kenneth Tomlinson, Disgraced former chairman of the Corporation for Public Broadcasting, in November 2004 in Baltimore, told PBS officials, "They should make sure their programming better reflected the Republican mandate." Tomlinson later said that his comment was in jest and that he could not imagine how remarks at a fun occasion were taken the wrong way. A report whose results were publicized in November 2005 sharply criticized Tomlinson for the way he used CPB resources to "go after" this perceived liberal bias.

Left-wing critics dislike PBS affiliates' dependence on corporate sponsorships and some are uncomfortable with shows such as Wall $treet Week which they see as promoting a corporate outlook without any corresponding series featuring opposing views from labor unions. For example, one of PBS' documentaries, Commanding Heights, strongly supports globalization while painting labor unions as socialist organizations.

Some of its documentaries on Islam and the Arab world, such as Empire of Faith, have been attacked as either fawning or factually challenged. Individual programs, particularly those dealing with the subject of homosexuality, have been the targets of organized campaigns by those with opposing views including United States Secretary of Education Margaret Spellings.

Kenneth Tomlinson, who took over in 2003, began his tenure by asking for Karl Rove's assistance in overturning a regulation that half the CPB board have practical experience in radio or television. Later he appointed an outside consultant to monitor the regular PBS program NOW with Bill Moyers. Told that the show had "liberal" leanings, Moyers eventually resigned after more than three decades as a PBS regular, saying Tomlinson had mounted a "vendetta" against him. Subsequently, PBS made room for conservative commentator Tucker Carlson, and Journal Editorial Report with Paul Gigot, an editor of the Wall Street Journal editorial page. On November 3, 2005 PBS announced the resignation of Tomlinson and the investigations of improper financial dealings with consultants.

New networks

PBS has also spun off a number of TV networks, often in partnership with other media companies: PBS YOU (ended January 2006, and largely succeeded by American Public Television's Create network), PBS KIDS (ended October 1, 2005), PBS KIDS Sprout, and PBS DT2 (a feed of HDTV and letterboxed programming for digitally equipped member stations), along with packages of PBS programs that are similar to local stations' programming, the PBS-X feeds. PBS Kids Go! is promised for September, 2006. Some or all are available on many digital cable systems, on free-to-air TV via communications satellites, as well as via DirecTV direct broadcast satellite. With the transition to terrestrial digital television broadcasts, many are also often now available as "multiplexed" channels on some local stations' standard-definition digital signals, while DT2 is found among the HD signals.

13

Radio and Standards of Ethics

The radio broadcasters are responsible for the image of their individual radio program, radio station and its support structures. How the broadcasters conduct themselves on the radio, at the station or elsewhere reflects not only their own personality but also the integrity of the radio station. Every radio should approve its own ethical standards. The following are selected examples of the ethical standards that participants in radio should adhere to. A radio's standards of ethics and conduct apply to every person representing the radio.

Conducting the Broadcast

1.Prepare for The Program

A radio program must present new ideas, information and points of view. Hence, an announcer should always read, research and secure information from reliable sources. He/she must organize the program well before going on air.

2. Do Research

The broadcaster should look for new and useful information. A person cannot give new, interesting and comprehensive information if it is not researched and available. Radio requires a lot of fresh information every minute of airtime. A broadcaster can only inspire other people if he/she has something new or interesting to offer. The most persistent researcher and inquirer will some day end up as the most reliable source of information for other people.

3. Keep a Good Taste

The broadcaster should always choose wholesome topics, language, jokes and presentation. Obscenity, blasphemy, profanity and vulgarity have no place in broadcasting, much less in a broadcast. Curse words are forbidden. Listeners, especially children and youth, should always be able to uphold the announcer as a model of propriety in action and language.

4. Tell the Truth

The announcer/reporter must report only facts gathered from reliable sources. If information has not been adequately researched and verified, the broadcasters should avoid using it on the air. If unverified information needs to be aired for the sake of forewarning the people, the announcer should clearly identify those pieces of information that have not been checked for veracity.

5. Verify Information

The announcer should seek and check all information with the most credible sources such as libraries, books, knowledgeable persons, competent authorities, involved persons and the records of the event in question. Half-truths or distortions of the truth should not be allowed on the air.

6. Be Fair

A reporter shall avoid introducing his/her own bias, prejudice, partiality, inclination or personal belief when reporting an event or describing a situation. Objectivity shall never be compromised.

7. Maintain the Innocence of the Accused

Dealing with allegations and accusations always requires utmost care and integrity. The accuser should be clearly identified, including his/ her position and relation to the accused as well as clarifying his/her, possibly biased, viewpoint. A broadcaster shall bear in mind that a person is presumed innocent unless proven guilty. Cases pending in court are subjudice, that is, merits of the case cannot be discussed in public, particularly in the media. Reporting the records and facts of the case being tried is, however, allowed.

8. Respect the Rights of Everybody

The urge, and even the right of the community to know, is not a license for the announcer to breach a person's privacy. Information withheld by a person for personal or family reasons should not be transgressed in the name of public information. A reporter should respect off-therecord information confided and entrusted to him/her by an interviewee.

9. Prefer the Positive/Constructive Approach

A positively minded announcer/reporter will find at least ten interesting and useful pieces of information for every major unsavory conflict. When dealing with a problem, the most important aspect is the discussion of solutions, suggestions, recommendations and possibilities for resolution.

10. Determine Hearsays, Gossips, And Rumors

There is a lot of unfounded information, rumor, hearsay, gossip and chatter delivered to radio station personnel. It is always tempting to repeat them on the air. However, all information should be validated before it is aired. It is better to take time and validate information than be the first one to disseminate disinformation. The latter may also have legal consequences.

Conduct within the Operational Framework

Be a Team Player

A member of the radio station shall treat his/her co-workers as team mates. He/she must therefore participate in evaluation and discussions regarding programs. He/she must encourage his/her team mates to assess and criticize his/her own work. All members of the team must be willing to accept constructive criticism. They must abide by the decisions and recommendations of management.

Respect Decisions

The members of the radio shall respect the administrative mechanisms and policies put in place by the CRC. Policies, rules and regulations approved by the management shall be fully complied with.

Be Prompt and Punctual

An announcer shall come to the studio no less than 10 minutes before broadcast time. In the case of a known reason for non-arrival he/she should inform his/her station manager at least a day before the broadcast, or earlier. Only in an emergency situation may an announcer be absent without advance notice.

Be Cooperative

Every announcer/reporter shall help a member who is placed in a difficult situation. He/she should offer additional information, contacts and materials to a fellow broadcaster in need.

Be Ready for Pinch-Hitting

It shall be standard procedure in live programs for the previous announcer to deputize for an announcer who does not arrive, or who fails to arrive in time.

Observe Proper Conduct in Studio Premises

No person shall be allowed to carry firearms inside the studio, irrespective of whether the person is a member of the police or military. It is a violation of the integrity of the radio to appear at the station under influence of alcohol or drugs, or to drink or use drugs at the station.

Any immoral or illegal activities within the station shall be considered an infringement of station's rules and regulations. The members of the radio shall not bring personal guests or relatives to the station who have not been advised about proper decorum with respect to sanitation, order, silence, and non-tampering of equipment as well as the importance of maintaining a clean environment. Guests shall not in anyway distract the broadcasters, interfere in studio operation, disrupt broadcasting activities, pilfer the station property and equipment or behave in any way that is prejudicial to the radio station.

Children must always be accompanied by adults at the station.

Care for Studio Equipment

Every member of staff should help preserve the equipment and property of the radio station.

Only the trained, qualified and authorized staff must operate studio equipment.Equipment should never be left "switched on" when not being used. It shall be the obligation of every user to clean, repack, cover and replace the equipment in its original position, rack or storage bin after usage.

The radio management should impose regulations regarding the proper use of equipment. Systems of usage and borrowing should be in place. A user's and borrower's [if allowed] log should be maintained in the studio.

No piece, or part of, studio equipment may be removed from the premises without written approval from the station manager or another designated person.

Equipment removed from studio premises shall be returned promptly. Any malfunction, breakdown, loss or abnormality in the set up of equipment should be reported immediately to proper authorities, together with pertinent notations on date, time and cause.

Conduct Outside the Studio Station

The conduct of a member of the radio station in the community will reflect on the image of the whole station.

How he/she treats his/her family, neighbors, friends, associates and the members of his/her community is a manifestation of what kind of person he/she is. A radio station's personality is therefore required to live a good community and family life in order to qualify as a reformer and development initiator.

It is a violation of the station policies for an unauthorized member of the station to solicit or receive funds, favors, or concessions in the name of the station, or program, for personal benefit.

Solicitation for Advertisements and Funds

Only officially designated persons may solicit donations, contributions, grants or advertisements for either the radio station or individual programs. It will be considered misrepresentation for any staff member, volunteer, member of the CRC or any one who has not been given written authority to solicit or receive funds for the station. Civil and criminal responsibility may be assessed against him/her.

The station must not receive funds from illegal sources such as operators of gambling dens, advertisers, drug pushers, illegal loggers, smugglers, environment polluters

14

Television Technology

Television is a telecommunication system for broadcasting and receiving moving pictures and sound over a distance. The term has come to refer to all the aspects of television from the television set to the programming and transmission. The word is derived from mixed Latin and Greek roots, meaning "far seeing".

History of Television

The origins of what would become today's television system are traced back as far as the discovery of the photoconductivity of the element selenium by Willoughby Smith in 1873, and the invention of a scanning disk by Paul Nipkow in 1884. All practical television systems use the fundamental idea of scanning an image to produce a time series signal representation. That representation is then transmitted to a device to reverse the scanning process. The final device, the television, relies on the human eye to integrate the result into a coherent image again.

While electromechanical techniques were developed prior to World War II, most notably by Charles Francis Jenkins and John Logie Baird, all-electronic television systems relied on the inventions of Philo Taylor Farnsworth, Vladimir Zworykin and others to produce a system suitable for mass distribution of television programming.

Commercial broadcast programming, following years of experimental broadcasts seen only in a few specially-equipped homes, occurred in both the United States and the United Kingdom before World War II.

The first television broadcasts with a modern level of definition (240+ lines) were made in England in 1936. Television did not become commonplace in United States homes until the middle 1950s. While North American over-the-air broadcasting was originally free of direct marginal cost to the consumer (i.e., cost in excess of acquisition and upkeep of the hardware) and broadcasters were compensated primarily by receipt of advertising revenue, increasingly television consumers obtain their programming by subscription to cable television systems or direct-to-home satellite transmissions. In the United Kingdom, on the other hand, the owner of each television must pay a licence fee annually which is used to support the British Broadcasting Corporation.

Elements of a Television System

The elements of a simple television system are:

— An image source - this may be a camera for live pick-up of images or a flying spot scanner for transmission of films

— A sound source.

— A transmitter, which modulates one or more television signals with both picture and sound information for transmission.

— A receiver (television) which recovers the picture and sound signals from the television broadcast.

— A display device, which turns the electrical signals into visible light and audible sound.

Practical television systems include equipment for selecting different image sources, mixing images from several sources at once, insertion of pre-recorded video signals, synchronizing signals from many sources, and direct image generation by computer for such purposes as station identification. Transmission may be over the air from land-based transmitters, over metallic or optical cables, or by radio from synchronous satellites. Digital systems may be inserted anywhere in the chain to provide better image transmission quality, reduction in transmission bandwidth, special effects, or security of transmission from theft by non-subscribers.

Display Technology

Thanks to advances in display technology, there are now several kinds of video displays used in modern TV sets:

CRT: The most common displays are the ubiquitous direct-view CRTs for up to 40in (100cm) (in 4:3) and 46in (115cm) (in 16:9) diagonally. These are still the least expensive, and are a refined technology that can still provide the best overall picture quality. As they do not have a fixed native resolution, in some cases they are also capable of displaying sources with a variety of different resolutions at the best possible image quality. The frame rate or refresh rate of a typical NTSC format CRT TV is 60 Hz, and for the PAL format, it's 50 Hz. A typical NTSC broadcast signal's visible portion has an equivalent resolution of about 640x480 pixels. It actually could be slightly higher than that, but the Vertical Blanking Interval, or VBI, allows other signals to be carried along with the broadcast.

Rear projection: Most big-screen TVs (up to over 100 inch (254 cm)) use projection technology. Three types of projection systems are used in projection TVs: CRT-based, LCD-based, and DLP(reflective micromirror chip) -based. Projection television has been commercially available since the 1970s, but could not match the image sharpness of the CRT; current models are vastly improved, and offer a cost-effective large-screen display. A variation is a video projector, using similar technology, which projects onto a screen.

Flat panel LCD or plasma: Modern advances have brought flat panels to TV that use active matrix LCD or plasma display technology. Flat panel LCDs and plasma displays are as little as 4in (10cm) thick and can be hung on a wall like a picture or put over a pedestal. Some models can also be used as computer monitors.

Signal Connections

The number of ways to connect a video device to a television has increased over the years:

— *HDMI* - a 19 or 29-pin industry-supported digital interface which supports standard, enhanced, or high-definition video, plus multi-channel digital audio on a single cable. The video signal is backward-compatible with DVI. Increasingly common on displays, DVD players, and high-end PC graphics cards. Copy protection is implemented using HDCP.

— *DVI* - a 17 to 29-pin connector that carries digital video signals, designed to carry HDTV but also used in current DVD players and latest digital displays. Copy protection is available using HDCP.

— *Component video* - three separate RCA jacks (colored red, green and blue) carry three analog video signals, one brightness (luminance) and two colors (chromas), and is usually referred to as "Y, B-Y, R-Y", "Y Cr Cb" (interlaced) or "Y Pr Pb" (progressive), or YUV. Audio is not carried on this cable. This connection provides for picture quality superior to S-Video and is typically used in home theater for DVDs, satellite and analogue HDTV;

less common in Europe but is starting to become more widely available.

—   *SCART* - a large 21 pin connector that may carry analog signals consisting of: one video signal composite video; or two video signals S-Video; or for picture quality similar to component video, three signals of separate red, green and blue or RGB; or for best picture quality, four video signals of separate red, green, blue and sync or RGBS; plus right and left line-level audio channels; along with a number of control signals including an aspect-ratio flag (e.g. widescreen). This system has been standard in Europe since mid-1980s for all consumer electronics, which meant that RGBS was available on even the earliest PAL DVD players and satellite receivers. Japan uses a 21 pin RGB connector which is visually similar to SCART but with different pin configurations. This connector is not used in the U.S.

—   *S-Video* - small round connector with two separate analog video signals, one carrying brightness (luminance), the other carrying color (chroma). Also referred to as Y/C video. Provides most of the benefit of component video, with slightly less color fidelity. Use started in the 1980s for S-VHS, Hi-8, and early NTSC DVD players to relay high quality video before component was available. This will sometimes, completely incorrectly, be referred to as an S-VHS connector. Audio is not carried on this cable.

—   *Composite video* - The most common form of connecting external devices, putting all the analog video information into one signal. Most televisions provide this option with a yellow RCA jack or occasionally a BNC connector. Audio is not carried on this cable, though two separate cables with similar red and white RCA jacks for right and left line-level audio are commonly bonded to composite video cables.

— *Coaxial RF* - All audio channels and picture components are transmitted through one coaxial cable and modulated on a radio frequency. Most TVs manufactured since the 1970s provide a coaxial connection, and this is the type of cable typically used for cable television.

Although still found on VHS tape-players, most modern DVD players and other video devices no longer supply an RF output, so very old TV sets made before composite video jacks became commonplace will need a modulator device. NTSC sets use a 75 ohm F-connector; most PAL sets use a 50 ohm Belling Lee. Most set-top TV antennas have a 300 ohm impedance, so to connect them to a coaxial input requires an inexpensive matching transformer to avoid signal degradation.

— *300 ohm twin-lead* - The predecessor to coaxial cable, generally a flat insulated cable with a pair of wires separated by 0.5 inch, found on NTSC television sets from 1940 to about 1985, and originally used to connect rabbit ears to a receiver. Connection to the set was by connecting the wire to a pair of screws on the back of the television set.

Nominal impedance was 300 ohms; connecting an older set to cable or VCRs requires an inexpensive matching transformer to avoid signal degradation due to impedance mismatch. Twin-lead wiring is sensitive to nearby metal objects. Long runs must be properly supported away from metal objects and should be mounted with a loose twist in the cable.

— *Fiber optic* - The latest in connections and only on extremly new and high quality TVs, fiber optics use a laser to transmit data along a glass fiber. Used for sound and/or video, can be found on newer TVs, high end video editing systems, as well as in high end computer systems. Can be referred to as S/PDIF digital-audio format.

Aspect Ratios

Aspect ratio refers to the ratio of the horizontal to vertical measurements of a television's picture. Mechanically scanned television as first demonstrated by John Logie Baird in 1926 used a 7:3 vertical aspect ratio, oriented for the head and shoulders of a single person in close-up.

Most of the early electronic TV systems from the mid-1930s onward shared the same aspect ratio of 4:3 which was chosen to match the Academy Ratio used in cinema films at the time. This ratio was also square enough to be conveniently viewed on round cathode-ray tubes (CRTs), which were all that could be produced given the manufacturing technology of the time. The BBC's television service used a more squarish 5:4 ratio from 1936 to 3 April 1950, when it too switched to a 4:3 ratio.

In the 1950s, movie studios moved towards widescreen aspect ratios such as CinemaScope in an effort to distance their product from television. Although this was initially just a gimmick, widescreen is still the format of choice today and square aspect ratio movies are rare. Some people argue that widescreen is actually a disadvantage when showing objects that are tall instead of panoramic, others say that natural vision is more panoramic than tall, and therefore widescreen is easier on the eye.

The switch to digital television systems has been used as an opportunity to change the standard television picture format from the old ratio of 4:3 (approximately 1.33:1) to an aspect ratio of 16:9 (approximately 1.78:1). This enables TV to get closer to the aspect ratio of modern widescreen movies, which range from 1.78:1 through 1.85:1 to 2.35:1. There are two methods for transporting widescreen content, the better of which uses what is called anamorphic widescreen format. This format is very similar to the technique used to fit a widescreen movie frame inside a 1.33:1 35mm film frame. The image is compressed horizontally when recorded, then expanded again when played back. The anamorphic widescreen 16:9 format was first introduced via European PAL-Plus television broadcasts and then later on "widescreen" DVDs; the ATSC HDTV system uses straight widescreen format, no horizontal compression or expansion is used.

Recently "widescreen" has spread from television to computing where both desktop and laptop computers are commonly equipped with widescreen displays. There are some complaints about distortions of movie picture ratio due to some DVD playback software not taking account of aspect ratios; but this will subside as the DVD playback software matures.

Furthermore, computer and laptop widescreen displays are in the 16:10 aspect ratio both physically in size and in pixel counts, and not in 16:9 of consumer televisions, leading to further complexity. This was a result of widescreen computer display engineers' uninformed assumption that people viewing 16:9 content on their computer would prefer that an area of the screen be reserved for playback controls or subtitles, as opposed to viewing content full-screen.

The television industry's changing of aspect ratios is not without teething difficulties, and can present a considerable problem. Displaying a widescreen aspect (rectangular) image on a conventional aspect (square) display can be shown:

— in "letterbox" format, with black horizontal bars at the top and bottom

— with part of the image being cropped, usually the extreme left and right of the image being cut off (or in "pan and scan", parts selected by an operator)

— with the image horizontally compressed

A conventional aspect (square) image on a widescreen aspect (rectangular) display can be shown:

— in "pillar box" format, with black vertical bars to the left and right

— with upper and lower portions of the image cut off (or in "tilt and scan", parts selected by an operator)

— with the image horizontally distorted

A common compromise is to shoot or create material at an aspect ratio of 14:9, and to lose some image at each side for 4:3 presentation, and some image at top and bottom for 16:9 presentation. In recent years, the cinematographic process known as Super 35 (championed by James Cameron) has been used to film a number of major movies such as Titanic, Legally Blonde, Austin Powers, and Crouching Tiger, Hidden Dragon. This process results in a camera-negative which can then be used to create both wide-screen theatrical prints, and standard "full frame" releases for television/VHS/DVD which avoid the need for either "letterboxing" or the severe loss of information caused by conventional "pan-and-scan" cropping.

Television Add-ons

Today there are many television add-ons including Video Game Consoles, VCRs, Set-top boxes for Cable and Satellite reception, DVD players, or Digital Video Recorders (including personal video recorders, PVRs). The add-on market continues to grow as new technologies are developed.

Advertising

Since their inception in the USA in 1940, TV commercials have become one of the most effective, most pervasive, and most popular methods of selling products of many sorts, especially consumer goods. U.S. advertising rates are determined primarily by Nielsen Ratings.

Programming

Getting TV programming shown to the public can happen in many different ways. After production the next step is to market and deliver the product to whatever markets are open to using it. This typically happens on two levels:

Original Run or First Run - a producer creates a program of one or multiple episodes and shows it on a station or network which has either paid for the production itself or to which a license has been granted by the producers to do the same.

Syndication - this is the terminology rather broadly used to describe secondary programming usages (beyond original run). It includes secondary runs in the country of first issue, but also international usage which may or may not be managed by the originating producer. In many cases other companies, TV stations or individuals are engaged to do the syndication work, in other words to sell the product into the markets they are allowed to sell into by contract from the copyright holders, in most cases the producers.

In most countries, the first wave occurs primarily on free-to-air (FTA) television, while the second wave happens on subscription TV and in other countries. In the U.S. however, the first wave occurs on the FTA networks and subscription services, and the second wave travels via all means of distribution.

First run programming is increasing on subscription services outside the U.S., but few domestically produced programs are syndicated on domestic FTA elsewhere. This practice is increasing however, generally on digital-only FTA channels, or with subscriber-only first run material appearing on FTA.

Unlike the U.S., repeat FTA screenings of a FTA network program almost only occur on that network. Also, affiliates rarely buy or produce non-network programming that isn't intensely local.

Social Aspects

Alleged dangers

Paralleling television's growing primacy in family life and society, an increasingly vocal chorus of legislators, scientists and parents are raising objections to the uncritical acceptance of the medium. For example, the Swedish government imposed a total ban on advertising to children under twelve in 1991. In the U.S., the National Institute on Media and the Family (not a government agency) points out that U.S. children watch an average of 25 hours of television per week and features studies showing it interferes with the educational and maturational process.

Fifty years of research on the impact of television on children's emotional and social development (Norma Pecora, John P. Murray, & Ellen A. Wartella, Children and Television: 50 Years of Research, published by Erlbaum Press, June, 2006) demonstrate that there are clear and lasting effects of viewing violence. In a recent study published in the journal Media Psychology, the research team demonstrated that the brain activation patterns of children viewing violence show that children are aroused by the violence (increased heart rates), demonstrate fear (activation of the amygdala-the fight or flight sensor in the brain) in response to the video violence, and store the observed violence in an area of the brain (the Posterior Cingulate) that is reserved for long-term memory of traumatic events.

A 23 February 2002 article in Scientific American suggested that compulsive television watching was no different from any other addiction, a finding backed up by reports of withdrawal symptoms among families forced by circumstance to cease watching.

A longitudinal study in New Zealand involving 1000 people (from childhood to 26 years of age) demonstrated that "television viewing in childhood and adolescence is associated with poor educational achievement by 26 years of age". In other words, the more the child watched television, the less likely he or she was to finish school and enroll in a university.

The changes in TV equipment and programming has been noted as one of the largest changes known to people because it was vital to people in the past as well as in the present.In Iceland, television broadcasting hours were restricted until 1984, with no television programs being broadcast on Thursday, or during the whole of July.

Television's biggest social aspect is the fact that it allows users to instantly view content that may be occuring far away from where they are. Television has been a major contributor in the process of globalization. The Earth's residents can be linked by the programming they watch; but like the internet, television has been taken advantage of as a perfect medium for advertising and the spreading of thoughts and ideas.

Technology Trends

In its infancy, television was an ephemeral medium. Fans of regular shows planned their schedules so that they could be available to watch their shows at their time of broadcast. The term appointment television was coined by marketers to describe this kind of attachment.

The viewership's dependence on schedule lessened with the invention of programmable video recorders, such as the Videocassette recorder and the Digital video recorder. Consumers could watch programs on their own schedule once they were broadcast and recorded. Television service providers also offer video on demand, a set of programs which could be watched at any time.

Both mobile phone networks and the internet are capable of carrying video streams. There is already a fair amount of internet TV, while mobile phone TV is planned to become mainstream, if it can be effectively sold, early in 2006.

Digital television (DTV) is a telecommunication system for broadcasting and receiving moving pictures and sound by means of digital signals, in contrast to analog signals in analog (traditional) tv. It uses digital modulation and data digitally compressed which is decoded by specially designed television sets or special by special receivers. Digital television has several advantages over traditional TV, such as superior image and audio quality, smaller channel bandwidth, better reception, and special services such as multicasting (more than one program on the same channel), electronic program guides and interactivity.

All digital TV variants can carry both standard-definition television (SDTV) and high-definition television (HDTV). All early SDTV television standards were analog in nature, and SDTV digital television systems derive much of their structure from the need to be compatible with analog television. In particular, the interlaced scan is a legacy of analog television.

Attempts were made during the development of digital television to prevent a repeat of the fragmentation of the global market into different standards (that is, PAL, SECAM, NTSC). However, once again the world could not agree on a single standard, and hence there are three major standards in existence: the European DVB system and the U.S. ATSC system, plus the Japanese system ISDB. Note: For cable, in addition to ATSC standards, the SCTE standard is used to describe Cable out-of-band metadata.

Most countries in the world have adopted DVB, but several have followed the U.S. in adopting ATSC instead (Canada, Mexico, South Korea). Korea has adopted S-DMB for satellite mobile broadcasting.

There could be other specialized high-resolution digital video formats in the future for markets other than home entertainment. Ultra High Definition Video (UHDV) is a format proposed by NHK of Japan that provides a resolution 16 times greater than HDTV.

Bandwidth

In current practice, HDTV uses 1280 × 720 pixels in progressive scan mode (abbreviated 720p) or 1920 × 1080 pixels in interlace mode (1080i). SDTV has less resolution (640 × 480 or 704 × 480 pixels with NTSC, 768 × 576 or 1024 × 576 with PAL in 4:3 and 16:9 aspect ratios respectively), but allows the bandwidth of a DTV channel (or "multiplex") to be subdivided into multiple sub-channels. The TV stations can use subchannels to carry multiple broadcasts of video, audio, or any other data, and can distribute their so-called "bit budget" as necessary, such as dropping one sub-channel down to a lower bitrate in order to make another one available to show higher quality video. Often, this is done automatically, using a statistical multiplexer (or "stat-mux").

In DVB-T, broadcasters can choose from several different modulation schemes, allowing them the option to reduce the transmission bitrate and make reception easier for more distant or mobile viewers.

Today most viewers receive digital television via a set-top box, which decodes the digital signals into signals that analog televisions can understand, but a slowly growing number of TV sets with integrated receivers are already available. Access to channels can be controlled by a removable smart card, for example via the Common Interface (DVB-CI) standard for Europe and via Point Of Deployment (POD) for IS or named differently CableCard. Some signals carry encryption and specify use conditions (such as "may not be recorded" or "may not be viewed on displays larger than 1m in diagonal measure") backed up with the force of law under the WIPO Copyright Treaty and national legislation implementing it, such as the U.S. Digital Millennium Copyright Act.

Suitability for Audience

Almost since the medium's inception there have been charges that some programming is, in one way or another, inappropriate, offensive or indecent. In addition, a lot of television has been charged with presenting propaganda, political or otherwise, and been pitched at a low intellectual level.

15

Impact of Television

Since the beginning, there have been mixed reactions to television and it was E.B. White who wrote "I believe that television is going to be the test of the modern world, and in this new opportunity to see beyond the range of our own vision, we shall discover either a new and unbearable disturbance of the general peace or a saving radiance in the sky. We shall stand or fall by television, of that I am sure." . White was correct, it would either be beneficial or detrimental to society. Ever since the first television station was licensed in 1941, our lives have been effected by the presence of television. However, this effect is not for the negative since it is used from simple means of entertainment to a widely used, invaluable, source of information. It is also an excellent aid in preparing children for school and assisting in educating children after they have begun school.

Every day millions of people turn to their televisions as a form of escape from the pressures and stress of day to day life. The television, to them, serves the purpose of entertaining them for a half hour or an hour at a time. This is the purpose of sitcoms, such as the popular NBC produced shows Friends and Fraiser, each appealing to different audiences, but both comedy bases for purposes of entertaining. Humor is not the only approach used in television entertainment. Shows, such as NYPD Blue, use thick plot lines and heavy drama to draw the viewer in.

Entertaining society through this media has become a multibillion dollar industry. Top movies like Jurassic Park, which grossed 390 million dollars, bring millions of people to movie theater, which are basically large televisions, for the soul purpose of entertainment. Movies are not restricted only to theaters since they are available on video cassette and even broadcasted into millions of homes each day. The privilege of television as entertainment should be used, but not abused. For instance, watching six hours of television every night, stopping only to eat and sleep does not promote and active lifestyle, however, on the other end of the spectrum, never watching any television does not expose a person to a vast array of entertainment and information.

Television is able to show different roles in society and therefore people are able to better understand others experiences and responsibilities. Along with this idea, people should know and understand current events of the world to help them better understand the effects of these events on society. Television has become the fastest media, reporting on today's event, as opposed to yesterday's events written about in a news paper.

Since there is not an area in this country, or an area in the world that does not receive a television signal, this, along with the fact only 2% of the population does not have a television, ensure that this is an extremely assessable media. Society has taken advantage of this by broadcasting the days news and information, regardless of which part of the world it took place in, over television signal so that 98% of the society can view it and become informed. This is not to say that television is the best source for news and information, but it is the most current.

Documentary show are very informative on one particular chosen subject. These shows help society better understand the world around them. For instance, a documentary show about the wars in the middle east can explain why there is a war and more importantly, the effects on the residents in this area. When a documentary is shown two stories are told; the verbal information presented and the progression of pictures. An emotion can be portrayed very effectively by means of pictures. The viewer now is not only told that the children in the middle east are left without food and shelter, he/she is able to see the children suffering. This aspect of television makes it an invaluable asset to today's society, and especially beneficial to children.

Studies estimate that before the age of 18, children have watched fifteen to twenty thousand hours of television. What kind of impact does this have on a child's ability to learn? In a survey of seven hundred fifty 10-16 year olds it was revealed that 82% of them confirmed that television can teach young children the difference between right and wrong. United States congress concluded that television has the capacity to effect society in a positive way by educating and informing children. "Studies show that television can effectively teach children special skills, assisting in preparing for formal schooling, as well complement skills taught in classroom.

For example, programs such as Sesame Street and Mr Roger's Neighborhood have been shown to enhance attentiveness and perceptual abilities." For younger children, viewing educational programs or cartoons can increase academic performance. As little as a half and hour per day can improve test scores on a variety of subjects. Although it has been argued that television tends to a reduction in reading and verbal skills, shows such as Sesame Street are addressing the issue by showing words to improve reading and encourage viewers to read along with the characters. It has been shown that there is actually a demand for more educational and informative programs for children.

Society has been effected and will continue to be effected, not only by television, but by media in general. Television is a constant form of entertainment and excellent source of information that is assessable by millions of people. The education content in children television is beneficial to preschoolers and students alike. However, television has been the blame for many of societies faults because it is easy to contribute it to violence and a social lack of initiative. Television is such a small part of a much larger picture and its benefits far outweigh its faults. The idea of television as an informative and education media must be embraced in the future to receive its full benefits. Even the thought of a society without television is incomprehensible to many.

Television is one of the most prevalent media influences in kids' lives. According to the Young Canadians In A Wired World Survey, almost 80 per cent of Canadian kids watch at least one hour of TV each day. How much impact TV has on children depends on many factors: how much they watch, their age and personality, whether they watch alone or with adults, and whether their parents talk with them about what they see on TV. To minimize the potential negative effects of television, it's important to understand what the impact of television can be on children. Below you will find information on some areas of concern.

Violence

Over the past two decades, hundreds of studies have examined how violent programming on TV affects children and young people. While a direct "cause and effect" link is difficult to establish, there is a growing consensus that some children may be vulnerable to violent images and messages.

Researchers have identified three potential responses to media violence in children:

— Increased fear-also known as the "mean and scary world" syndrome Children, particularly girls, are much more likely than adults to be portrayed as victims of violence on TV, and this can make them more afraid of the world around them.

— Desensitization to real-life violence

Some of the most violent TV shows are children's cartoons, in which violence is portrayed as humorous-and realistic consequences of violence are seldom shown.

— Increased aggressive behaviour

This can be especially true of young children, who are more likely to exhibit aggressive behaviour after viewing violent TV shows or movies.

Parents should also pay close attention to what their children see in the news since studies have shown that kids are more afraid of violence in news coverage than in any other media content. Fear based on real news events increases as children get older and are better able to distinguish fantasy from reality.

Effects on Healthy Child Development

Television can affect learning and school performance if it cuts into the time kids need for activities crucial to healthy mental and physical development. Most of children's free time, especially during the early formative years, should be spent in activities such as playing, reading, exploring nature, learning about music or participating in sports.

TV viewing is a sedentary activity, and has been proven to be a significant factor in childhood obesity. According to the Heart and Stroke Foundation of Canada almost one in four Canadian children, between seven and 12, is obese. Time spent in front of the TV is often at the expense of more active pastimes.

A Scientific American article entitled "Television Addiction" examined why children and adults may find it hard to turn their TVs off. According to researchers, viewers feel an instant sense of relaxation when they start to watch TV-but that feeling disappears just as quickly when the box is turned off. While people generally feel more energized after playing sports or engaging in hobbies, after watching TV they usually feel depleted of energy. According to the article "this is the irony of TV: people watch a great deal longer than they plan to, even though prolonged viewing is less rewarding."

As well as encouraging a sedentary lifestyle, television can also contribute to childhood obesity by aggressively marketing junk food to young audiences. According to the Canadian Paediatric Society, most food advertising on children's TV shows is for fast foods, candy and pre-sweetened cereals. Commercials for healthy food make up only 4 per cent of those shown.

A lot of money goes into making ads that are successful in influencing consumer behaviour. McDonald's, the largest food advertiser on TV, reportedly spent $500 million on their "We love to see you smile" ad campaign.

Sexual Content

Kids today are bombarded with sexual messages and images in all media-television, magazines, advertisements, music, movies and the Internet. Parents are often concerned about whether these messages are healthy. While television can be a powerful tool for educating young people about the responsibilities and risks of sexual behaviour, such issues are seldom mentioned or dealt with in a meaningful way in programs containing sexual content.

According to a 2001 study from the Kaiser Family Foundation, entitled Sex on TV, three out of four prime time shows contain sexual references. Situation comedies top the list: 84 per cent contain sexual content. Of the shows with sexual content, only one in ten included references to safe sex, or the possible risks or responsibilities of sex. In shows that portrayed teens in sexual situations, only 17 per cent contained messages about safe and responsible sex.

16

Television News

Television news refers to the practice of disseminating current events via the media of television. News Bulletins are programmes lasting from seconds to hours that provide updates on world, national, regional or local news events. Television channels may provide news bulletins as part of a regular program that is aired daily or more often at standard times. Less often, television shows may be interrupted or replaced by "news flashes" to provide news updates on current events of great importance or sudden events of great importance.

A newscast typically consists of the coverage of various news events and other information, either produced locally by a radio or television station, or by a broadcast network. It may also include such additional material as sports coverage, weather forecasts, traffic reports, commentary and other material that the broadcaster feels is relevant to their audience.

In some parts of the world there are 'rolling news' TV channels that broadcast news 24 hours a day. Television news consists of several different elements, introduced by a news presenter or presenters. The presenters read 'links' and do interviews.

Most news stories come in the form of short 'packages'. These are pre-recorded reports usually lasting from one to five minutes. News reporters gather and edit together interview clips, pictures and their own 'pieces to camera' to tell a story. They script and record a 'voice-over' to explain the pictures and link the elements together.

Some stories are done as live reports. This can be a reporter on the scene of a story either being interviewed by a studio presenter (sometimes known as a 'two-way'), a reporter interviewing one or more other people, or simply live pictures and sound of an event. The sound and pictures are sent back to the TV station via fixed cable links, bounced off a satellite from a vehicle carrying a satellite dish (a 'sat truck'), or sent through microwave radio transmissions from a vehicle carrying a microwave transmitter. With the growth of "rolling news" channels the use of live material has increased enormously and TV reporters are now often judged as much on their ability to perform live in front of a camera as on their package-making or writing skills.

TV news programs are put together by producers, who decide what goes in and what gets left out, and how long and in what form each story is presented. They put together 'running orders' - a list of the stories in what they decide is the right order. A separate news editor is often responsible for co-ordinating the gathering of material.

News Values

News values determine how much prominence a news story is given by a media outlet. In practice such decisions are made informally by editors on the basis of their experience and intuition, however analysis shows that several factors are consistently applied across a range of news organizations. In 1965, Galtung and Ruge enumerated these factors. The following list is based on their analysis that remains influential today.

Impact

— *Threshold:* A big story is one that has an extreme effect on a large number of people. Where the immediate effect of an event is more subtle, the threshold may be determined by the amount of money involved.

— *Frequency:* Events that occur suddenly and fit well with the news organizations schedule are more likely to be reported than those that occur gradually or at inconvenient times of day or night. Long-term trends are not likely to receive much coverage.

— *Negativity:* Bad news is more exciting than good news.

— *Unexpectedness:* If an event is out of the ordinary it will have a greater effect than something that is an everyday occurrence. As Charles A. Dana famously put it: "if a dog bites a man, that's not news. But if a man bites a dog, that's news!"

— *Unambiguity:* Events whose implications are clear make for better copy than those that are open to more than one interpretation, or where any understanding of the implications depends on first understanding the complex background in which the events take place.

Audience Identification

— *Personalisation:* Events that can be portrayed as the actions of individuals will be more attractive than one in which there is no such "human interest."

— *Meaningfulness:* This relates to the sense of identification the audience has with the topic. "Cultural proximity" is a factor here — stories concerned with people who speak the same language, look the same, and share the preoccupations as the audience receive more coverage than those concerned with people who speak different languages, look different and have different preoccupations.

— *Reference to elite nations:* Stories concerned with global powers receive more attention than those concerned with less influential nations.a

— *Reference to elite persons:* Stories concerned with the rich, powerful, famous and infamous get more coverage.

Pragmatics of Media Coverage

Political speeches, inquiries and court cases lend themselves to media coverage because they are predictable and provide an ongoing narrative with which the audience becomes familiar. Here, Sen. Joe McCarthy holds up a list of alleged communist sympathizers.

— *Consonance:* Stories that fit with the media's expectations receive more coverage than those that defy them (and for which they are thus unprepared). Note this appears to conflict with unexpectedness above. However, consonance really refers to the media's readiness to report an item. The story may still violate the audience's expectations, although today's media savvy audiences are not easily impressed by pre-prepared cliches.

— *Continuity:* A story that is already in the news gathers a kind of inertia. This is partly because the media organizations are already in place to report the story, and partly because previous reportage may have made the story more accessible to the public (making it less ambiguous).

— *Composition:* Stories must compete with one another for space in the media. For instance, editors may seek to provide a balance of different types of coverage, so that if there is an excess of foreign news for instance, the least important foreign story may have to make way for an item concerned with the domestic news. In this way the prominence given to a story depends not only on its own news values but also on those of competing stories.

News Source

A news source is a person, publication or other record or document that gives information. Examples of sources include: official records, publications or broadcasts, officials in government or business, organizations or corporations, witnesses of crime, accidents or other events, and people involved with or affected by a news event or issue.

Reporters are expected to develop and cultivate sources. This applies especially if they regularly cover a specific topic, known as a "beat". However, beat reporters must be cautious of becoming too close to their sources.

Reporters often but not always give greater leeway to sources with little experience. For example, sometimes a person will say they don't want to talk, and then proceed to talk. If that person is not a public figure, reporters are less likely to use that information.

Journalists are also encouraged to be skeptical without being cynical ("If your mother says she loves you, check it out.") As a rule of thumb, but especially when reporting on controversy, reporters are expected to use multiple sources.

Embargo

In journalism and public relations, an embargo (sometimes called a press embargo) is an agreement or request that a news organization refrain from reporting certain information until a specified date and/or time, in exchange for advance access to the information. For example, if a government official is preparing to make a short speech announcing a policy initiative at 1:00 pm, the official's staff might transmit expanded details of the initiative to news organizations several hours ahead of the scheduled announcement, with a notice indicating that the contents are embargoed until 1:00. This gives the news organizations time to research and prepare complete stories that are ready to be disseminated when the embargo is lifted. In theory, press embargoes reduce inaccuracy in the reporting of breaking stories by reducing the incentive for journalists to cut corners in hopes of "scooping" the competition.

Embargoes are typically used by government or corporate representatives working in publicity or public relations, and are often arranged in advance as part of a formal or informal agreement. Sometimes publishers will release advance copies of a book to reviewers with the agreement that reviews of it will not appear before the official release date of the publication. Complex scientific news might also require advance notice with an embargo. Governments also have legitimate reasons for imposing embargoes, often so as to prevent news reports being an unfair or undue influence over votes in legislative bodies. Artists' names and locations of performances are sometimes embargoed pending the official announcement of the scheduled performance tour.

Sometimes publicists will send embargoed press releases to newsrooms unsolicited in hopes that they will respect the embargo date without having first agreed to do so.

News organizations sometimes break embargoes and report information before the embargo expires, either accidentally (due to miscommunication in the newsroom) or intentionally (to get the jump on their competitors). Breaking an embargo is typically considered a serious breach of trust and can result in the source barring the offending news outlet from receiving advance information in the future.

Unidentified Sources

Most sources are not confidential. At least in the United States, most news organizations have policies governing the use of anonymous sources. Critics sometimes cite instances of news organizations breaking these policies. Research indicates that anonymous sourcing undermines credibility however, there are instances that many journalists believe call for anonymous sourcing.

Whether anonymous sources are used may depend on:

— Whether the information is available any other way.

— If getting the information out serves a greater good.

— Whether or not competing news outlets might do so.

Many news organizations require use of anonymous sources to be approved by someone senior to the reporter. Some also require the reporter to tell a senior person the identity.

In the United States, anonymous sources are used more in Washington than by smaller news organizations.

The George W. Bush administration and the Washington press corps has been criticized for the use of background briefings for which no source is identified.

Sometimes, though rarely, sources are impersonal or unknown. Neil Sheehan received the complete text of the Pentagon Papers on his doorstep, left there by an unknown individual, later revealed to be Daniel Ellsberg. Sources may also engage in disguise and/or voice alteration, nicknames, aliases, or simply not mention their identity, as attempts to ensure their anonymity. In some cases, this may be due in part to lack of trust between sources and reporters or their news organizations. In reality, few journalists will accept information from an anonymous source, though they may pretend to have done so in order to protect the source's identity, or to protect themselves in case a court later orders them to name the source.

Journalists can usually count on the support of their editors and publishers when refusing to identify a confidential source. Some courts have upheld the sanctity of the informal privacy agreement between a journalist and his/her sources as a matter of unofficial confidence, in the belief that the confidential nature of the journalist-source relationship underpins the existence of a free press.

In some cases, courts will break the notion of reporter-source privilege, and demand a reporter reveal their source under pain of contempt of court. Often, reporters will resist such demands. In the 2005 Plame affair, New York Times reporter Judith Miller was jailed for 85 days for refusing to identify vice presidential aide Lewis Libby as her source until he gave her a personal release of confidentiality. In the United States, some states have shield laws which protect journalists by statute, rather than relying on courts to find a common law justification.

17

TV Reporting

Good reporters first must learn to write, but just being able to write well does not guarantee that a person will make a good reporter. Many additional skills and abilities, unrelated to writing, are required.

Although print and broadcast reporters need many of the same skills, broadcast news reporters face challenges not encountered by their print counterparts, or even by broadcast journalists of the recent past. Electronic News Gathering (ENG), which relies on videotape or digital equipment and microwave technology, places demands on TV reporters that were unknown when reporters filmed stories and had the luxury of writing their scripts while the film was being developed. Broadcast journalists today need to think faster and to prepare their reports more rapidly, often while the story is still going on around them. They also need to learn about the different types of assignments they are likely to cover and the best way to perform them.

Basic Reporting Skills

The most important skill a reporter needs is accuracy. At first, this may not appear to be a skill, but being accurate requires a lot of attention-checking, and double-checking information demands concentration. Errors usually creep into copy when reporters become too relaxed. Nothing should be assumed or taken for granted. If information cannot be confirmed, it should not be used without some kind of attribution.

Reporters also must develop news judgment. They must understand what news is and be able to recognize that certain stories are more important than others. That skill sometimes takes time to develop. Reporters must also be curious, showing an interest in everything and everyone making news-whatever the reason.

Reporters must be concerned, sometimes alarmed, often angered, and always caring about the major problems that face the communities and world in which we live. Reporters often can do little to correct injustice or unfairness, or the misery, suffering, and critical problems of certain segments or groups in our society, but they should have a desire to do so. Their weapons are enlightenment and information.

Reporters must be determined and persistent in their search for facts and details. Reporters must be aggressive, walking a thin line between tenacity and belligerence. For many people entering journalism, some of these characteristics seem to come naturally, whereas others need to be developed. Let's look at these qualities in detail.

Accuracy

Most of the blame for the inordinately high level of inaccurate in reporting during events is placed on

(1) the record amount of media coverage;

(2) the apparent need to be first with every bit of information, regardless of its value and questionable accuracy;

(3) the new technology that encourages broadcast journalists to go live before they have sufficient time to think;

(4)   the manipulation of the media by a variety of entities, including but not limited to the prosecution, police, and the defence; and

(5)   the incredible, unprecedented use of unidentified and unreliable sources.

The attitude during coverage often is: "If the story is wrong, we'll correct it later. . . but let's air it before someone else does"-a certain formula for disaster.

News Judgment

Let us try and perhaps define news judgment, which isn't easy. Even professional journalists have difficulty explaining the term. Different people have different news judgments. News judgment can also be related to the audience you are trying to serve. "The editors of The Times Off India and The Hindustan Times will see news differently," he said. "They each will ask, "Is this a story my readers will care about and want to know about?"" Each channel, publication has its own ideology, and the news judgment to a large extent will be governed by this ideology.

Curiosity

For curious people, one of the rewards of reporting is the joy of discovering things. Discovering something "first" is the best reward of all. But discovering information is not always as exciting as depicted on the TV programs based on broadcast news. To hold a network primetime audience, these programs must come up with some imaginative story ideas each week. In the real world, few reporters get caught up in the kind of sensational situations and intrigue depicted on sitcoms and TV dramas.

Most reporting assignments are fairly routine. Reporters spend a lot of time covering murders, lots of fires, plenty of elections, more news conferences than they would care to remember, accidents of all kinds, and hundreds of feature stories. That is the real world of broadcast news. The fact that most reporters do not deal with crooked politicians, track down terrorists, or go to bat for someone on death row who they are convinced is innocent does not mean that reporting is dull. There is an endless assortment of stories to satisfy most people's curiosity, and there are opportunities to explore previously unknown subjects. Getting the answers, finding out about things - and learning and growing along the way-are part of the excitement of reporting. These are some of the reasons why the profession is so compelling.

When reporters arrive at the newsroom for work, they never know what stories they will be covering, and that is an exciting concept for curious people. Most reporters will tell you that they could not imagine any kind of work that they would rather do.

Persistence

A good reporter hates taking "no" for an answer. Learning how to get people to talk to you when they may not want to is a skill. Getting them to tell you things they don't want to requires even more skill.

Aggressiveness

Most reporters seem to agree that they try to be aggressive without being obnoxious. They criticize reporters who shout and shove microphones into people's faces, demanding answers to their questions. Most politicians, police officials, lawyers, and others who deal with the media on a daily basis are accustomed to a certain amount of badgering into the press. They would probably be disappointed and feel neglected if the news corps was not surrounding them when there's a story to tell. But the reporter who runs down the street after a newsmaker's car and shoves a microphone into the open window is out of line. More than one reporter has lost a microphone that way when the irritated person rolled up the window.

Fairness

It is often argued that it is not possible for anyone to be completely objective. This may be true. Everyone has certain biases and prejudices, but reporters must learn to leave out their personal feelings when they start writing or delivering news. Objectivity for a journalist really means "fairness"; it means honestly giving both sides of an argument, controversy, or debate. Reporters can tell when their report on a controversial issue has been successful because both sides of the issue accuse them of being partial to the other.

Staying Well-informed

Reporters cannot function well unless they are well informed. Being well informed does not mean just having a good education; it means taking the time to know what's going on around you. Journalists must constantly add new material to their knowledge. One of the best ways to stay well informed is to read.

Reading the news wire and the Internet extensively is an immediate way to know what is going on. Reporters should also read the local newspaper (or all of them if they work in a city with more than one) and at least one national paper every day. Weekly news magazines are a useful source of additional information, as are books, particularly nonfiction bestsellers.

Research

All good reporters do research because they want to know as much as possible about a story before trying to cover it. The Internet has made the research task tremendously easier than when reporters had to dig through libraries and morgues to find information. Research sources are many and varied : getting information through contacts, stringers, news wires, agencies related to a particular issue, publications and books and PR agencies.

It is also a good idea to get on mailing lists. Many organizations are happy to add a reporter's name to their lists, and just getting on some mailing lists automatically places your name on many others. Much of the information distributed by these groups has limited news value because it is public-relations material, but it is useful for alerting you to the positions certain organizations take on issues. Many of the groups are dedicated to worthwhile causes. Almost all of them, and thousands of other organizations too, will have Websites.

Working with the Team

Reporting the news is a team effort. Getting along with colleagues is essential. Young reporters just beginning their careers should watch and listen to the seasoned staff members. Seeking their advice lets them know that they are appreciated. When that happens, there is little that they will not do to help a reporter, which is important when the reporter needs a cameraperson to skip lunch or a tape editor to spend an extra 30 minutes in the morgue looking for "Just the right file footage" for a story. It is also important to remember that reputations follow reporters from station to station.

News managers like team players. They hire reporters who have demonstrated in previous positions that they are cooperative and eager to lean and grow TV news is fundamentally the pursuit of right pictures. And, "who is in charge of gathering those pic-tures? Of course", the reporter. Be it in the field or in the studio, a major chunk of pictures is the product of reportorial" efforts. No doubt, the reporter sees through the eyes of his cameraman who mayor may not be assisted by a recordist and a lightman, and so on.

Most of the time the reporter accompanies the cameraman. But on occasions, he takes the backseat allowing his cameraman to take charge. Suppose you are assigned to cover a heavy snowfall in Kulu Manali in Himachal Pradesh. This valley being totally cut off by any form of surface transport, road or rail, the only way to get to the spot is by helicopter, which is a two-seater, one seat for the pilot. Will you take even a second to decide as to who should occupy the only passenger seat?. Your" cameraman" will board the chopper and you will utilize your time "at the airport in collecting some necessary information for your narration. Here the rule is: "Camera comes first". Not only is the camera first in, it is also first out. This is so because the pictures are of no good if they do not reach to a place where they can be edited into a story before the telecast deadline.

Television reporters are thus required to be much more than mere reporters. They must also, be on-the-spot producers, directors and logisticians. They must know how to get to the story, how to shoot it, how to write it and how to get it back to the transmission point. In newspaper and radio, the reporter works alone. Though other people are present at various stages, the final product, the story, is essentially the work of a single person. But not so in television TV news is a team effort, each member of the team contributing to what is finally telecast. A reportorial effort is actually the combined work of an assignment editor, a reporter, a cameraman, a producer, a scriptwriter, and a tape editor. Then you have the studio crew of over a dozen technical personnel.

Thus a TV reporter must be capable of working smoothly with other team members. This is not like the "thought for the day" from your school teacher who churned out a slogan a day. This is real. TV reporters are on call round-the-clock round-the-week. They are expected to be reachable anytime, anywhere, even when they are honeymooning.

All this is not out of choice, but because of the television's need for relevant pictures. The aftermath of an event is sometimes useful for constructing a story, but more often is simply not good enough to stand up to the cut-throat competition permeating the television news business. The pictures are wanted now, the interviews are wanted now. The reporter's phone is ringing now. Reporters in print an_ radio can gather stories by telephone but TV reporters must go on the spot. Thus, to the time spent in purely journalistic functions such as researching, covering, scripting and recording a story must be added the traveling time, the editing time, and the time to protect any breaking angles for the late night or next morning telecasts. It is normal for TV reporters to work over 12 hours a day, often without a proper meal.

Sometimes, the fruits of your initiatives are reaped by the reporters of rival channels or by the other media print or radio. Supposing you are able to extract an answer from the media savvy BJP leader Mrs Sushma Swaraj on the party's strategy on the construction of Ram Mandir (Temple) in Ayodhya, the resulting sound bite is not your exclusive property. Anyone present in the news conference would be free to use it.

Still at other times, the presence of the camera and microphone makes the news team an easy target of "abuse and attack"-the Aaj Tak correspondent Ashutosh was allegedly slapped by the BSP chief Kansi Ram when relentlessly pursued for a sound bite by the former. Unaware of all this and the fact that TV news is nine parts preparation and hard work and only one part screen appearance, many young recruits are attracted to reporting with the same desires as the actors and models-to be loved and recognized by the public. A good number of such neophytes soon start detesting the pressures order which they have to feed the ever-hungry news, machine: to rush to the airport to catch planes in order to meet the deadlines, eating whatever is available mostly without proper time to finish a meal, waiting outside Parliament for a politician to turn up and say a few words about the ongoing event, and so on.

However, not all reporters come to TV news for the sake of glamour and (a little) more money than their print counterparts. Perhaps they embrace television reporting for its inherent excitement of witnessing the momentous events as they unfold. It is this pursuit of excitement by such reporters that brings to us daring coverages like the Gulf War, the Falklands War and the Bosnia Conflict. "Are you still sure you want to stick to TV news reporting? If yes, in you there is a Captain M.N. Mulla (of 1971 war with Pakistan) who chose to sink with his naval ship rather than desert it. Now over to the pleasant side of reporting. Don't you enjoy those moments when your landlord, neighbors or even parents know that you have become something to "reckon" with or take pride in? But that is just a fraction of what you feel when greeted by your executive producer or colleagues. This is so because only the people in your profession know the heavy odds against which you delivered a good package.

Once a reporter is on the job, he has to face competition not only from the reporters of the rival channels, but also from the reporters of the same newsroom. Getting a lead story is like getting the lead story on the first page of a newspaper. Do you get such a chance everyday? No. But occasionally, yes. You get there by out-reporting your colleagues. For this you come to the edit meeting with your own story ideas instead of waiting for a story to break.

For routine coverages, the producer of the newscast gives "daily briefings" to the reporters. After this, every reporter is expected to go through as much background material as he can within as little time as possible, sayan hour or so. But the meeting with the producer is not entirely in the nature of being "do-this-and-do-that". As already discussed, each member of the team is expected to come with his or her own story ideas in his or her respective beats, and convince the producer about the same.

Immediately after clinching an assignment, you have to make efforts to ensure the necessary" logistics" - identifying interviewees, calling on them to fix appointments, and briefing your cameraman about the story, its contents, mood, and the time it is likely to be allotted in the newscast. Maybe you will get time to talk to your cameraman only after boarding the taxi taking you to the location of the shoot. Never mind. This is the case most of the times. In any case, you are expected to gather details of the story and the visual possibility of each story element before you reach the location.

Next comes the "interview-setting" which is as important as the story itself: a factory owner inside the factory (where the background shows the production process) rather than his plush office (which makes a dull viewing); an auto mechanic taped while peeping out from underneath a jacked-up taxi in his garrage; a doctor in his clinic; and a journalist shot in the backdrop of his newsroom activities make for reliable and newsworthy pictures. However, for broadcast quality pictures and sound bites, you should ensure that there is enough light and that the ambient sound is not distracting. True, office interviews are unavoidable sometimes.

Electronic News Gathering

Electronic News Gathering (ENG) is a broadcasting (usually television) industry acronym which stands for electronic news gathering. It can mean anything from a lone reporter taking a single camcorder out to get a story to an entire television crew taking a satellite truck on location to do a live report for a newscast. In its early days, the term ENG was used by newsroom staff to differentiate between the

NG (newsgathering) crews that collected tv news with traditional film cameras and the new ENG crews who collected tv news with new electronic analogue tape formats like low band U-matic. The requirement for the differentiation stems from the radically different methods of post-production involved in video versus film. Film needed to be processed before editing, unlike tape where footage could be edited fairly quickly, thus dramatically reducing the turn-around time for a story. The use of film in newsgathering virtually disappeared by the mid 1980s.

ENG originally referred to the use of point-to-point terrestrial microwave signals to backhaul the remote signal to the studio. In modern news operations, however, it also includes SNG (satellite news gathering) and DSNG (digital satellite news gathering). ENG is almost always done using a specially modified truck or van such as those made by Frontline or Wolfcoach. Terrestrial microwave vehicles can usually be identified by their masts which can be extended up to 50 feet (15 m) in the air (to allow line-of-sight with the station's receiver antennas), while satellite trucks always use a larger dish that unfolds and points skywards towards one of the geostationary communications satellites operated by companies such as PanAmSat, SES Americom or IntelSat.

In the U.S. there are ten ENG video channels set aside in each area for terrestrial microwave communications, with frequency coordination typically done by the local Society of Broadcast Engineers chapter rather than the FCC. In Atlanta for example, there are two channels each for the four news TV stations, one for CNN, and another open for other users on request, such as GPB. It is worth noting that this situation is in flux, as the FCC is currently seeking to auction off some of the 2 GHz frequency bands.

18

TV New Editing

Editing is the process of preparing language, images, or sound for publication through correction, condensation, organization, and other modifications. A person who edits, especially professionally or as a hobby, is called an editor.

Professionals may specialize in the editing of writing, still images, cinema/video, sound recordings, and music recordings. These areas sometimes overlap depending on the project. For example, language editors may comment on or make alterations to graphics and photographs embedded in a job that mostly comprises language; sound editors may make alterations in the linguistic text of, for example, a sound interview, to improve the intended meaning or reduce the duration of an item.

The top editor sometimes has the title executive editor or editor-in-chief (the former is replacing the latter in the language). This person is generally responsible for the content of the publication. The exception is that newspapers that are large enough usually have a separate editor for the editorials and opinion pages.

The executive editor sets the publication standards for performance, and is responsible for assuring the highest standards of ethical conduct in the process of gathering and presenting information, as well as for motivating and developing the staff. The executive editor is also responsible for developing and maintaining the publication budget. In concert with the publisher and the operating committee, the executive editor is responsible for strategic and operational planning.

Technical editing involves reviewing text written on a technical topic, and identifying errors related to the use of language in general or adherence to a specific style guide.

This activity ensures that documentation is of good quality. In large companies, experienced writers are dedicated to the technical editing function; in organizations that cannot afford dedicated editors, experienced writers typically peer-edit text produced by their relatively less experienced colleagues.

It helps if the technical editor is familiar with the subject being edited, but that is not always essential. The "technical" knowledge that an editor gains over time while working on a particular product or technology does give the editor an edge over another who has just started editing content related to that product or technology. In the long run, however, the skills that really matter are attention to detail, the ability to sustain focus while working through lengthy pieces of text on complex topics, tact in dealing with writers, and excellent communication skills.

Editors in the visual mediums, who may be described as film or video editors, perform a variety of tasks. Assistant editors and production assistants perform preliminary screening and logging of motion picture footage; senior editors are responsible for creative placement of scenes and shots, structural placement of major elements and organization of the entire presentation. Other editors are involved with assembly of the final product and preparation for distribution.

Motion pictures have many sound editors, this team works with various aspects of the picture or program's sound designers. These editors construct tracks consisting of assembled pre-recorded dialogue, the audio mixing in of typewriters?) You must have your material well organized before you start, because once committed to paper, changes are difficult to make. As we will see, nonlinear editing is more like working with a sophisticated word processor.

The concept behind linear editing is simple: one or more tapes containing the original footage are transferred (recorded) segment by segment onto a tape in a video recorder. In the process, the original segments can be shortened and rearranged, bad shots can be removed, and audio and video effects can be added.

The source machine(s) contain the original footage and the edit recorder, which is controlled by an edit controller, is used to record the final edited master. (A lot of terms here, but they make sense, if you think about it.)

The person doing the editing uses an edit controller (such as the one shown here) to shuttle tapes back and forth to find the beginning and ending points of each needed segment. These reference points are then entered into the edit controller as either control track marks or time code numbers. You can then turn things over to the edit controller, which uses the precise beginning and ending points you've entered to roll and cue the tapes and make each edit. In simple linear editing systems the in and out points are referenced by pulses recorded on the tape-

30 per second in NTSC video. The method of editing that locates and marks segments based on a count of control track pulses is referred to as control track editing. Control track editing has two major shortcomings. First, it relies on mechanical equipment to maintain an accurate count of thousands of control track pulses.

For devices that are subject to mechanical variations this can be difficult, because during editing you are constantly shuttling tapes forward and backward at varying speeds as you find and mark in and out points for edits. If equipment loses count just for a fraction of a second, an edit sound effects, foley and music to achieve the desired effec for the motion pictures and television programs.

Linear Editing

Linear editing is nothing but to make a copy of the selected portions from the shot tapes onto another tape called the master tape in the recorder. It can be compared to manual type writing that is, it needs to be done in the final sequence otherwise every time there is a change an entire sequence will need to be redone.

The simplest form of linear editing is called assemble editing or deck to deck. This is when you copy only the "good" parts of a tape over to a new tape. Assemble editing systems often include titlers (character generators) or special effects generators to make the videos more fun to watch. A/ B roll editing is when we edit from two or more video sources. An A/B roll system often includes a digital mixer, to let us cut, fade, dissolve and wipe from source A to source B. Insert editing is when we splice in a different scene, or video only, into the middle of an existing video tape. Only very expensive, high end editing decks are capable of insert editing. Today, linear editing means deck to deck. The quality of your linear editing is dependent on the editing capabilities of your decks. For the best results you need special editing decks with flying erase heads, special editing jacks, pre-roll and time codes. These decks often cost $1000 or more.

Linear Editing Systems

Linear editing systems require edits to be made in a linear fashion; i.e., in a 1-2-3 sequence. In a typical project this would mean that you would start by editing in the countdown leader, followed by scene one, followed by scene, two, etc. This type of editing can be likened to writing a term paper with a typewriter. (Remember point will end up being off by a few video frames-which will destroy a carefully timed edit.

Savvy editors keep an eye on the digital tape counter as tapes are shuttled back and forth. If the counter freezes for a split second when the tape is moving, the equipment has momentarily lost an accurate count of control pulses. Problems generally come down to either less-than-perfect videotape condition or a less-than-perfect control track.

The second disadvantage of simple control track editors relates to the ability to replicate and make adjustments to your original edit decisions at a later time.

Since the control track count is kept in the volatile memory of computer chips, when the machine is turned off or reset, all edit decision information is lost.

These counter references are "relative" to where you started the counter and not "absolute" (i.e., recorded on the tape itself). Therefore, they do not remain accurate when the tapes are reloaded at a later time.

The only way to insure accuracy is when exact locations are referenced from permanent information on the tape. This is possible with SMPTE time-code. When time-code is used, exact scene locations remain consistent, even when tapes are used in different machines at different times. As you can see, simple control track editing has a number of shortcomings. Even so, it remains the fastest way to assemble and edit a simple video project.

Insert and Assemble Editing

There are two types of edits you can make in linear editing. When you use assemble editing you add video and audio segments, one after another like links on a chain, complete with the associated control track. As we've noted, the control track is difficult to record with unerring precision with each and every edit. Any timing error during this basically mechanical process results in a glitch in the video.

For this reason, assemble editing is not the preferred approach. It's used primarily when a few segments need to be spliced together in a hurry.

Insert editing requires an extra step; you must first "lay down" (record) a stable control track over the entire area you plan to use on the edited master tape. If you think that your final project will be five minutes, you record six or more minutes (just to be sure) of a video signal (generally just black). You then have a consistent (uninterrupted) control track on your final tape that should translate into a stable playback. During editing, you "insert" the video and audio segments you want over the prerecorded control track. Since you are not trying to record a new control track as you add each video segment, the process results in a more stable playback.

Within the time constraints of whatever audio and video has been recorded on the edited master, it's also possible to insert (substitute) new video and audio at a later time. It's not possible, however, to lengthen or shorten parts of the edited master, something you can easily do with...

Use of Time Code

Although we've mentioned time-code previously, we now need to more fully explore its role in the editing process. SMPTE/EBU time-code (or just " time-code") is an eight-digit code that allows you to specify, among other things, precise video and audio editing points. A designated time-code point (set of numbers) cannot vary from one editing session to another, from one machine to another, or even from one country to another.

Editing instructions like, "cut the scene when Whitney smiles at the camera," leave room for interpretation-especially if Whitney tends to smile a lot. Plus, there is the very real possibility that different takes of the same scene will become confused. But even though a tape may be four hours long, "00:01:16:12" refers to one very precise point within that total time.

Breaking the Code

Although a string of eight numbers like 02:54:48:17 might seem imposing, their meaning is very simple: 2 hours, 54 minutes, 48 seconds and 17 frames. Since time-code numbers move from right to left when they are entered into an edit controller, you must enter hours, minutes, seconds and frames, in that order.

By entering only six numbers instead of eight, the machine assumes "00 hours," since the combination of numbers entered would only (as they move from right to left) reach to the minutes designation. If there is anything tricky about time-code, it's the fact that you don't add and subtract from a base of ten the way you do with most math problems.

The first two numbers are based on 24 hours (military time). The minutes and seconds range from 00 to 59, just the way they do on any clock, and the frames go from 00 to 29. (Recall there are 30 frames per second in NTSC video. The PAL and SECAM systems use 25 as a base.) Thirty frames, like 5/5 of a mile, would be impossible to display, because 30 frames in NTSC equal one second. Likewise, "60 minutes" would be impossible in time-code (but not necessarily impossible on CBS). So, as an example, the next frame after 04 hours, 59 minutes, 59 seconds and 29 frames would change the counter to: 05:00:00:00.

Now let's look at some problems. If one video segment is 8 seconds, 20 frames long, and a second segment is 6 seconds, 19 frames long, the total time of the two segments added together would be 15:09.

8 seconds, 20 frames, plus

6 seconds, 19 frames

= 15:09

Note in this example that as we add the total number of frames we end up with 39. But, since there can be only 30 frames in a second, we add one second to the seconds' column and we ending up with 9 frames. (39 minus 30 = 09 frames). Adding 9 seconds (8 plus the 1 we carried over) and 6 gives us 15 seconds, for a total of 15:09.

Let's look at this question. If the time-code point for entering a video segment is 01:22:38:25, and the out-point is 01:24:45:10, what is the total time of the segment?

Segment out-point - 01:24:45:10

segment in-point - 01:22:38:25

= total segment time - 00:02:06:15

Getting the answer is just a matter of subtracting the smaller numbers from the larger numbers. Note that since we can't subtract 25 frames from 10 frames we have to change the 10 to 40 by borrowing a second from the 45. For people who regularly do time-code calculations, computer programs and small hand held calculators are available. A computer pop-up time-code calculator called WTCC is available for free downloading on the Internet.

Drop-Frame Time-code

Basic SMPTE/EBU time-code assumes a frame rate of 30 per- second in NTSC video. Although that's a nice even number, it actually only applies to black and white television. For technical reasons, when the NTSC color television was introduced, a frame rate of 29.97 frames per second was adopted. This frame rate is also used in the U.S. version of DTV/HDTV. Although the difference between 30 and 29.97 may seem insignificant, in some applications it can result in significant timing problems. If you assume a rate of 30 frames per second instead of 29.97, you end up with a 3.6-second error every 60 minutes.

Since broadcasting is a to-the-second business, a way had to be devised to correct this error. Just lopping off 3.6

seconds at the end of every hour was not seen as a practical way of doing this-especially from the viewpoint of a sponsor that gets a commercial cut off at the end of a show as a result.

So how do you fix this error? Well, 3.6 seconds equals extra 108 video frames each hour (3.6 times 30 frames per second). So, to maintain accuracy, 108 frames must be dropped each hour, and done in a way that will minimize confusion. Unfortunately, we're not dealing with nice even numbers here. First, it was decided that the 108-frame correction had to be equally distributed throughout the hour. (Better to lose a bit here and there instead of everything all at once.) If you dropped 2 frames per minute, you would end up dropping 120 frames per hour instead of 108. That's nice and neat, but it's 12 frames too many. But, since you can't drop half frames, this is as close as you can get by making a consistent correction every minute. So what to do with the 12 extra frames? The solution is every 10th minute not to drop the 2 frames. In one hour that equals 12 frames, since there are six ten-minute intervals in an hour. So, using this approach you end up dropping 108 frames every hour-exactly what you need to get rid of.

Since the frame dropping occurs right at the changeover point from one minute to the next, you'll see the time-code counter on an editor suddenly jump over the dropped frames every time the correction is made. For example, when you reach 01:07:59:29, the next frame would be 01:08:00:02. In drop-frame time-code frames 00 and 01 don't exist. Maybe this is not the most elegant solution in the world, but it works, and now it should be obvious why it's called drop-frame time-code. For non-critical applications, such as news segments, industrial television productions, etc., drop-frame isn't needed. However, if you are involved with producing 15-minute or longer programs for broadcast, you should use an editor with drop-frame capability. On most edit controllers you will find a switch that lets you select either a drop-frame or non-drop frame mode. Software programs typically have a drop-down box where you can select the approach you want. When you use the drop-frame mode, a signal is added to the SMPTE/EBU time-coded video that automatically lets the equipment know that drop-frame is being used.

User Bits

There is room within the time-code signal for a bit of extra data. Specifically, there are 32 bits of space called user bits where a small bit of information can be entered. This can be used to trigger equipment, or to simply record abbreviated user data, such as reel numbers, recording dates, camera information, etc. User bits are limited to four letters or eight digits-which, admittedly, isn't much in the way of data. Not all equipment will record or read user bits, so you need to check out this feature if you plan to use it.

Adding Time-code

Time-code is not an inherent part of the video signal; it must be recorded on the videotape as the production is being shot-or, in some cases, when the tape is being reviewed. The same goes for user bits, which are a part of time-code. These time-code numbers can be used to organize and specify segments on a videotape or hard drive, as well as to calculate total times. Editing equipment will also use the numbers to correctly cue and edit the segments you've selected-and, if needed, to recall the segments at a later time.

Recording Time-code

Time-code can be recorded on videotape in two ways: as part of an audio signal, or as part of the video signal.

Longitudinal time-code (LTC)

Time-code consists of 2,400 bits of information per second in the NTSC system and 2,000 bits of information in the PAL and SECAM systems. Although it's digital information, it can still be recorded on audio track , an address (time-code) track, or a cue track. When it's recorded in this way it's referred to as longitudinal time-code (LTC). Although the longitudinal system of time-code has been greatly improved in recent years and it's the easiest to record, it can have three major weaknesses. First, it can only be reliably read off the tape on most VCRs when the tape is moving. This can be a problem when you are constantly starting and stopping the tape during the editing process. Second, when a videotape is copied, the audio track can suffer a loss of signal quality that will make the high speed digital pulses unreliable-especially when the videotape is shuttled back and forth at various speeds during editing.

To solve this problem a jam sync process is required to regenerate the longitudinal time-code as a new copy of the tape is being dubbed (copied). Finally, if the time-code is recorded at too high a level, it can cause cross talk, which results in a obnoxious "whine" in the program audio. Longitudinal time-code requires a VTR with well-aligned recording heads, excellent audio capabilities (wide band amplifiers and broadband reproduce heads), and well-aligned tape guides-not to mention a near perfect time-code signal to start with. Otherwise, when the tape is shuttled at high speeds, the machine will lose count of the pulses.

VITC Time-Code

VITC (vertical-interval time-code) and other systems that record time-code with the video heads have many advantages over the longitudinal system. Since VITC is recorded by the video heads, it's less likely to be affected by the variety of technical problems that can plague LTC. VITC time-code is also always visible-even when the tape is in the pause mode. VITC is recorded in the area of scanning lines 10 and 20 in the so-called vertical blanking interval of each video field. This means that the signal is recorded four times per frame a bit of redundancy that lowers the chance of things getting messed up due to dropouts, or whatever. And, if that isn't enough, there is built-in error checking (CRC error checking code) that ends up making the process pretty much fail-safe. When VITC time-code is used, it should be recorded as the video is shot. Otherwise, you will have to copy the entire tape over in order to add the time-code. You will lose video quality in this process unless you are doing the copying from uncompressed digital video.

Of course, during the editing process you are bringing together a variety of segments, all of which have different time- codes. That could look a bit weird when you watch the resulting e-code on playback-not to mention throw-editing equipment into fits. tim The solution is jam sync, where the time-code is regenerated as part of the editing process. The time-code generator will take its cue from the first segment, and then resynchronize the code with each edit so that the edited master contains a smooth time-code progression. In the words of one editor, "Jam-sync with VITC isn't optional, it's mandatory."

With any video segment involving time-code, you need to have enough time-coded leader preceding the actual segment you want to use so that equipment will have an opportunity to "pick up the count." Systems vary, but some editors suggest up to 20 seconds. This isn't a lot when the editing machine is speeding backwards to find a time-code number to cue up a segment.

Time-code numbers, which reverse in time, can really confuse an editing system. If you stop a recording session, you need to make sure that when the time-code resumes you are going forward in time. Don't for some reason start with a time-code that jumps back in time. The latter could easily result at some point in reproducing the same code you recorded earlier. This means that during editing the system might easily come up with the wrong segment-and refuse to get the right one for you.

Time-Code Display

Some editing systems have small time-code displays on the top of the edit controller, as shown here. More sophisticated editing systems superimpose the time-code numbers over the video, itself. In the latter case the time-code numbers may be either temporarily superimposed over the video (keyed-in code), or they may become a permanent part of the picture (burned-in time-code).

In the case of keyed-in code, an electronic device reads the digital time-code information from the tape and generates the numbers to be temporarily keyed (superimposed) over the video. The disadvantage of this approach is that you can only see the code if you are using special equipment, such as an appropriate editing system.

Once the time-code-numbers have been burned in (permanently superimposed into the video), the video and time-code can be viewed on any VCR. Although this approach requires making a special copy of the tape, it can be an advantage if you want to use a standard VCR to review tapes at home or on location and make notes on the segments.

Logging Your Tape

Before you start editing you have to discover what and where the scenes are you are going to use in your program. The logging of your tapes is all-important regardless of what editing system you use, because this "SHOT/SCENE LOG", will be used in every editing system.

There are three different logs kept on the tape themselves, depending on the tape format.

1. *Time code*- time code is a number on the tape, which tells you the exact location of any frame on the tape. This number is on all the digital tapes.

2. *Time and Date*- this is the time hour-minute- and sometimes second the tape was made.

Again the tape format will determine this. On the older VHS cameras you had to turn it on, and the date would be showing on the screen, on the newer DV formats this is embedded/hidden on every frame and can be used. This is a fast way to find a clip.

3.   *Tape Counter-* this number is the least accurate, especially when you are changing the tape from one player to another. It depends upon the tape being completely rewound to have any degree of accuracy.

If you are making a serious video, you will have a shot-log sheet in the field when you shoot the footage, and you will write the following on the sheet:

1.   Time code number - the start and the ending number of the scene

2.   The date and time of day

3.   The description of the scene

4.   The script page and line numbers

5.   Make appropriate notes about the scene.

Non-linear Editing

Non-linear editing for film and television postproduction is a modern editing method that involves being able to access any frame in a video clip with the same ease as any other. This method was inherent in the cut and glue world of film editing from the beginning but, in the world of analogue film, editing was a destructive process. It was also linear. Non-linear, non-destructive methods began to appear with the first digital images.

Video and audio data are first digitized to hard disks. The data is either recorded directly to disk or is imported to disk from another source. Once on disk they can be edited on a computer using any of a wide range of software.

In Non-linear editing, the original source files are not lost or modified during editing. Professional editing software saves the decisions of the editor in an "Edit decision list" (EDL) (which can be interchanged with other editing tools). Many generations and variations of the original source files can exist without needing to store many different copies. This allows for very flexible editing. It also makes it easy to change cuts and undo previous decisions simply by editing the edit decision list (without having to have the actual film data in many different copies). Loss of quality is also avoided due to not having to repeatedly re-encode the data when different effects are applied.

Compared to the linear method of tape-to-tape editing, non-linear editing offers the flexibility of film editing, with random access and easy project organization. With the edit decision lists, the editor can work on low-resolution copies of the video. This makes it possible to edit both broadcast quality and high definition quality very quickly on normal PCs which do not have the power to do the full processing of the huge full-quality high-resolution data in real-time.

The costs of editing systems have dropped such that non-linear editing tools are now within the reach of home users. Some editing software can now be accessed free as web applications, some, like Cinelerra, can be downloaded free of charge, and some, like Microsoft's Windows Movie Maker and Apple Computer's iMovie come included if you buy the appropriate operating system.

A computer for non-linear editing of video will usually have a video editing card, video capture card for capturing analog video or a FireWire socket for capturing digital video from a DV camera, as well as video editing software. Modern web based editing systems can take video directly from a camera phone over a GPRS or 3G mobile connection, and editing can take place through a web browser interface, so strictly speaking a computer for video editing does not require any installed hardware or software beyond a web browser and an internet connection.

Various editing tasks can then be performed on the imported video before it exported to another medium, or MPEG encoded for transfer to a DVD.

The first truly non-linear editor, the CMX 600, was made in the early 1970s by the CMX Corporation, a joint venture between CBS and Memorex). It recorded & played back black-and-white analog video recorded in "skip-field" mode on modified disk pack drives the size of washing machines. These were commonly used to store data digitally on mainframe computers of the time. The 600 had a console with 2 monitors built in. The right monitor, which played the preview video, was used by the editor to make cuts and edit decisions using a light pen. The editor selected from options which were superimposed as text over the preview video. The left monitor was used to display the edited video. A Digital PDP-11 computer served as a controller for the whole system. Because the video edited on the 600 was in black and white and in low-resolution "skip-field" mode, the 600 was suitable only for offline editing.

Various approximations of non-linear (editing systems) were built in the '80s using computers coordinating multiple laser discs, or banks of VCRs. Computer processing advanced sufficiently by the late '80s to enable true digital imagery, and has progressed today to provide this capability in software on personal computers.

An example of computing power progressing to make non-linear editing possible was demonstrated in the first all-digital non-linear editing system to be released, the "Harry" effects compositing system manufactured by Quantel in 1985. Although it was more of a video effects system, it had some non-linear editing capabilities. Most importantly, it could record (and fully apply effects to) 80 seconds (due to hard disk space limitations) of full broadcast-quality uncompressed digital video encoded in 8-bit CCIR 601 format on its built-in hard disk array.

Non-linear editing with computers as we know it today was first introduced by Avid in 1988 with the Avid/ 1, the first in the line of their Media Composer systems. It was based on the Apple Macintosh computer platform (Macintosh II systems were used) with special hardware and software developed and installed by Avid. The Avid/1 was the first system to introduce modern concepts in non-linear editing, such as timeline editing and clip bins.

The video quality of the Avid/1 (and later Media Composer systems from the late 80s) was somewhat low (about VHS quality), due to it using a very early version of a Motion JPEG (M-JPEG) codec. But it was enough to be a very versatile system for offline editing, and to revolutionize video and film editing, quickly becoming the dominant NLE platform.

Although M-JPEG became the standard codec for NLE during the early 1990s, it had drawbacks. Its high computational requirements ruled out software implementations, leading to the extra cost and complexity of hardware compression/playback cards. More importantly, the traditional tape workflow had involved editing off tape, often in a rented facility. When the editor left the edit suite he could take his confidential video tapes with him. But the M-JPEG datarate was too high for systems like Avid on the Mac and Lightworks on PC to store the video on removable storage, so these used fixed hard discs instead. The tape paradigm of keeping your (confidential) content with you was not possible with these fixed discs. Editing machines were often rented from facilities houses on a per-hour basis, and some productions chose to delete their content after each edit, and then redigitise it again the next day, in order to guarantee the security of their content. In addition, each NLE system had storage capacity limited by its hard disc capacity.

These issues were addressed by a small UK company, Eidos plc (which later became famous for its Tomb Raider video game series). Eidos chose the new ARM-based computers from the UK and implemented an editing system, launched in Europe in 1990 at the International Broadcasting Convention. Because it implemented its own compression software designed specifically for non-linear editing, the Eidos system had no requirement for JPEG hardware and was cheap to produce. The software could decode multiple video and audio streams at once for real time effects at no extra cost. But most significantly, for the first time, it allowed effectively unlimited quantities of cheap removable storage. The Eidos Edit 1, Edit 2 and later Optima systems even allowed the editor to use any Eidos system, rather than being tied down to a particular one, and still keep his data secure. The Optima software editing system was closely tied to Acorn hardware, so when Acorn stopped manufacturing the Risc PC in the late 1990s, Eidos stopped selling the Optima system; by this time Eidos had become predominantly a games company.

Another leap came in the late 90s with the launch of DV-based video formats for consumer and, more importantly, professional use. With DV came IEEE1394 (Firewire/iLink), a simple, inexpensive, accessible and native way of getting video into and out of computers. The video no longer had to be converted from an analogue signal to digital data - it was recorded as digital to start with - and Firewire offered a very straight forward way of capturing the signal without the need for additional hardware or compression. With this innovation, editing suddenly become a more realistic proposition for standard computers with software-only packages. It enabled real desktop editing producing high-quality results with a fraction of the cost of other systems.

More recently the introduction of highly compressed HD formats such as HDV has continued this trend - making it possible to edit HD material on a standard PC running a software-only editing application.

Avid has held on to its market leading position, its major new competition coming in the form of other, cheaper software packages, notably Premiere and later Final Cut Pro. Since its introduction in 2000, Final Cut Pro has come to be the main NLE software to compete with Avid today in terms of number of users. Avid is still considered the industry standard, with the lion's share of feature films, television programs, and commercials created with its NLE systems. For example, Avid products - including technologies from its Digidesign audio division, and Softimage 3D animation subsidiary, were used in the creation of every film nominated in the Best Picture, Directing, Film Editing, Sound Editing, Sound Mixing, Visual Effects, and Best Animated Feature categories of the 77th Annual Academy Awards, held in 2005. In addition, Avid systems were the overwhelming NLE choice of the 2004-2005 Primetime Emmy Award nominees – with more than 50 shows in eleven major categories created on one or more Avid systems.

Quality of Non-linear Editing

One of the primary concerns with non-linear editing has always been picture and sound quality. The need to compress and decompress video leads to some loss in quality. While improvements in compression techniques and disc storage capacity have reduced these concerns, they still exist.

With the more recent adoption of DV formats, quality has become an issue again: DV's compression means that manipulation of the image can introduce significant degredation. However this can be avoided by decompressing DV before making alterations and keeping the resulting video in an uncompressed format, thereby avoiding quality loss through recompression of the modified video images. Software-based editing systems are only able to capture and output DV video and have no capability to do this without the addition of specialist input/output hardware.

The range of user-friendly editing tools has given inexperienced people access to editing at high quality for the first time. While in the short term this may have negative consequences for average programme quality, the wider pool of experienced users it creates will be a benefit in the long run.

19

TV Anchoring

The concept of an anchor has undergone a sea change and news broadcast anchors are no longer just news presenters but people who understand news and also fulfill other roles at the desk or as reporters. If you have talent and start working in a relatively small market, you may reach the anchor desk quickly. You will still, however, have to prove you are ready for that job by impressing the news director with your reporting ability.

Not all reporters become anchors; some good reporters do not have the special talent required to anchor news. Similarly, some anchors make awful reporters. Ask news directors what they look for in reporters and anchors and most will tell you credibility. They want people who are believable, people who come across as knowledgeable about and comfortable with what they are doing.

Jeff Puffer, a voice coach for one of the nation's major broadcast consulting firms, Frank Magid Associates, says he knows many "reliable anchor reporters with good potential who just don't seem comfortable in the anchor chair. In person they're spontaneous and charming. But on the air they're wooden, with unnatural speech rhythms and awkward inflection." Puffer says that when he's instructing anchors and reporters, he expects them "to show two qualities in their reading: intelligence and genuine sensitivity." He says he looks for "emotion that is appropriate for the story, the person, and the occasion. They know what they're reading and that they're thoughtfully weighing the facts as they speak." Puffer says: "I always want them to say it with feeling, not artificially, but with sensitivity and maturity."

It is not always easy for anchor-reporters to accomplish these goals, and those who coach people in delivery techniques use a variety of methods. Puffer says he doesn't concentrate on speech pathology material such as breathing, diction, and resonance. "We're involved in matters relating to interpretation, making the voice sound spontaneous and conversational, like an ad-lib, Puffer admits that his methodology could be called "unconventional or unorthodox," but, he says, "given what we have been finding in neuroscience research, we know that the whole of human intelligence is not just the left side of the brain, the intellectual side. It's also intuition, artistry, abstractions, pattern recognition, and the like."

Roles of News Presenters

A news presenter is, broadly speaking, a person that presents a news show on television, radio or the Internet. The term is not commonly used by people in the industry as they tend to use more descriptive, and sometimes country-specific, terms.

A newsreader is a presenter whose role it is to read the news. In modern times, technology enables journalists to broadcast from relevant locations, reducing the role of the central presenter to that of a newsreader. The term is the most common one for a news presenter outside of the United States and Canada.

Since the 1980s some broadcasters have moved away from using newsreaders, many of whom were simply actors who delivered a script written by others and who played no part in news gathering. Stations such as the BBC and RTÉ instead moved to use newscasters.

A newscaster is a presenter of a news bulletin who is himself or herself a working journalist and news gathering, and a participant in compiling the script to be delivered in a news bulletin.

The American use of the term is presumed to have been coined (or borrowed from English) in the 1980s to distinguish active journalists from newsreaders, the previous type of news presenter.

However in the UK, ITN's presenters are referred to as newscasters (and have been since the 1950s), whilst those working at the BBC are called newsreaders.

A news anchor is a television personality who presents material prepared for a news program and at times must improvise commentary for live presentation. The term is primarily used in the United States and Canada. Many news anchors are also involved in writing and/or editing the news for their programs. Sometimes news anchors interview guests and moderate panels or discussions. Some provide commentary for the audience during parades and other events.

The term anchor was coined by CBS News producer Don Hewitt. CBS cites its first usage as being on July 7, 1952 to describe Walter Cronkite's role at the Democratic and Republican Party National Conventions. The term may have been in reference to the "anchor leg" of a relay race.

A common dogma among the general public equates "news" and "news media" with "journalism", and this typically carries over to news anchors as well — associating media personalities with journalists — much to the consternation of many print journalists. In the current age of mass media and consolidation, news anchors tend to be viewed as belonging to the infotainment or news trades, rather than to the journalism profession. There is a spectrum and scale however — the quintessential national news anchors from early days of television news tended to come from experienced backgrounds in print journalism. Since then, television news has largely been an entity in its own right, where print and television journalism can be viewed as divergent trades.

Adding to the distinction between journalists and anchors and reporters are "human interest", personality, or celebrity news stories, which typically are directed by marketing departments based on a demographic appeal and audience share. Its commonly accepted that anchors are also media personalities, who may even be considered celebrities.

The very nature of corporate network news requires its media personalties to use their public appeal to promote the networks investments, just as network broadcasts themselves (morning shows, TV news magazines) schedule self-promotional stories, in addition to advertising. Critics might go so far as to view anchors as a weak link in the news trade, representing the misplacement of both the credit and the accountability of a news journalism organization —hence adding to a perceived erosion of journalistic standards throughout the news business.

In popular culture, the corporate news anchor is viewed as an archetype of the status quo and bland superficiality of corporate news media. As public people, they tend to receive an excess measure of social (and financial) reward for the hard work of "true" journalists behind the scenes.

North American news anchors are frequently imitated and lampooned people who are hired more for their looks on TV than for any skill at journalism or intelligence. This kind of character is the subject of long running gags on Saturday Night Live, SCTV, and the UK-produced The Muppet Show and the subject of sitcoms like Mary Tyler Moore, Murphy Brown, and NewsRadio.

One-Way Communication

Puffer says the difficulty in broadcast training is the "no interactive environment." He points out that there is "no give and take, it's largely one way. The result of that strained environment is that the communicators do not automatically use all their self-expression when looking into a camera or speaking on mike as they would in a face-to-face dialogue." Puffer adds: "What we try to do is restore that quality and feeling in the delivery. We try to trigger that part of the brain that is responsible for artistry, abstraction, etc."

Puffer also notes that he's not trying to make a person's voice sound like someone else's. "We all have developed and cultivated a wealth of knowledge regarding what is appropriate interpersonal communication over the years," he says. "We all know the tools; we know how loud to speak; how to emphasize and articulate our words; how to use our face and eyes with accompanying gestures; no one has to tell us how to do these things. The idea," Puffer adds, "is to tap into those resources and help bring them into the environment that is not interactive, like the broadcast studio."

Getting Help with Your Delivery

If you are having problems with your voice, diction, and delivery, it's a good idea to deal with the problems while you are in college. Speech and debating courses sometimes help, but if you have serious problems, you may need a voice coach. Voice coach Carol Dearing advises students who are intent on being in front of a microphone or camera to "do all they can to prepare themselves before they leave college." She says that without professional help, some students "fall into habit patterns that will work against them."

Listening to Yourself

In is always a good idea to read your copy aloud because your ear catches mistakes and detects poorly constructed copy that your eye misses. Similarly, reading aloud alerts you to any problems you have with pronunciation, articulation, and awkward speech patterns.

Getting Pronunciation Help

Newscasters should avoid using words that are difficult to pronounce. The mind understands the meaning of many words, but sometimes it has trouble relaying the pronunciation to the tongue, which causes newscasters to stumble over their copy. Tricky words and phrases invite trouble. Sometimes writers and anchors have no choice, however. Proper names, for example, cannot be changed. Spelling them correctly does not guarantee that they will be pronounced correctly. The writer of a newscast must identify the correct pronunciation of any difficult names in a script.

Reporters should ask the people whom they are interviewing for the proper pronunciation of their names. Names of towns also should be checked if there is any doubt. If a job takes you to a new part of the country, it is a good idea to seek out someone who has lived in the area for some time. Colleagues who have been working at the station will be able to help, and someone at the local library or historical society will probably be happy to answer questions about the pronunciation of nearby towns or local family names.

The wire services send out pronunciation guides to their customers these are particularly useful when covering national and international stories. If your news operation is computerized, the guides should be stored for future use. It is not always necessary to use the names of foreign dignitaries. If you do use them, it is a good idea to refer to the dignitaries by their titles during the rest of the story, particularly if the names are unusually difficult to pronounce. When using difficult names, write them phonetically in the copy to help the person who will be reading the script.

Dictionaries, which give the proper pronunciation of words as well as their meanings, are invaluable tools. Several dictionaries of pronunciation are also available for purchase, and most newsrooms keep copies on hand. If you are unsure about the pronunciation of a word, look it up.

Pacing

What else can you do to improve your delivery? pacing is important. Using a pause to get attention when you want something you just said "to sink in. . . . A pause can be very telling, provided you know something." When you writes for yourself use a lot of ellipses (series of three dots). to remind yourself that that is supposed to be a pause. Also capitalize certain words. . . because you want to hit that particular word for it to work. Also it's important to remember when you are on the air that you're talking to somebody, which means that you have to be conscious at all times that there's somebody there, you can't assume people are listening; you "have to get their attention, you don't automatically have it."

Marking Copy

Most newscasters mark copy to help them remember when to pause or to emphasize certain words. They mark the copy as they read it aloud, which also helps them control their breathing. Long sentences require extra breath, so newscasters must either pause more often or rewrite the sentence. Otherwise, they sound as though they are running out of breath. Often, inexperienced newscasters try to speed up their delivery when they realize that they might have trouble getting through a complicated sentence, but that's a poor solution. If you find yourself leaning toward this solution, rewrite your copy until you can read it at a normal pace. use slash marks to indicate pauses and underline words that you wishes to emphasize.

Some anchors use a double underline for words that require extraordinary emphasis. Other anchors use all caps for words they wish to stress. Some anchors use ellipses to indicate pauses, and others use dashes. Some anchors like their scripts typed in all caps, whereas others prefer upper- and lowercase (which, according to studies, is easier to read).

Characteristics of Successful Anchors

People watch people. They don't watch helicopters or satellites and they prefer to watch people they like and are comfortable with, so you have to build a relationship with the viewers and make them comfortable with you. It's also important for anchors to be involved in the production of the show. Either write a little of the newscast yourself or be involved in the reporting.

It is important for anchors to understand that there is more to the job than looking and sounding good on the air. They also should be involved in the community through personal appearances or charity work. It's important for anchors to be working journalists. They should be able to handle a school board meeting or a foreign story with equal ease.

Most news directors use the same language when they speak about successful anchors, and words like credibility, honesty, and genuine keep cropping up, along with concern and caring about what's going on in the community. Another common denominator is that successful, top-rated anchors are all genial people who are well liked by their co-workers and their viewers. If you have a good voice, learn to use it properly. Get accustomed to reading your copy aloud before you go in front of a microphone. In addition to alerting you to grammatical errors or awkward phrases you may have missed, reading your copy aloud helps you discover that certain words and names in the copy are hard to pronounce. If so, add the phonetic spellings next to or above the difficult names and places. Last, reading your copy aloud gives you the opportunity to determine what words you want to emphasize and how you can use pacing effectively.

1. Read a few newspaper stories silently and then read them into a tape recorder. Make a note of the things you discovered were a problem in the copy only after reading it aloud. After making appropriate changes in the copy, read the story into the tape recorder a second time, and note any improvements.

2. Write a one-minute radio script based on information from a newspaper or newspaper wire. Then read the script into a tape recorder. Listen to the recording, and make notes on anything that you did not like about your reading, such as inflection, breathing, pitch, or pace.

3. Do a second reading, but this time mark your copy before doing so. After reading, note whether your delivery improved.

4. Go through a newspaper or newspaper wire copy and find words that are unfamiliar to you. Look up the words in a dictionary for meaning and pronunciation and in a pronunciation guide if one is available. Write the words phonetically along with the rest of the sentences, and read them into a tape recorder. Then replay the tape for other members of your class, and note whether they understood the meaning of the words.

5. After you have noted the words that fellow students did not understand, find synonyms for them and record the sentences with the new words.

Handking Telepromoters

As you all by now would know that the television news or programme production involves a lot of people who directly or indirectly becomes the part of the production. It will be of immense help for you to know, how to work with the producer or the anchor with ease as well understand the working of basic tools like the teleprompter if you are the anchor.

Now that you have a clear picture of what you're dealing with, think like a football or basketball coach and put together a game plan that maximizes those strengths in every show. Make sure you give a toss to a breaking live shot that could fall apart any minute to the anchor that can ad-lib out of it when the signal goes to hash. Give the most important local stories to the anchor that's a good writer. If your anchor can't get to a generic live shot at :00:01 without looking panicked, then give them some video: 10-: 15 before the shot and wipe to your generic live. This may sound simplistic, but in charting your strengths and weaknesses you may find a better way to present your stories. I'm not trying to say that a job in front of the camera is more difficult than producing, just different. Very different. So to help you understand your subordinates, here are some rules for their care and feeding.

Protect Your Talent

While making the list you may have written, "dumb as a post" for one of your anchors. Sadly, you may be right on the money. But if you knowingly let your anchor go into a show with copy that's going to trip them up or let a director take a shot that makes them look stupid, you'll not only damage your relationship with your anchors, but you'll damage their image to the viewers. Watch your talent closely during the broadcast. Do they look their best? Their image is your image.

Protect your talent from the morons that call on the phone after the broadcast. Be friendly, and always side with them. If it was awful, say he/she didn't mean it and they're terribly sorry. Remember you're a family. Don't side with anyone against the family. If it's really bad, dump the call to the news director. That's what they get paid for.

Get out the Pampers

Anchors are Babies. Even the most experienced, professional anchors can and will act like toddlers. They'll count the number of stories they're reading, get peeved when there's no water on the set, or blame others when they make a mistake. We all have stories, but the bottom line is you're the producer. You've got to be firm but you also have to care about what makes them happy. Granted, this can get ridiculous, so sometimes discipline is the way to go. However, if making sure some P.A. has water on the set for your anchor all the time makes your anchor better, do it. Your broadcast will benefit and so will you. Also, the occasional "liked the way you read that story on the homeless" goes a long way. You might find the sentiment returned.

It's important to remember that most anchors are terribly insecure. However, they're strong enough to take a risk and put whatever talent they have on the line every night. If the broadcast goes in the crapper, they often hear about it two hours later at the grocery store. Imagine if you had to explain to the produce clerk at the Safeway why video of a monkey riding a horse came up on the mayor's obit. You, the director, the font op., the tape op., or the audio person can make the mistake, but to the viewer, it's the anchor that's accountable. So when it does happen, and they handle it well, make sure you let them know. Your babies may act like children, but they can make you look very good if you treat them right and that pays off next time you're looking for a job.

Get to Know Your Talent

You're coaching a team. Find out about your players. How they feel about the station, you, and the broadcast. An hour over a few cups of coffee could save you a month's worth of headaches and heartache. You might be shocked to learn they know a lot more about things than they let on. These days an anchor team may get a new producer every six months to a year. To them that's like getting a new mother or father. Know what they like and don't like. Find out how to get the most out of them. Chances are they'll tell you. Here are a few good questions:

What are your interests/background? Is there a special topic or story you want to write or read most often? Should I remind you when there are ten/five minutes to the open? Do you feel like you're getting enough/too many reads? How's the pacing of the broadcast? How can it be improved? What can I do to make you more comfortable on-air?

You'll be amazed at what you can learn from an hour with your talent outside the station. If you show them you care, they'll usually do the same. Many times they'll recommend you to their friends and contacts, and you'll end up with a better job when you leave.

When filming anyone - actor or "real person" - who must deliver a long passage of script straight to camera, it's hard to beat a teleprompter. The on-camera talent can read even a lengthy monologue from the teleprompter and it appears they aren't reading at all. On larger productions freelance teleprompter operators with their own equipment are the norm. They will generally want the copy to be delivered on a computer disk several days in advance of the shoot. On some of the older teleprompter models, the copy must typed in by hand and then printed on a special roll of paper. These work fine until you must change more than a word or two of the copy. Today most Teleprompters are built around computers and monitors. This eliminates the tedious process of retyping the copy and allows for copy changes right on the set. As you watch a Rajdeep Sardesai or a Deepak Chaurasia anchor his bulletins, watch his eyes carefully. Sometimes you can see them moving left and right as he reads from the teleprompter. Almost everyone who delivers this much copy uses a teleprompter and this slight eye movement is rarely objectionable. Moving the camera and teleprompter farther away from the person reading could minimize it, but this would change the composition of the shot. And the person reading would need to have very good eyesight to read from that distance.

Teleprompter Tips

— Rehearsals save time and money

— Before the shoot give the actor or on-camera speaker a printed version of the script. It's best to rehearse the script out-loud because the printed word and spoken word can be two very different things. If there are any names or terms that could have more than one pronunciation, you'll have time to decide which pronunciation is correct or most appropriate.

— While lighting and other preliminaries are underway, let the actor and teleprompter operator rehearse from the actual teleprompter. An experienced operator knows to vary the speed of the scrolling text to keep up with, but never rush, the anchor. A smart operator can even deal with a bit of improvisation from the anchor.

— Some things which read just fine on paper, needed to be rewritten so they sounded right.

Tips for Narrators

Narrators often have several tricks to keep their voices at peak performance. They range from snake oil to prescription drugs. Here are a few, first, and most important is proper hydration.

Drink lots of clear liquids, preferably water. Although it is nice to have a bottle of water to moisten a dry throat during a recording, proper hydration occurs long before the session. Hot liquids of any kind will help open your sinuses with steam, Avoid coffee, though. It is too hot, too sugary, too creamy or too strong. Some vocal coaches recommend swishing any drink in your mouth to minimize extremes of hot or cold on your throat.

These last two narrator tricks are less superstitious and more technical. Many people produce lip-smacking sounds as they speak. A quick way around this is to rub on some lip balm. Not only will it reduce the smacking sounds, it has an aromatic quality that can help clear sinuses. As the "voice" speaks into the microphone, you may find the sound too aggressive or full of distracting mouth sounds (odd pops and gurgles). Simply reposition the microphone so the narrator addresses it at a 45-degree (or greater) angle. You may also try positioning the mic from above the narrator, pointing down at their mouth. You will be surprised at how this will change the character of the sound, hopefully for the better.

Camera Prompters

Working and types People who work in front of the camera use various prompting methods to aid them in their on-camera delivery. Most prompters (often referred to as TelePrompTers or Teleprompters after the original manufacturer) rely on a reflected image of the words, which are visible in a mirror in front of the camera lens. The side view of a camera prompter illustrates how this works. The video image from the video monitor (displaying the text to be read) is reflected into a half-silvered mirror mounted at a 45-degree angle to the lens. The image of the text as seen by the prompter camera is electronically reversed left-to-right so that the mirror image will appear correct.

Since the mirror is only half-silvered, it ends up being a "two-way mirror." First, it reflects the image from the video prompter screen, allowing the talent to read the text. Second, being semitransparent, the mirror allows much of the light from the scene being photographed to pass through its surface and go into the camera lens. When the talent looks at the prompter mirror to read the text, it appears as if they are looking right at the camera lens, and, therefore, at the audience.

In order not to give the appearance of constantly staring into the camera lens, most on-camera people who use prompters periodically glance at their scripts, especially as a way of emphasizing facts and figures. Some on-camera people prefer large pasteboard cue cards with the s written out with a bold black marker. This approach has definite limitations. Not only does the use of cue cards require the aid of an e person (a card puller), but the talent must constantly look slightly off to the side of the camera to see the cards. Plus, since the cards can't be reused, the approach ends up being rather expensive.

Many news reporters working in the field simply rely on handheld note cards or a small notebook containing names, figures and basic facts. Reporters typically memorize their opening and closing on-camera comments and then speak from notes (or even read a fully written script) while continuing with off-camera narration. Some field reporters have mastered the technique of fully writing out the script, recording it on an audio cassette machine, and then playing it back in a small earphone while simultaneously repeating their own words on camera. Although this technique demands practice, concentration, and reliable audio playback procedures, once mastered, it can result in highly effective on-camera delivery. Even so, a camera prompter (Teleprompter) is the most relied upon form of prompting, especially for long on-camera segments. There are two types of camera prompters: hard copy and soft copy.

Hard Copy Prompters

The first type of on-camera prompter, what became known as a hard copy prompter, uses long rolls of paper or clear plastic. When paper is used, the on-camera script is first typed in large letters in short (typically, two to four-word) lines. The paper is attached to two motor driven rollers and the image is picked up by a video camera and displayed on a video monitor, as previously illustrated. The script has to be scrolled at a carefully controlled speed while the talent reads the text. Either a prompter operator or the talent, himself or herself, regulate the speed of the prompter by means of a handheld control. Hard copy prompters have now largely been replaced by soft copy prompters.

Soft Copy Prompters

Soft copy prompters bypass the hard copy phase and display the output of a computer, much the same as the computer-monitor displays the text you are reading right now. This approach has several advantages.

First, because the text is a direct, electronically generated image, it is sharp and easy to read. Revisions are easy to make without the legibility problems associated with crossing out words or phrases on paper and penciling in last-minute corrections.

Once the script is entered into the computer it can be electronically reformatted and displayed in a standard prompter format-narrow lines with large bold letters as shown below. If a color video prompter monitor is used, the text can be color-keyed to set off the words of different speakers, or special instructions to the talent (which are not meant to be read aloud).

Issues In Using Prompters

When using cue cards or any type of on-camera prompting device there is always the important issue of the compromise involved in the camera-to-subject distance. If the camera is placed close to the talent (making it easy for them to read the prompter), the constant left-to-right reading movement of their eyes can be distracting to an audience. Moving the camera back and zooming in reduces this problem by narrowing the left-to-right motion of the eyes; but, at the same time, the extra distance makes the prompter harder to read. The solution is to work with the talent to arrive at an acceptable compromise, and then hold to the agreed upon camera distances throughout productions.

20

Television Interviews

The most typical response o a news producer to an issue is, 'let's talk to someone'. This 'talking to someone' does have its advantages, especially in view of the uncertainty about many items of the newscast. The interview item has the flexibility of being extended or shortened depending upon the availability of the edited news stories ready for transmission. But the flexibility of interview items apart, there are occasions when a story is better told by the reporter on the spot or the anchor 'in the studio.

Thus, before proceeding for an interview it is better to ascertain the following things:

1. Is there no better alternative to an interview?

2. If no, are you talking to the right 'persons?

3. If so, what do you ask?

4. And finally, what do you expect from the interview?

Given that everything is in order, have you done your homework by going through the minimum required background material? Or you will start your interview with something like "what should I ask you ?". True, the interviewee is quite likely to-know more about the subject, but you should at least know what you want from. the interviewee. Or else, be ready to look foolish on air or be used by the, interviewee to his advantage, or both.

Put yourself in the shoes of the interviewee and what you find are: there is a thousand watt light shining into your eyes, a reporter gunning his mike towards you, and the cameraman aiming his fancy equipment at you.

This much to drive the point that a reporter must be able to put the interviewee at ease, to make him unconcerned about the electronic paraphernalia around him. You cannot be at ease with a doctor who hesitates while giving an injection. Similarly, nothing makes an interviewee more uncomfortable than a confused reporter who does not know what he wants from the subject. However, on the other end, there are interviewees professionally trained to deal with media people. They know the type of answers a reporter likes most for the purpose of editing back at the station. Also, there are politicians who divulge only that much information which suits them most, whatever questions the reporter may ask. Again, there are public officials who place themselves in positions, relative to the camera, that display their most flattering angles. In such a situation, the TV reporter should not forget that he or she is in-charge, not the interviewee. The reporter should tell the interviewee politely but firmly where to stand, but not what to say. In fact, such a situation often turns into a battle of wits in which neither side wants to lose its cool.

In television, journalistic judgement and writing ability alone are not enough. Unlike his print or radio counterpart, a TV reporter has to 'get to the point at once, as directly and curtly as practicable. His questions should be so designed as to produce compact answers, because the video cannot be compressed, though it can be cut. As a TV interviewer you have to think quickly to follow up topics outside any originally planned structure of the interview and organise your thoughts in a way that leads to logical, step-by-step answers. This is important in view of the fact that the newsroom is likely Jo select two or three questions and answers which follow a rational pattern. Any attempt to produce a relaxed atmosphere by putting one or two 'warm up' questions is at best a waste of time. Next comes the phrasing of questions. Putting a long question or wrapping up more than one question together is most likely to be counter-productive.

Phrasing of Questions

The long questions may not be properly understood or the wrapped-up questions may give an opportunity to the clever interviewee to seize on the one that suits him most, ignoring the rest. Alternatively, an inexperienced interviewee may be unsure of which question to answer first. General questions of 'the truth is at stake' variety are likely to produce lengthy and wide-ranging answers which interest only the interviewee-and a few others. In sum, a focussed approach to questions is a must to produce the real 'sound bites'. However, this -is not enough. You have to take care not to come up with small interjections during the answers. Such interjections overlap with the answers and are difficult to be edited. Even if they do not overlap, they fail to register on the screen long enough.

Stereo-type Questions

Though it is difficult to do without some cliche questions and differential phrases meant to soften up the interviewee, it is advisable to use them very cautiously. In television, journalistic judgement and writing ability alone are not enough. Unlike his print or radio counterpart, a TV reporter has to get to the point at once, as directly and curtly as practicable. His questions should be so designed as to produce compact answers, because the video cannot be compressed, though it can be cut. As a TV interviewer you have to think quickly to follow up topics outside any originally planned structure of the interview and organize your thoughts in a way that leads to logical, step-by-step answers. This is important in view of the fact that the newsroom is likely to select two or three questions and answers which follow a rational pattern. Any attempt to produce a relaxed atmosphere by putting one or two 'warm up' questions is at best a waste of time.

Next comes the phrasing of questions. Putting a long question or wrapping up more than one question together is most likely to be counter-productive. The long questions may not be properly under clever interviewee to seize on the one that suits him most, ignoring the rest. Alternatively, an inexperienced interviewee may be unsure of which question to answer first. General questions of 'the truth is at stake' variety are likely to produce lengthy and wide-ranging sum, a focused approach to questions is a must to produce the real 'sound bites'. However, this is not enough. You have to take care not to come up with small interjections during the answers. Such interjections overlap with the answers and difficult to be edited. Even if they do not overlap, they fail to register on the screen long enough.

Another point to be remembered about any interview is the growing practice of trying out questions in a 'dry run' without the camera. Many newsrooms ban this, unless that is a condition for the interview itself. However, a brief discussion about the scope of the interview is in order. In fact, the interviewee can ask for such an information as a matter of right.

Follow up Questions

Some experienced people, especially politicians, are smart enough to evade a difficult question by saying some anecdotes in the popular language, which may be even difficult to translate into English or even standard Hindi, and so on. Others may stick doggedly to their prepared texts. Such interviewees can be chased with intelligent follow-up questions until their evasion becomes too obvious. But what if you yourself do not listen to the answers and instead, stick to the prepared list of questions?

Most of the interviews do not end up as what they were expected to be. So sticking to the prepared list of questions is not of much help, though the list itself is necessary to avoid missing any important question.

However, if the answer is of no consequence and the interviewee speaks non-stop ignoring your hints to finish, you better interject when the inflexion of the subject's voice is downward. But it is good to start it all over again if the question is misunderstood. Don't wait for the answer to end. Just call out 'cut' to stop the camera and discuss the question properly before restarting the shoot.

News Interviews

There are five major types of interviews depending upon the number of interviewees and the situation in which the interviewee and the interviewer are placed. The most common of these is the 'set piece' interview which is conducted with the advance permission of the interviewee. In this case, the reporter gets enough time to prepare questions and make the necessary arrangements for the interview.

A set piece may be conducted at the newsmaker's own place (party office, Parliament, factory, nursing home, the place of residence, and so on), in or from the studio, to be telecast live or recorded for a broadcast scheduled later in the day or even a week. Next to the set piece interview is the eye witness, or spot interview which is conducted on location from the people present at the time of occurrence of the event. This type of interview demands very speedy identification of those willing and able to talk about the experiences of events to which they were witnesses. The questions are more about facts rather than opinions: what did you see, where were you when the event took place, what did you do on seeing this, and so on. In the third category, the' quickie', both the reporter and the newsmaker are hard pressed for time. This is a hit-or-miss affair and is a common sight on daily newscasts.

For example, the leader of the opposition emerging out of his chamber in Parliament and on the way to his waiting car. The reporter is in a hurry to catch him before another MP, this time of the, ruling party, might reach the parking area in a minute or two. So before the ruling party MP arrives, the reporter asks a few questions of the leader of the opposition about, say the presentation of the Prasharati Bill in the Lok Sabha. The routine questions are: 'What is going on?', 'What next?', etc. Even the refusal to say anything is worth while showing, if it conveys the motive and the manner of the rebuff. '

In this type of interview, the reporter literally waits at the doorsteps or outside some building in order to have a few words about an event in which the newsmaker is a participant. Normally, such an interview is only 2 to 3 questions long and is usually held standing up, the CD of the newsmaker hastily framed against a neutral background and the reporter using a hand mike. Even for such short duration interviews, reaction cutaways serve as good editing tools. Here the camera need not be moved radically. You can move only in the correct direction for a matching cutaway. And, the correct direction is the opposite of what the interviewee had been, looking to from the camera's point of view.

A word about the position of the mike. Since you are pressed for time, matching the direction of the mike may claim a few precious seconds or minutes. So it is better to avoid the mike when framing the reaction cutaway. Or alternatively, you must pretend to thrust the mike back and forth as you did during the interview.

In the fourth category, the 'group interviews'. A reporter is required to interview more than one person at a time: the co-winners of an award, the parents of the kidnapped child, and so on. The fact that interviewees share an interest in the issue at hand makes a case for showing them together in the same shot. But fulfilling this need creates some technical problems. There won't be enough microphones to wire each interviewee. Thus you have to position your mike in a way that it captures sound from different directions. This. also means that the location must be quiet. The camera may not always be precisely on the specific interviewee who spontaneously comes up with his response, thus forcing the camera operator to readjust his shot which may cause a brief loss of focus. Thus a number of cutaways would be required in addition to the standard reaction shot of the reporter: These cutaways should be of three types:

1. The reporter in close-up, looking in each direction because some members of the group were looking left, others right.

2. Each member of the group in close-up, listening silently to the rest.

3. The entire group from behind, as the reporter listens first turning his or her attention from left to right, holding for' a moment then turning from right to left.

The same type of shots are necessary in case of stand-up interviews of two or more persons where the reporter holds a hand mike. In this case, the reporter should be seen turning his or her attention as well as the mike in each direction.

Finally the 'Vox Pop' (vox populi) which aims at gathering opinions of the members of the general public, normally on an issue of common interest, e.g., rising food prices, budgetary cut in kerosene oil prices, etc. This type of interview calls for the same question to be put in the same way to different people So that the answers can be edited without inserting the face of the interviewer. This also helps in maintaining the flow of the interviews, each of which do not last more than a few seconds.

These five broad categories may be said to include all kinds of interviews, including press conferences which are organised to avoid separate interviews to different channels and various media. News conferences take the choice of location entirely out of the hands of the newsteam which has to contend with whatever light is available.

Here, the camera-operator has to be fully relied upon for supplying good pictures and sound quality to make the result as satisfactory as possible. And, there is no reason why the camera-operator will not do his or her best. After all, 'the camera operator too fails if the report is junked. '

Studio Interviews

Live studio interviews in newscasts have the merit of being flexible. Those which are not getting anywhere can be shortened, while the lively ones can be extended by dropping some less important items of the newscast. At times, live interviews also become handy for filling up any vacant space in the programme either because of slow news flow or because of some sudden technical snag in any area.

The outcome of studio interviews depends largely on the judgement and the ability of the interviewer. The techniques of interview being the same as elsewhere, except that the interviewer has to be much more alert and be briefed deeply and accurately. The third quality, possibly as important as the other two, is an 'acute sense of timing'. The interview must not be so fast that the few seconds of the allotted time still remain to be filled up, neither should it be so slow that some of the important aspects remain to be covered and the interview has to be cut short abruptly. Experienced interviewers like Prannoy Roy and Rajat Sharma are able to extract the very last ounce of value from their interviews right up to the end of the closing seconds.

The interviewer is helped in this regard by the floor manager, positioned out of vision, who keeps on giving him signals about the passage of time as the interview progresses. The most crucial time is the final minute of the interview. At the start of the last 15 seconds, the interviewer is signalled to wind up the interview and when the last second ends, the floor manager signals to stop the interview immediately. Various signals to. indicate the different time segments of the interview are almost the same the world over. For example, drawing a finger across in a cut-throat motion shows that the show must be halted forthwith.

The increasing number of live news interviews have been matched by a corresponding advance in production technology which is capable of linking the interviewer in the studio with the interviewee elsewhere. This is also known as 'down the line' interview.

In case of live news interviews between two people, most studios prefer using three cameras: one concentrating on each participant (for his or her medium close-up and close-up shots) and the third to provide a range of two-shots. The cameras trained on the two participants can also be moved to provide a variety of over-the-shoulder shots.

The subject of an interview should be looking at the reporter. The camera is recording a conversation between two people who should normally be looking at each other. To look into the camera would look unnatural.

The reporter is required to pause between the end ,of the interviewee's answer and the start of his next question. A second's' silence is good enough as an editing tool, reducing the possibility of 'upcutting' either participant's words. But if the interviewee is' very hard to deal with and speaks nonstop, you interrupt as fast as possible when he (the interviewee) pauses because of losing his breath momentarily.

If you choose not to take notes during an interview in order to make the interviewee feel at ease, you may forget some important points while recording your narration.

However, to get the best results you may carry a pocket audio cassette recorder to keep a separate record of the interview. You can also use this cassette to check the exact wording of reverse angle questions after the interview.

Ideally the reporter should not suggest contents of a statement to the interviewee. For further details, check with your producer. The interviewee doesn't need to answer the reverse questions because the camera is shooting just the back of his head. At times, the second hearing of the question will cause the interviewee to recall some important point he forgot to make during the interview. In this case, if the reporter also feels the same and the time permits, the camera should be set up again in its former position before the interview resumes.

Though one eye direction or profile cannot be said to be better than the other, when several interviews are recorded in connection with the same subject, some interviewees should be looking right, others left. This gives a kind of visual variety and is especially effective in presenting the conflicting views of two people by editing together their sound bites. It appears as if they were talking one-to-one.

The reporter must correct the interviewee when the latter makes an inaccurate remark through a slip of tongue. He can do this by stopping the interview momentarily. You may say, "Hold on a second, sir, you said the confidence vote is on Friday. But the Lok Sahba secretariat has fixed it for the next Thursday". The newsmaker should be grateful to you, if he does not want to put his foot in his mouth.

However, if an interviewee, say a Lok Sabha MP says the total number of his party's MPs incorrectly because he or she is unaware of it, you need not correct the interviewee. In fact, the latter's wrong statement itself becomes a matter of news.

Ethics of Interviewing

News interviews; be it for TV, radio or print, continue to be the most talked about and controversial aspect of all the news items taken together. The prime reasons being:

(a) The alleged misrepresentation of contents during the editing of interviews.

(b) Intrusion into the privacy of the interviewee.

(c) The reporter's attitude towards his or her subject.

Editing: Most of the public figures are well aware that not all that they say is going to find time on TV. So they restrict themselves to the main points which are capable of turning into juiciest sound bites. However, the people inexperienced in the ways of TV do complain about their facts being misrepresented. The best way to get over such complaints is to tell the interviewee right in the beginning that the newsroom is under no obligation to air the whole or even part of the interview. The interviewee has also the right to know the context and purpose of interview. He or she should also be informed whether divergent opinions are sought on the same subject.

Intrusion: If you ask penetrating questions of the newly bereaved who are still too shocked to comprehend what they are saying, that would amount to being unjust to the interviewees. But many of the bereaved, like parents of those killed in the Uphar Cinema tragedy, are willing to talk to - the camera either to vent their anger at the callousness of the concerned authorities or as an attempt to help prevent similar tragedies elsewhere. However, there are people who do not want to talk about anything under similar circumstances. You cannot demand answers from them as a matter of right. Their privacy must be respected. But here also, putting questions with tact and empathy can beget best results. In any case, the victims of crime must not be gruelled into feeling that they are 'victims twice over':

first at the hands of the criminal, and next the media. This is especially true of the victims of sexual abuse.

Attitude towards the Subject: The worst charge against most Star Television interviewers is that they often compel their subjects into admitting things which are damaging to the latter. How do the interviewers do so? By relentless questioning bordering on interrogation. Some interviewers are also alleged to be more interested in projecting their egos than getting genuine answers to their questions. On the other hand, there are interviewees like Shri Laloo Prasad and Har Kishen Singh Surjeet who have the knack of answering any awkward question in a way that suits them. They know very well that the questions they are being asked are connected with the area in which they are experts and the interviewer under the constant pressure of deadlines would be happy with a 'colourful' sound bite. Moreover, very few reporters are sure of their ground to put intelligent questions-either they are not properly briefed or they have not done their homework properly, or both. However, an interviewer who' has done his ground work and is well-briefed should be able to extract something worthwhile by putting intelligent questions with tact and sympathy. If you bully the interviewee, it is quite possible that he or she will win the sympathy of the viewer. On the other hand, the interviewee's refusal to answer and his or her facial expressions speak volumes for themselves. Finally, about purpose of this discussion. The caution about editing, intrusion and attitude is mostly relevant in the case of . programmes broadly grouped as 'current affairs'.

Transcribing

Back from the shoot you do not start working on the final script immediately. This is so because what you conceived about your story before the shooting will not be what you actually get after the shooting is over. It may be better or worse but never the same. It is for this reason that you need to reacquaint yourself with the shot material. For this, you mark the time codes at which the shots you would -like to include in the story are located in the tape. This is what is called lagging. Mast of the freshers are 'likely to be assigned the job of lagging at the start of their careers. For those who have no 'understanding of television as a medium and who are straight from print or radio, logging is very helpful.

Once you develop a knack for shots, you can identify-the desired shots even when the player is an fast forward made. Now you note only the shots you need and also. where a particular, sequence of shots begins: Far example, in a story an firing in the Kargil sector along the line of control (LOC), you might heed to' note the time codes where the following sequences begin: hospital where the victims of firing are admitted; the damaged school building where many of the villagers have taken shelter; general view; of the villagers living outside their homes far fear of fresh firing the firing from across the border with the wild track, and so. on.

It is the audio equivalent of logging, though lagging is far easier than transcribing. This is so. Because transcribing cannot be done on fast forward made. Listening to. an interviewee's wards is a slaw and monotonous job. But in order to. select the most 'colourful' and 'opinionated' sound bites you need to go through this painful process. But the burden can be, reduced to. a great extent by making short rates - at the time at the interview First you scribble the' order of questions' when the Interview is a progress. This will help you locate the selected. bites back at the editing table. But make sure that your noting down the questions does not distract the interviewee who may feel that you are not paying attention to what he is saying. Also, you should make sure that you do not miss out the follow. up questions which you had not planned before the shoot.

Next to the identification of sound bites is the question of 'how' the words were spoken. Did the interviewee make awkward pauses or did he have severe speech impediments like interspersing his words with Errs, Ums, and running his words together? In such situations, you may have to settle for less problematic bites, sometimes with relatively weak contents. From the preceding discussion it does not follow that you do not take the sound bites of speakers who suffer from one or the other type of speech problems even if it means supering the 'translated' version of their spoken words on the screen.

Could you afford to drop the words of E.M.S. Namboodiripad even if your story demanded his sound bites? Obviously not. He had severe speech problems. He repeated the first syllable of the opening word of a sentence to an intolerable degree, yet his sound bites _re used when necessary. Similarly, Sunil Gavaskar had the habit of running his words together till the last days of his career in the test cricket. But he needed to be interviewed. In fact, such situations are not rare. This only drives the point that the time codes of awkward pauses and other problematic bits of interview need to be noted all the more carefully. It is helpful in selecting alternative start and end points if there are less unclear or better sound bites elsewhere in the interview.

Recording

Before you record the narration for a field report, you have to write II yourself. It comes at the end of a long exacting day spent in gathering the right pictures. And, the conditions under which you may have to write your narration are usually not at all ideal. The newscast deadline may be a few minutes away. A courier boy might be waiting to leave with the tape containing your narration. Moreover, you may be without a desk, a chair or a typewriter. You think this is too much? No, hold on. There may be no roof on your head. How will you do your job! You might scribble your narration in a note-book while seated in your crew car or O.B. Van, where you will record as well. If you have the capacity to concentrate on writing your narration even on a 'stock-trading floor', you have the right stuff for reporting.

But for the factual details of narration, memory alone cannot be depended upon. Why? You shoot here, interview there, and so on, collecting a mass of raw footage and information. An accurate account of all this-persons and locations shot on the tape-is called a dope-sheet. The dope-sheet helps you recall and organise your story elements quickly. Also, you will have no time to review the mass of shot material when reporting from the field.

There is still another reason for keeping an accurate record of the footage. Suppose you shoot an accidental fire in your district collectorate and then proceed to cover a news conference by a visiting minister. During the press conference, you get a call on your cell phone. This is from the newswriter handling your fire story. He wants to know which of the two interviewees is the Chief Fire Officerthe man with the stripped bush shirt or the one without moustache? If you had sent a dope-sheet identifying who is who, your newsroom could be saved from losing valuable editing and writing time. If there is nothing so distinguishing about the interviewee you can mention who spoke first or what were their relative positions-left, right' or centre. Yet verbal identification on the tape itself would be another way of sharing information with the members of your team.

Identification on Tape: The technique of verbal identification is also helpful in informing your tape editor, which 'take' of your PTC voice-over, is okay. A take is synonymous with a try. On camera closer may be identification usually by the reporter as 'Closer, Take One' If he or she fumbles, the identification (ID) become 'Closer, Take.

Visual Identification: Some newsrooms want their reporters to hold up the equivalent number of fingers in front of the camera for the purpose of identifying the number of takes. This. allows the tape editor to locate the correct take (which you have noted on your dope-sheet) by picture only on a fast forward mode. This saves a few critical minutes of editing time just before the news deadline.

Closing Pad: At the end of a PTC (openers, bridge or closer), you need a Duffer of silence and picture, to make up for the delay in punching the following segment or item of the newscast. Thus, at the end of a closer; especially after signing off, the reporter remains motionless, eyes still directed at the camera, for about five 'seconds. During this is period the reporter should not be winking his eyes or scratching his head. This is true for live as well as recorded PTCs. The term 'closing pad' is so caned because the reporter himself acts as the 'pad' to 'cover' any delay in-roll cues or punching-of the next item.

Recording Techniques

1. To maintain the uniformity of sound, you should use the 'same mike for narration as you used in your interviews and PTC. This is to avoid the differences in sound quality from mike to mike.

2. Unwanted background noise is to be avoided to the maximum extent possible. Beware that certain closed places give worse sound quality than open places. For recording indoors, choose a room with carpeting drapes, which absorb sound. Conversely, tiled surfaces bounce back the sound in your mike, giving an echo-effect.

3. When recording in windy conditions, 'use a windscreen or a handkerchief around the mike. Otherwise, a gentle breeze over your mike can sound like cyclone to the recording head of the camcorder.

4.   Don't move the mike cable during recording because this movement may produce crackle on the tape.

5.   And finally, don't kiss the mike. Love it sure, but at' a distance of 6 to 18 inches from your lips, depending upon the type of mike and the strength of your voice.

Reporter as a Performer

Besides journalistic abilities and a minimum mastery over television techniques, a TV reporter should posses two other qualities which are basic to the medium itself: a reasonably presentable appearance and a clear diction. This does not mean that actor-like-looks and compete-like-diction are the inthings in TV news. In contrast, the preference is for people who look and sound as though they lead real lives off screen. In sum, the viewers want a reporter as someone who belongs to their neighbourhood and yet who enters the screen with a style of his (or her) own, This means the reporter should be able to perform to the TV camera.

The Way You Speak: A natural style of delivery, i.e. words spoken at an even pace and with emphasis and pauses, is not something reserved for star performers. Most of the news people can attain this by preparing for it. Practice reading with a tape recorder and being one's own ruthless critic while hearing the replay are very helpful. Even voice coaches can be consulted if problems persist. But non-existent full-stops in the middle of sentences and running one word into another can be checked by careful practice and paying attention to what the team members point out in good (or bad) spirit.

At Ease with Camera: Some reporters are naturals for new_ camera, but most are not. Many of those who are uncomfortable with the camera start passing tongues between dry lips, their necks become stiff. You can add any number of body movements-sitting on the edge of the chair, handtwitching and so on-and facial expressions that result from nervousness when faced with the camera. Here again, the only remedy is the close scrutiny of personal performances (recorded on a VHS tape) and efforts to get over the shortcomings.

At times you have to bear with the ego-trips of your production staff when they point out a genuine flaw in your performance in order to 'show you down'. Never mind, this happens everywhere and TV is no exception.

If you have worked in a newspaper, you may recall your first encounter with a veteran paster who' advised' you on a feature page layout that finally landed you with a good reprimand from the news editor. So is the case in TV news. Only the names and functi6ns change,' attitudes remaining the same.

A Sense of Dressing: The most important thing about dress is to 'avoid clothes and colours which the majority of the viewers would consider inappropriate Uncombed hair or two day beard would not be allowed. by 'any TV news producer except when the situation demands so, e.g., covering the. civil war "in Afghanistan. Similarly, an open-necked bush-shirt and jeans would be quite appropriate 'When covering the terrorist operations in Kashmir during the summer while a formal shirt and tie would be required for a studio interview.

As for female reporters; necklaces, beads and long ear rings; are best avoided as' their movements and the lights reflected from them cause distraction. Lapel badges also' divert the viewers' attention When' tend to 'be divided between deciphering what is written on the badges and listening to what is being said' in the news programme.

Finally, about some technical limitations. The sensitive electronic cameras fail accept certain striped or checked patterns (which cause strobing),'and some colours (especially shade of blue) create 'holes; through which studio backgrounds can be seen.

Steps of Effective Interview

One of the most basic building blocks of journalism is the interview. It sounds obvious, but reporters have to talk to people to learn what's really going on. More than that, however, journalists need to include people's voices in their stories to make those stories come alive. Interviewing takes preparation and skill. It's not just a matter of going out with a question and coming back with a sound bite.

Decide whom to interview

— Talking to "the usual suspects" all the time can make stories predictable and flat. The trick is to choose unexpected sources, or to get the usual suspects to say unexpected things.

— Ask these questions to decide whom you'll talk to: Who is most directly involved in this story? Who is the central character? Who is most affected by what is happening in this story? Who is in conflict in this story? Who might have more information about this story? Who could help me find the right person to speak to for this story?

— Ask these questions to decide if you have chosen the right source: How does this source know what he or she knows? (Is this person in a position to know these things-either personally or professionally?) How can I confirm this information through other sources, through documents? How representative is my source's point of view? (Is this just one person who complains loudly about the landlord, because he or she has a personal problem? Or is this the most articulate voice speaking for an entire group that has serious, legitimate problems?)

Persuade reluctant sources

— They don't have time. Offer a more convenient time or place. Say you'll drive to work with them in the morning and talk along the way. Be prepared to limit the amount of time you need, if this is an important source.

— They're afraid. They think you will make them look bad. Be clear about why you want to talk to them and why the story needs their point of view. If they are just anxious about talking to a reporter, work hard at being a real person so they can relax. Don't use the "interview" word. Just say you want to talk to them, but be clear that it will be on camera.

— They don't know what to say. Maybe you have chosen the wrong source. Or maybe you have not been clear about what you are seeking. Focus on what the person does want to say, so you can draw them out. If you are dealing with children or victims of trauma, take special care.

— They are being protected. You have to get through a secretary or a public relations officer to the person you want. Write a letter directly to the source. Call during lunch or after business hours-you may find that person at his desk without a secretary to run interference. Some reporters have been known to just show up at the office or at a location where the person will be (the parking lot, a football game). Cultivate the person who is standing in your way. Sometimes they will even take your case, if you are polite but persistent. Use an intermediary-- someone who knows that source and can put in a good word for you.

— Start from the premise that public officials should talk to you, and that you have a right to know. Appeal to their sense of public service. If they say no comment, ask what they thought the last time they read a story with a no comment in it. Did they think the person was hiding something? Wouldn't they rather provide some information to set the record straight? Appeal to their sense of importance. Tell them you really need their point of view, that they can contribute something no one else can.

Prepare for interviews

— Research the person. Ask others about the person; see what has been written about them already. If it's a famous person, you don't want to ask a question that the person has answered hundreds of times unless you can ask it in a very different way. Use the Internet, clipping files, talk to other journalists who have interviewed that person.

— Research the subject. You need to know what you are talking about. This establishes your credibility from the start. Check clip files, the Internet, colleagues. The more you know, the better the questions and the better the answers, the better the story. But don't assume that because something has been published it must be true. Use your research as background, not as fact.

Know your purpose

— Know what you hope to accomplish in each interview. Do you need factual information or the person's reactions to a situation, or are you looking for a deeper understanding of the person? This will guide you in planning and preparing questions.

— Picture the best possible outcome for each interview. Then ask yourself what problems may arise and how you will get over them? For example, know what you will do if the person wants to go off the record.

Going on a Shoot

— Some journalists innately possess a visual sense-that is, the ability to fathom a story visually-much before they come to TV news. But not many are born with this visual sense. Most of them have been trained into dealing with facts, ideas and words. Yet for the, converts to TV news, it is a professional necessity to familiarize themselves with the camera angles and techniques that will enable them to illustrate their words with pictures. Though they mayor may not handle the camera themselves, they must oversee that the pictures so taken best illustrate the story element they wish to describe.

— A few reporters, who are fresh from print or radio, resist learning the nuances of the new medium, but only to realize their folly a little later. Any way, better late than never.

Before going on a shoot

— In small newsrooms and outstation units, TV journalists operate the camcorder themselves. But even at large stations and networks, they must at least be familiar with the equipment in order to know , what it is capable of doing. Thus before going on a shoot do take the following steps:

— Test or make sure the camera-operator tests the camera and the recorder. Is the camera battery fully charged? Is the spare battery fully charged? Is the tape fresh? Is it running smoothly in the recorder? Test the microphone and its cables for hum or noise. Is the recorded sound clear and unmuffled? Test the picture playback on a colour monitor for its true colours and sharpness. If the colours are not true, take a new White Balance.

— If all the above tests yield negative results, send the equipment for skilled repairing.

Shooting a news event

There are certain tips for shooting a news event no matter what type or brand of cquipment is used.

1. *Steady Shots*: Steady shots are crucial to news. To ensure this the camera has to be kept steady. Once a shot is framed, zooming in and out is almost forbidden. Then what about the 'movement' that is so characteristic of a TV show? Yes, the 'movement' is added in editing, not in shooting. This means you frame. a shot and then hold it. For a change of shot, stop the camera, reframe the shot, then switch on the camera. For long steady shots, use a tripod.

2. *Wild Track*: It is always better to shoot with natural sound or the wild track than without it. This is so to lend credence to the story. Anchor voice over (AVO) stories are usually run with the wild track under the anchor's voice.

3. *Adequate Light*: Make sure there is enough light. Most outdoor and many indoor locations have enough natural light for routine news coverage. However, to avoid any light related deficiency, you should keep a camera mounted light with you. It is better if you carry a stand-mounted fill-light, to fill any dark areas of a scene, such as space behind an interviewee.

4. *Tape Replacement*: You should know how much tape time is left on a cassette. Suppose the Prime Minister is holding a press conference on an important foreign policy issue, and your tape runs out just when he makes the most important statement. Most of the times such a mishap can be avoided by timely replacement of the tape. No matter, if the old tape had ten minutes left on it at the time you replaced it with a fresh one.

21

Soap Operas

A soap opera is an ongoing, episodic work of fiction, usually broadcast on television or radio. This genre of TV and radio entertainment has existed long enough for audiences to recognize them simply by the term soap. What differentiates a soap from other television drama programs is their open-ended nature. Plots run concurrently, intersect, and lead into further developments. An individual episode of a soap opera will generally switch between several different concurrent story threads that may at times interconnect and affect one another, or may run entirely independent of each another.

Each episode may feature some of the show's current storylines but not always all of them. There is some rotation of both storylines and actors so any given storyline or actor will appear in some but usually not all of a week's worth of episodes. Soap operas rarely "wrap things up" storywise, and generally avoid bringing all the current storylines to a conclusion at the same time. When one storyline ends there are always several other story threads at differing stages of development. Soap opera episodes invariably end on some sort of cliffhanger.

Evening soap operas sometimes differ from this general format and are more likely to feature the entire cast in each episode, and to represent all current storylines in each episode. Additionally evening soaps and other serials that run for only part of the year tend to bring things to a dramatic end of season cliffhanger. Some of the larger, disaster cliffhangers that affect a large proportion of the cast sometimes serve to bring all current storylines together.

Origin of Soap Opera

The soap opera form originated on U.S. radio in the 1930s, and expanded into television starting in the 1940s. They normally "air" during the daytime, hence the alternative name, daytime serial drama. Radio soap operas began in Chicago in 1930 when WGN broadcast the fifteen minute drama Painted Dreams, about the trials of an Irish-American widow and her daughter. By the start of World War II there were dozens of popular soap operas.

The first concerted effort to air continuing drama on television occurred in 1946 on the DuMont television series Faraway Hill. Soap operas were introduced to network television in 1949, with NBC's short-lived These Are My Children, followed by NBC's Hawkins Falls in June 1950 and CBS's two year run of The First Hundred Years in December 1950. Two long-running soaps, Search for Tomorrow and Love of Life, started broadcasting in 1951. Guiding Light began on radio in 1937 and first aired on television in 1952.

The term "soap opera" originated from the fact that when these serial dramas were aired on daytime radio, the commercials aired during the shows were largely aimed at housewives. Many of the products sold during these commercials were laundry and cleaning items, and included a jingle praising the product. This specific type of radio drama came to be associated with these particular commercials, and this gave rise to the term "soap opera" — a melodramatic story that aired commercials for soap products. Though soap operas are still sponsored by companies such as Procter & Gamble, the diverse demographic groups that soap operas attract have caused other advertisements for such things as acne medication and birth control, appealing to a much younger audience.

Characteristics of Soap Opera

Most soaps follow the lives of a group of characters who live or work in a particular place, or focus on a large, extended family. The storylines follow the day-to-day lives of these characters. In many soap operas, in particular daytime serials in the United States, the characters are generally more handsome, beautiful, seductive, and wealthy than the typical person watching the show. This is true to a lesser extent in soap operas from Australia and the United Kingdom which largely focus on more everyday characters and situations, and are frequently set in working class environments. Many Australian and UK soap operas explore social realist storylines such as family discord, marriage breakdown or financial problems, and sometimes include significant amounts of comedy.

Romance, secret relationships, extra-marital affairs, and genuine love has been the basis for many soap opera storylines. In US daytime serials the most popular soap opera characters, and the most popular storylines, often involved a romance of the sort presented in paperback romance novels. Soap opera storylines sometimes weave intricate, convoluted, sometimes confusing tales of characters who have affairs, meet mysterious strangers and fall in love, and who commit adultery, all of which keeps audiences hooked on the unfolding story twists. Australian and UK soap operas also feature a significant proportion of romance storylines.

In soap opera storylines, previously-unknown children, siblings and twins of established characters may emerge, and unexpected calamities disrupt weddings with unusual frequency. Much like comic books—another popular form of linear storytelling—a character's death is not guaranteed to be permanent without an on-camera corpse, and sometimes not even then. The death of Dr. Taylor Forrester on The Bold and the Beautiful seemed permanent as she had flatlined on-camera and even had a funeral. But when actress Hunter Tylo returned to the show in 2005, the "flatlining" was explained away with the revelation that Taylor had actually gone into a coma.

In addition, the musical soundtrack used for a soap opera uses a style that instantly identifies it as belonging to soap operas. Soaps aired during the golden age of radio usually used organs to produce most of their music (because they were cheaper than full-blown orchestras). The organists from the radio serials moved over to television, and were heard on some serials as late as the 1970s.

Like the storylines themselves, soap opera soundtracks were overblown and melodramatic. An instantly recognizable characteristic of a soap (one that has been spoofed and imitated many times) consists of a scene where a character delivers a shocking revelation. At that moment a single, blaring organ chord resonates on the soundtrack, emphasizing this dramatic moment.

Organ music was abandoned by the serials during the 1960s and 1970s to be replaced by pre-recorded library music, mostly created by synthesizers.

Soaps Operas around the World

Soaps in the United States

The American soap opera The Guiding Light started as a radio drama in January 1937 and subsequently transferred to television. With the exception of several years in the late 1940s when Irna Phillips was in dispute with Procter & Gamble, The Guiding Light has been heard or seen every weekday since it started, making it the longest story ever told. Other American soaps that have been telecast for more than thirty years (and are still in rotation) include As the World Turns, General Hospital, Days of Our Lives, One Life to Live, All My Children, and The Young and the Restless. Due to the shows' longevities, it is not uncommon for multiple actors to play a single character over the span of many years. It is also not uncommon for a single actor to play several characters on other shows over the years. Actors such as Robin Mattson, Roscoe Born and Michael Sabatino have played no less than six soap roles. As actors transition between soap roles, it is not uncommon nowadays to be dropped from contract status to recurring status, a part of contract negotiations which is almost completely unique to U.S. soaps.

In the USA, the shows purely known in the vernacular as soap operas are broadcast during daytime. In the beginning, the serials were broadcast as fifteen-minute installments each weekday. In 1956, the first half-hour soaps debuted, and all of the soaps broadcast half-hour episodes by the end of the 1960s. When the soap opera hit a fever pitch in the 1970s, popular demand had most of the shows, one by one, expanded to an hour in length (one show, Another World, even expanded to ninety minutes for a short time). More than half of the serials (and all of the pre-'80s hour-long serials on the air today) expanded to the new time format by 1980. Today, eight out of the nine American serials air sixty-minute episodes each weekday.

Port Charles used the practice of running 13-week "story arcs", in which the main events of the arc are played out and wrapped up over the 13 weeks, although some storylines did continue over more than one arc. According to the 2006 Preview issue of Soap Opera Digest, it was briefly discussed that all ABC shows might do telenovela arcs, but this was rejected.

Many soaps, in the beginning of television, found their niches in telling stories in certain environments. The Doctors and General Hospital, in the beginning, told stories almost exclusively from inside the confines of a hospital. As the World Turns dealt heavily with Chris Hughes's law practice and the travails of his wife Nancy who, when she tired of being "the loyal housewife" in the 1970s, became one of the first older women on the serials to become a working woman. The Guiding Light dealt with Bert Bauer (Charita Bauer) and her endless marital troubles. When her status moved to that of the caring mother and town matriarch, her children's marital troubles were then put on display. Search for Tomorrow told the story, for the most part, through the eyes of one woman only: the heroine, Joanne (Mary Stuart). Even when stories revolved around other characters, she was almost always a main fixture in their storylines. Days of Our Lives first told the stories of Dr. Tom Horton and his steadfast wife Alice. In later years, the show branched out and told the stories of their five children.

In contrast to these shows was Dark Shadows (1966-1971) which featured supernatural characters and dealt with fantasy and horror storylines. Its characters included the vampire Barnabas Collins, the witch Angelique, and various ghosts and goblins, both friendly and malevolent.

Prime time serials were just as popular as those in daytime. The first real prime time soap opera was ABC's Peyton Place (1964-1969), based in part on the original 1957 movie (which was itself taken from the 1956 novel). The popularity of Peyton Place prompted rival network CBS to spin off popular As the World Turns character Lisa Miller Grimaldi into her own evening soap opera entitled Our Private World in 1965. Our Private World ended in 1966 and the character of Lisa returned to As the World Turns.

The structure of the Peyton Place with its episodic plots and long-running story arcs would set the mold for the prime time serials of the 1980s when the format reached its pinnacle.

The successful prime time serials of the 1980s included Dallas, Dynasty, Knots Landing and Falcon Crest. These shows frequently dealt with wealthy families and their personal and big-business travails. Common characteristics were sumptuous sets and costumes, the presence of at least one glamorous bitch-figure in the cast of characters, and spectacular disaster cliffhanger situations. Unlike daytime serials which where shot on video in a studio using the multicamera setup, these evening series were shot on film using a single camera setup and featured much location-shot footage, often in picturesque locales. Dallas, its spin-off Knots Landing, and Falcon Crest all initially featured episodes with self-contained stories and specific guest stars who appeared in just that episode. Each story would be completely resolved by the end of the episode and there were no end-of-episode cliffhangers. After the first couple of seasons all three shows changed their story format to that of a pure soap opera with interwoven ongoing narratives that ran over several episodes. Dynasty featured this format throughout its run.

The soap opera's distinctive open plot structure and complex continuity also began to be increasingly incorporated into major American prime time television programs. The first significant drama series to do this was Hill Street Blues, produced by Steven Bochco, which featured many elements borrowed from soap operas such as an ensemble cast, multi-episode storylines and extensive character development over the course of the series. The success of this series prompted other drama series and situation comedy shows such as St. Elsewhere, E.R., The West Wing and Friends to incorporate soap opera style stories and story structure to varying degrees.

The prime time soap operas and drama series of the 1990s, such as Beverly Hills 90210, Melrose Place and Dawson's Creek, focused more on younger characters. In the late 1990s and early 2000s many new prime time soap operas were produced for cable television, including Queer As Folk.

Evolution of Daytime Soaps

For several decades US daytime soap operas concentrated on family and marital upsets, legal dramas and romances. The action rarely left the interior settings within the fictional, medium-sized Midwestern towns in which the shows were set. Exterior shots, once a rarity, were slowly incorporated into the series Ryan's Hope. Unlike many earlier serials Ryan's Hope was set in an already-existing place, New York City, and outside shoots were used to give the series greater authenticity. The first exotic location shoot was made by All My Children, to St. Croix in 1978. Many other soaps planned lavish storylines after seeing the success of the All My Children shoot. Another World went to St. Croix in March 1980 to culminate a long-running storyline between popular characters Mac, Rachel and Janice. Search for Tomorrow taped for two weeks in Hong Kong in 1981.

During the 1980s, perhaps as a reaction to the evening drama series that were gaining high ratings, daytime serials began to incorpate action and adventure storylines, more big-business intrigue, and featured an increased emphasis on youthful romance and began developing supercouples. One of the first and most popular supercouples was Luke and Laura in General Hospital. Luke and Laura helped to attract both male and female fans. Even Elizabeth Taylor was a fan and at her own request was given a guest role in Luke and Laura's wedding episode. Luke and Laura's popularity led to other soap producers striving to reproduce this success by attempting to create supercouples of their own. With increasingly bizarre action storylines coming into vogue Luke and Laura saved the world from being frozen, brought a mobster down by finding his black book in a Left-Handed Boy Statue, and helped a Princess find her

Aztec Treasure in Mexico. Other soaps attempted similar adventure storylines, often featuring footage shot on location - frequently in exotic locales.

During the 1990s the mob stories and the action and adventure plotlines fell out of favour with producers due to overall lower ratings for daytime soap operas and the resultant budget cuts. In the 1990s soaps were no longer able to go on expensive location shoots to Argentina, France, Hawaii, Jamaica, Italy and Japan as they had in the 1980s. In the 1990s soaps increasingly focused on younger characters and social issues, such as Erica Kane's drug addiction on All My Children, the re-emergence of Viki Lord's Multiple Personality Disorder on One Life to Live, and Katherine Chancellor's alcoholism on The Young and the Restless. Other social issues included Breast Cancer, AIDS, and racism.

Perhaps to fill the niche, some newer shows have incorporated supernatural and science fiction elements into their storylines. One of the main characters in US soap opera Passions is Tabitha Lenox, a 300-year-old witch. Port Charles has featured a vampire character. Frequently these characters are isolated in one of the ongoing story threads allow a fan to ignore them if they do not like that element, a form of krypto-revisionism.

Characteristics of Modern Soaps

Modern U.S. daytime soap operas largely stay true to the original soap opera format. The duration and format of storylines and the visual grammar employed by US daytime serials set them apart from soap operas in other countries and from evening soap operas. Stylistically, UK and Australian soap operas, which are usually produced for evening timeslots, fall somewhere in-between US daytime and evening soap operas. Similar to US daytime soaps, UK and Australian are shot on videotape, and the cast and storylines are rotated across the week's episodes so that each cast member will appear in some but not all episodes. However UK and Australian soaps move through storylines at a faster rate than daytime serials, making them closer to US evening soaps in this regard.

American soap operas since the 1980s have shared many common visual elements that set them apart dramatically from other shows: Overhead spotlighting, or back lighting, is often placed directly over the heads of all the actors in the foreground, causing an unnatural shadowing of their features along with a highlighting of their hair. Back lighting was always a standard technique of film and television lighting, though it was mostly abandoned in the mid-to-late eighties due to its somewhat unnatural look. The technique has nevertheless persisted in soap operas.

The rooms in a house often use deep stained wood wall panels and furniture, along with many elements of brown leather furniture. This creates an overall "brown" look which is intended to give a sumptuous and luxurious look to suggest the wealth of the characters portrayed.

Daytime soap operas do not routinely feature location or exterior-shot footage. Often they will recreate an outdoor locale in the studio. Australian and UK daily soap operas invariably feature a certain amount of exterior-shot footage in every episode, this is usually shot in the same location and often on a purpose-built set, however they regularly include new exterior locations for certain storylines

The visual quality of a soap opera is usually lower than prime time television shows due to the lower budgets and quicker production times involved. This is also due to the fact that soap operas are recorded on videotape using a multicamera setup, unlike primetime productions which are usually shot on film and frequently using the single camera shooting style. Because of the lower resolution of video images, and also because of the intense emotions explored by soap operas, daytime serials feature a heavy use of closeup shots.

Soaps often reuse the same blocking techniques. For example, if a romantically involved man and woman are talking to each other face-to-face, one character will inevitably turn 180° and face away from the other character while they both continue to have a conversation. While this would virtually never happen in real life, and is not seen outside of US daytime serials, it is an accepted soap convention.

In US daytime soaps, when a scene is about to reach a temporary conclusion and the episode is to switch to a new scene with a different set of characters, one character in the currently concluding scene will often be shown in extreme closeup and deliver a shocking announcement. No other character will respond and there will be no dialogue for several seconds while the music builds before cutting to a new scene.

Additionally, in a construct unique to US daytime serials, the episode will frequently then return to this precise point in time after some intervening scenes, and the discussion will continue from the point where the revelation was made. Usually, however, when the discussion resumes the previously tense and dramatic mood created through music and closeup shots will have dissipated; the scene usually resumes in a relatively relaxed and sedate mode. The format of ending a scene to switch to other characters but to then return to the original scene at the precise time the viewer last left it is unique to US daytime serials.

Soaps in the UK

In the United Kingdom, soap operas are one of the most popular genres, most being broadcast during prime time. Most UK soaps focus on working-class communities. The most popular is ITV's Coronation Street (nicknamed Corrie), which regularly attracts the highest viewing figures for any programme.

Coronation Street has been a popular soap opera in the United Kingdom since the show was first aired in 1960(and still running, albeit with several cast changes over the years).Soap operas began on radio and consequently were associated with the BBC. The BBC continues to broadcast the world's longest-running radio soap, The Archers, on Radio 4. It has been running since 1951 nationally. It continues to attract over five million listeners, or roughly 25% of the radio listening population of the UK at that time of the evening.

In the 1960s Coronation Street revolutionised UK television and quickly became a British institution. Other soap operas of the 1960s included Emergency Ward 10 (ITV), and on the BBC Compact (about the staff of a women's magazine) and The Newcomers (about the upheaval caused by a large firm setting up a plant in a small town). However none of these came close to making the same impact as Coronation Street.

During the 1960s Corrie's main rival was Crossroads, a daily serial that began in 1964 and was broadcast by ITV at teatime. Crossroads was set in a Birmingham motel and while the series was popular, its purported low technical standard and bad acting was much mocked. By the 1980s its ratings had begun to decline and several attempts to revamp the series through cast changes and later, expanding the focus from the motel to the surrounding community, were unsuccessful, and Crossroads was cancelled in 1988.

A later rival to Corrie was ITV's Emmerdale Farm (later renamed Emmerdale) which began in 1972 in a daytime slot and had a rural Yorkshire setting. Increased viewing figures saw Emmerdale being moved to a prime-time slot in the 1980s. When Channel 4 began in 1982 it launched its own soap, the Liverpool based Brookside, which over the next decade re-defined the UK television soap. In 1985, the BBC's London based soap opera

EastEnders debuted and was a near instant success with viewers and critics alike. Critics talked about the downfall of Coronation Street, but this was put to rest in 1994 when the two serials were scheduled opposite each other, with Corrie winning handily. For the better part of ten years, the show has shared the number one position with Coronation Street, but the ratings for EastEnders reached an all-time low as of late 2004, allowing Corrie to regain the top spot.

Daytime soaps were unknown until the 1970s because there was virtually no daytime television in the UK. ITV introduced General Hospital, which later transferred to a prime time slot, and Scottish Television had Take the High Road, which lasted for over twenty years. Later, daytime slots were filled with an influx of old Australian soap operas such as The Young Doctors, The Sullivans, Sons and Daughters and eventually, Neighbours and Home and Away. These achieved significant levels of popularity. Neighbours and Home and Away were moved to early-evening slots and the UK soap opera boom began in the late 1980s. Later, 1992 saw the BBC launch Eldorado to alternate with EastEnders but it only lasted a year; however, this failure did not stop the ever-increasing prominence that soap operas would have in UK schedules.

In 1995 Channel 4 introduced Hollyoaks, a soap with a youth focus that would eventually fill the gap made by the outgoing Brookside. When Channel Five began in March 1997 it came with its own soap opera, Family Affairs which debuted as a five-days-a-week soap. In 2001 a new version of Crossroads was produced by Carlton Television for ITV, featuring a mostly new cast, but it did not achieve satisfactory ratings and was cancelled in 2003. Family Affairs, which was broadcast opposite the racier Hollyoaks, never achieved significantly high viewing figures and after several dramatic revamps of the cast, changes in style and even location, it was cancelled in late 2005.

UK soaps for many years usually only aired two nights a week. The exception was the original Crossroads, which began as a five days a week soap opera in the 1960s, but was later reduced. In 1989, things started to change when Coronation Street began airing three times a week (later expanding further to four in 1996), a trend which was soon followed by rival EastEnders in 1994 and Emmerdale in 1997. Family Affairs debuted as a five-days-a-week soap in 1997 and regularly ran five episodes a week its entire run.

Today Coronation Street (which began screening two episodes on Monday nights in 2002) and Hollyoaks both produce five episodes a week, while EastEnders screens four. In 2004 Emmerdale began screening six episodes a week leading to the concern that soap operas in the UK were at saturation level.

Today's UK soap operas are mainly shot on videotape in the studio using a multicamera setup. However UK soap operas feature a proportion of outdoors shot footage in each episode - usually shot on a purpose-built outdoor set that represents the community the soap focuses on.

Soaps in Australia

Title card from a 1975 episode of Number 96Australia has had quite a number of well known soap operas, some of which have gained cult followings in the UK and other countries. The majority of Australian soap operas are produced for early evening or evening timeslots. They usually produce two or two-and-a-half hours of new material each week, either arranged as four or five half-hour episodes a week, or two one-hour episodes. Stylistically they most closely resemble UK soap operas in that they are nearly always shot on videotape, mainly in the studio using a multicamera setup, with some location-shot footage in each episode. Like UK soap operas most Australian soaps focus on a mixed age range of middle-class characters.

The first successful wave of Australian evening soap operas started in the late 1960s with Bellbird produced by the Australian Broadcasting Corporation. This rural-based serial was a moderate success but built-up a consistent and loyal viewer base, especially in rural areas. The first big soap opera hit in Australia was the sex-melodrama Number 96 which began in March 1972, screening on Network Ten. Number 96 brought such rarely explored topics as homosexuality, adultery, drug use, rape-within-marriage and racism into Australian living rooms en masse. By 1973 it had become Australia's highest-rating show.

In 1974 the sexed-up antics of Number 96 prompted the creation of The Box, which rivaled it in terms of nudity and sexual situations. Produced by Crawford Productions, many critics considered The Box to be a more slickly produced and better written show than Number 96, and in its first year it was extremely popular. Meanwhile in 1974 the Reg Grundy Organisation created its first soap opera, and significantly Australia's first teen soap opera, Class of '74. Its attempts to hint at the sex and sin shown more openly on Number 96 and The Box meant it came under intense scrutiny of the Broadcasting Control Board who vetted scripts and altered whole storylines. By 1975 both Number 96 and The Box, perhaps as a reaction to declining ratings for both shows, de-emphasised the sex and nudity moving more in the direction of comedy. Class of '74 was renamed Class of '75 for its second year but ratings dwindled and this year would also be its last.

A feature film version of Bellbird entitled Country Town was produced in 1971 not by the Australian Broadcasting Corporation but by two of the show's stars, Gary Gray and Terry McDermott. Number 96 and The Box also had feature film versions, both of which had the same title as the series, released in 1974 and 1975 respectively. As Australian television was in black and white until 1975 these theatrical releases all had the novelty of being in colour. The film versions of Number 96 and The Box also allowed more explicit nudity than could be shown on television at that time.

Launched on the Nine Network in late 1976 was The Sullivans, a series chronicling the affects of World War II on a working-class Melbourne family. Produced by Crawford's this show was a ratings success and attracted many positive reviews. At around the same time Grundy's created a new teen-oriented soap, The Young Doctors, which also screened on Channel Nine starting late 1976. This show eschewed the sex and sin of Number 96 and The Box instead emphasising light-weight storylines and romance. It was also popular but unlike The Sullivans it was not a success with critics. Meanwhile in 1977 Number 96 would re-introduce nudity, with several much-publicised full-frontal nude scenes featured in an attempt to boost the show's plummeting ratings.

Bellbird, Number 96 and The Box were all cancelled in 1977; all had been experiencing declining ratings since 1975 and various attempts to revamp the shows with cast reshuffles or spectacular disaster storylines had proved only temporarily successful. Late that year they were replaced by such successful new shows as the Crawfords Produced Cop Shop (1977-1984) on Channel Seven, which was a meld of soap opera and police drama, and The Restless Years (1977-1981) on Channel Ten, which was another teen soap produced by the Reg Grundy Organisation. The Reg Grundy Organisation subsequently reached even higher levels of success with women's-prison drama Prisoner (1979-1986) on Network Ten, and melodramatic family saga Sons and Daughters (1981-1987) on the Seven Network. Both shows achieved high ratings in their first run, and unusually, found success in repeats after their original runs ended.

Neighbours is currently Australia's longest-running soap opera. The Young Doctors and The Sullivans ran on

Nine until 1982. Thereafter Channel Nine attempted many new soap operas, several produced by The Reg Grundy Organisation including Taurus Rising, Waterloo Station, Starting Out and Possession, along with Prime Time produced by Crawford's, but none were successful and most were cancelled after only a few months. The Reg Grundy Organisation also created Neighbours, a suburban-based daily serial devised as a sedate family drama with some comedy and lightweight situations, for the Seven Network in 1985. Produced in Melbourne at the studios of HSV-7, Neighbours rated well in Melbourne, Brisbane and Adelaide, but not in Sydney. Sydney was the only city where it was shown in the earlier 5.30 p.m. timeslot which put it up against hit dating game show Perfect Match on Channel 10, and Seven's Sydney station ATN-7 quickly lost interest in the show.

HSV-7 in Melbourne lobbied heavily to keep Neighbours going but ATN-7 managed to convince the rest of the network to cancel the show and instead keep ATN-7's own Sydney-based dramas A Country Practice and Sons and Daughters. After the network cancelled Neighbours it was immediately picked-up by Channel Ten. They revamped the cast and scripts slightly and from 20 January 1986 aired the series in the 7.00 p.m. slot. It initially attracted low viewing figures however after a concerted publicity drive Ten managed to transform the series into a major success, turning several of its actors into major international stars. The show's popularity eventually declined and it was moved to the 6.30 p.m. slot in 1992, yet the series retains consistent viewing figures in Australia and is still running today, making it Australia's longest-running soap opera.

The success of Neighbours prompted the creation of somewhat similar suburban and family or teen-oriented soap operas such as Home and Away (1988-) on Channel Seven and Richmond Hill (1988) on Channel Ten. Both proved popular, however Richmond Hill emerged as only a moderate success and was cancelled after one year to be replaced on Ten by E Street (1989-1993).

Meanwhile Nine had still failed to find a successful new soap opera. After the failure of family drama Family and Friends in 1990 they launched the raunchier and more extreme Chances in 1991, a series that would resurrect the sex and melodrama of Number 96 and The Box in an attempt to improve the show's chances of ratings success. However it too achieved only moderate ratings, although the increasingly bizarre storylines were much-discussed and the series continued into 1992 albeit in a late-night timeslot.

Several Australian soap operas have also found significant international success. In the UK starting in the mid 1980s daytime screenings of The Young Doctors, The Sullivans, Sons and Daughters and Neighbours achieved significant success. Neighbours was subsequently moved to an early-evening slot. Grundy's Prisoner began screening in the United States in 1979 and achieved high ratings in many regions there, however only the first three years of the series would be screened in that country. Prisoner was also screened in late-night timeslots in the UK beginning in the late 1980s, achieving enduring cult success there.

The show became so popular in the UK that it prompted the creation of two stage plays and a stage musical based on the show, all of which toured the UK, among many other spin-offs. In the late 1990s Channel Five repeated Prisoner in the UK. Between 1998 and 2005 Five ran late-night repeats of Sons and Daughters. During the 1980s the Australian attempts to emulate big-budget US soap operas such as Dallas and Dynasty had resulted in Taurus Rising and Return to Eden, two slick soap opera dramas with big budgets and shot entirely on film. Though their middling Australian ratings ensured they ran only a single season both programs were successfully sold internationally.

Other shows to achieve varying levels of international success include Richmond Hill, E Street, Paradise Beach (1993-1994), and Pacific Drive (1995-1997). Indeed these last two series were designed specifically for international sales. Channel Seven's Home and Away, a teen soap developed as a rival to Neighbours, has also achieved significant and enduring success on UK television.

Title card of headLand.Attempts to replicate the success of daily teen-oriented serials Neighbours and Home and Away saw the creation of Echo Point (1995) and Breakers (1999) on Network Ten, and more recently the Australian Broadcasting Corporation produced the rural-based Something in the Air (2000-2002). None of these programs emerged as long-running successes and Neighbours and Home and Away remained the most visible and consistently successful Australian soap operas in production. In their home country they both attract respectable although not spectacular ratings, and both continue to achieve significant ratings in the UK. This and other lucrative overseas markets, along with Australian broadcasting laws that enforce a minimum amount of local drama production for commercial television networks, help ensure that both programs remain in production. Neighbours, which is celebrated its 20th Anniversary in 2005, was aired on the U.S. channel Oxygen in March 2004, however it attracted few viewers, perhaps in part because it was scheduled opposite well-established and highly-popular US soap operas such as All My Children and The Young and The Restless, and due to low ratings it was cancelled shortly afterwards.

New Australian serial headLand premiered on Channel Seven in November 2005. This new series rose from the ashes of a proposed Home and Away spinoff that was to have been produced in conjunction with the UK's Channel Five, which screens Home and Away. The spin-off idea was cancelled after Channel Five pulled-out of the deal, which meant that the show could potentially screen on a rival UK channel, so Five requested that the new show developed as a stand-alone series and not feed off a series they own a stake in. The series premiered in Australia on 15 November 2005 but was not a ratings success and was cancelled 23 January 2006.

Indian Soap Operas

Indian soap operas are soap operas written, produced, filmed in India, with characters played by Indians, with episodes broadcast on a daily/weekly/semi-weekly basis on Indian television channels/channel chains (Star Network, Sony Entertainment, Sun Network, Doordarshan) that are not often limited to the Republic of India itself: often many "serials," as they're more commonly referred to as, are broadcast overseas in the UK, USA, and some parts of Europe, South Africa, and Australia.

Indian soap operas are often mass-produced under large production banners, with houses like Balaji Telefilms—run by Ekta and Shobha Kapoor, daughter and wife respectively to Hindi film star Jitendra—running the same serial in different languages on different television networks/channels.

The most common languages in which Indian serials are made in are: Hindi, Punjabi, Marathi, Gujarati, Bengali, Tamil, Kannada, Telugu, and Malayalam, though most often they contain a mix of the predominant language and English. This often creates and unintentional comic effect: a certain High School-themed serial on Star One has created a bizarre language of its own, a heavy mix of colloquial Hindi and corruptions of modern American slang, which, though fairly odd to understand at first, has created its own coterie of loyal fans devoted to using the very same 'language' in daily speech.

Indian serials are often stereotypical, both in storylines and in characters. The ideals of the quintessential Indian

Family are often given fanatical attention to, which lines being written in grand, melodramatic tones, drawing in references to events in the Mahabharata and the Ramayana, the typical Indian Woman, and other similar themes. Balaji Telefilms has often been frowned at for repeating the same essential storylines with different characters and sets (altering the sequence of events and their intensity) to create more and more serials.

One of the first serials created by the banner was Kyunki Saas Bhi Kabhi Bahu Thi (literally, Because the Mother-in-Law was once the Daughter-in-Law), the story of the fictional industrialist family Virani, the apple-of-their-eye son Mihir, and their loyal and subservient (i.e., quintessential) daughter-in-law, Tulsi, his wife. An almost immediate release was another serial called Kahaani Ghar Ghar Ki (loosely translatable as The Story of (all) our Homes), also a story about an industrialist family—albeit, the "Agrarwals"—also about the apple-of-their-eye son—this time, "Om", though it is essential to note that later in the series the lives of all the brothers of the families and their wives were dealt with extensively—and yet again, their loyal and subservient daughter-in-law, "Parvati." The storylines are loosely parallel, though the writers continually attempt to "shock" their audiences with rapes, extramarital affairs, murders, conspiracies, and kidnappings—in all serials, though at different points in time. A standard feature now is the 20-year-jump, where one epoch in the series ends at a stalemate and continues in the next episode with all the characters and surroundings twenty years older, the effects of ageing being shown by white dye in strands in the hair of the women of the family, and not-so-subtle hints of grey around the gentlemen's moustaches and sideboards.

Another slightly unreal aspect of the Indian serial is the "face-change operation". A typical scenario is one wherein an accident happens to one of the protagonists, with him/her waking up in hospital with a new face, one that is most often the result of the antagonist scheming with an evil plastic surgeon who creates an entirely new face for the hapless hero(ine). The protagonist invariably loses his/her memory, which leaves him/her vulnerable to the antagonist's schemes, and this, along with the 20-year-jump, helps create scenarios such as a missing darling son of the family now being one "converted" to one of the enemy camp, with further clichéd themes as the Indian Mother's Yearning for her Son helping to create about a month's worth of material, which inevitably ends in a reunion scene with lots of happy tears.

Dialogue in Indian serials, in addition to being largely melodramatic and filled with historical and religious references, is widely thought lacking as far as dialogue goes. If seen very carefully, one would notice that there is, in fact, little or no conversation that takes place during the 30-odd minutes of a typical Indian soap opera's episode. Actors' lines in scenes are often delivered one large monologue at a time (even longer in scenes of "conflict" between the protagonist(s) and the antagonist(s)), there are often dance scenes based on the exact same encountered in the parent film of the song (this being less parody and more of a filler, often seen during idle amorous fantasies of the "goof" of the cast), and features elaborate sound effects, which are actually repeated in different serials which are under the same banner.

For example, female antagonists often enter the room with screeching cat noises being played in the background, perhaps an allusion to the character's invariable cattiness; though often antagonists that are well-known and widely-spurned by the TV-seeing public often have their distinctive entrance sound effects: in the serial Kasauti Zindagi Kii, whenever the character 'Komolika', began to scheme and soliloquise and/or entered a room, a playful, almost vampish strain of gaudy music was played to an amorous play of her name. This was keeping in with the effect her heavy makeup, thick, bristly fake eyelashes, and garish contact lenses portrayed the character as.

Male antagonists that are young often have Indianised strains of rather obscure hip-hop songs working for them in the background, and those that are older often have deeply resonating kettle drums booming in the background.

Sex has never been dealt with on screen, although it is ironic considering so many characters are exposed as having extramarital affairs. There has never been a kiss, heterosexual or homosexual, in an Indian soap opera in any language in any form whatsoever. This is seen as being consistent to the extreme conservatism that India is filled with.

The camera often spins wildly from character to character during scenes in which shocking news is revealed, shaking vigorously when a character faints, and showing the same slap hitting the same cheek thrice during a confrontation, keeping in sync with the overall melodramatic touch most of the serials prefer to incorporate.

Indian serials first began with the introduction of the television set in Indian homes: the first soap opera on the State-run channel, Doordarshan (the only television channel that existed at that point in time), was Hum Log, a story of a family comprising of three generations. It was urban, it was middle-class, and it was new, and till today, it, along with Buniyaad, is considered among the best-made Indian serials to be seen by an Indian audience.

In the "old" Star TV channel of the Star Network, certain serials like Saans and Kora Kaagaz broke the mould and gained artistic as well as commercial success; serials on Zee TV like Taara and Banegi Apni Baat (which featured among the early work of renowned Hindi/Tamil actor Madhavan), too, were of the same privileged fate.

More recently serials on the Star One channel on the Star Network have seen to be largely different from the conventional, with Saturday Night Live-esque programmes like The Great Indian Comedy Show, stand-up shows like The Great Indian Laughter Challenge and game shows like Bluffmaster being of great popularity. However, it should be noted that in a purely technical sense game and comedy shows aren't really 'soap operas', and though alternatively-themed shows on crime (Siddhant), High School (Happy Go Lucky), and twentysomethings do exist and are relatively popular, a grand majority of Indian television shows are soap operas based on the Family-and-Marriage theme. Remix, an Extremely Popular Serial among Youngsters due to its uniqueness and variety brings much wanted relief to teens who got bored of watching Saas-Bahu Serials.

In public opinion, other serials that "broke the mould" at one point in time are Astitva: Ek Prem Kahani (Zee TV), Yeh Meri Life Hai (Sony Entertainment Television), etc.

Based on predictions made by celebrity astrologer/numerologist/tarot-card reader Sunita Menon, almost all serials made under the Balaji Telefilms banner are supposed to begin with a 'K', regardless of what language it's made in. This is believed to be Creative Head (Ekta Kapoor)'s 'lucky alphabet', and consequently, the K Phenomenon was born. Examples are Kyunki Saas Bhi Kabhi Bahu Thi, Kahaani Ghar Ghar Ki, Kasauti Zindagi Ki, Kkusum, Kavyanjali, Kahiin to Hoga, and so on.

An exception is, however, Hum Paanch, a comedy about a family of five sisters, their bent-on-their-getting-married but loving stepmother, and their father, who talks to their dead mother via a framed photograph hung on a living room wall. This is probably because the show was created and shown in an entirely different time—the late nineties—presumably before Ms Kapoor met Ms Menon. It is interesting to note that despite all the stereotypical content K-serials contain, they are all immensely popular with the masses, which is believed by some to be a result of the initial K.

No Indian serial so far has dealt with issues such as the legislative system, the medical system, rural issues, etc., and though some are set within legal/medical/rural contexts, it has storylines, once more, largely based on marriage and family, or rather, the concepts of marriage and family in the traditional Indian context.

Neither has an Indian serial dealt with homosexuality or AIDS, burgeoning issues in India that are being swept under the carpet by the moral police. An ironic fact, considering Ekta Kapoor, Creative Head of Balaji Telefilms, which is believed to produce the largest number of Indian soap operas, was quoted in a film magazine in an interview as saying one of her favourite shows was Queer as Folk (unavailable for purchase in India, incidentally), and that the actor who played Brian, Gale Harold, was one of her favourite TV drama actors.

However, in commercial terms, Indian serials almost always do well. Not many Indian serials ever end—and so, writers are forced to stretch storylines over a generation or more to cope with the lack of character-exploration/ situation-exploitation. Many Indian serials run for over five years, and, analogous to Bollywood film stars being deified to Godhood, many soap opera stars are treated with a demigod-like quality. The actress who played "Tulsi Virani" in Kyunki Saas Bhi Kabhi Bahu Thi, Smiti Irani, stood to be elected as MP in the 2004 General Elections from the Delhi constituency of Chandni Chowk, and it was hoped by her party, the BJP, that her popularity would help them out in that largely pro-Congress area. Unfortunately she lost, and the seat, along with the entire election, was won by a massive pro-Congress vote.

Bibliography

Archer, Gleason, *History of Radio to 1926*. NY: The American Historical Company, 1938.

Broadsky, Ira. *Wireless: The Revolution in Personal Telecommunications*. Norwood, MA: Artech, 1995.

Calhoun, George, *Digital Cellular Radio*, Norwood, MA: Artech, 1988, especially chapters 1-3.

Coe, Lewis, *Wireless Radio: A Brief History*. Jefferson, NC: McFarland, 1996.

Dunlap, Jr. Orrin E., *The Story of Radio*. NY: The Dial Press, Inc., 1935.

Garrard, Garry A., *Cellular Communications: World-wide Market Development*. Norwood, MA: Artech House, Inc., 1998.

Inglis, Andrew F., *Behind the Tube: A History of Broadcasting Technology and Business*. Boston: Focal, 1990.

Kraeuter, David W., *Radio and Television Pioneers: A Patent Bibliography*. Metuchen, NJ: Scarecrow Press, 1992.

_____,*British Radio and Television Pioneers: A Patent Bibliography*. Metuchen, NJ: Scarecrow Press, 1993.

Leinwoll, Stanley, *From Spark to Satellite: A History of Radio Communication*. NY: Scribner's. 1979.

Orr, William I., *Radio Handbook, Twenty-Third Edition*. Boston, MA: Butterworth-Heinemann, 1997.

Shiers, George (Ed), *The Development of Wireless to 1920*. New York: Arno Press "Historical Studies in Telecommunications," 1977.

Slotten, Hugh, *Radio and Television Regulation: Broadcast Technology in the United States*, 1920-1960 Baltimore: The Johns Hopkins University Press, 2000.

Wedlake, G. E. C., *SOS: The Story of Radio Communication*. New York: Crane, Russak, 1973.

Year-Book of Wireless Telegraphy and Telephony. London: The Wireless Press/Marconi, 1913-1925 (annual).

Yuzo Takahashi, "A Network of Tinkerers: The Advent of the Radio and Television Industry in Japan." *Technology and Culture* 41, no. 3, 460-84, July 2000.